Working, Shirking, and Sabotage

Michigan Studies in Political Analysis

Michigan Studies in Political Analysis promotes the development and dissemination of innovative scholarship in the field of methodology in political science and the social sciences in general. Methodology is defined to include statistical methods, mathematical modeling, measurement, research design, and other topics related to the conduct and development of analytical work. The series includes works that develop a new model or method applicable to social sciences, as well as those that, through innovative combination and presentation of current analytical tools, substantially extend the use of these tools by other researchers.

GENERAL EDITORS: John E. Jackson and Christopher H. Achen

Keith Krehbiel
Information and Legislative Organization

Donald R. Kinder and Thomas R. Palfrey, Editors
Experimental Foundations of Political Science

John Brehm
The Phantom Respondents: Opinion Surveys and Political Representation

William T. Bianco
Trust: Representatives and Constituents

Melvin J. Hinich and Michael C. Munger
Ideology and the Theory of Political Choice

John Brehm and Scott Gates
Working, Shirking, and Sabotage: Bureaucratic Response to a Democratic Public

R. Michael Alvarez
Information and Elections

David Austen-Smith and Jeffrey S. Banks
Positive Political Theory I: Collective Preferences

Working, Shirking, and Sabotage

Bureaucratic Response to a Democratic Public

John Brehm and Scott Gates

Ann Arbor

THE UNIVERSITY OF MICHIGAN PRESS

First paperback edition 1999
Copyright © by the University of Michigan 1997
All rights reserved
Published in the United States of America by
The University of Michigan Press
Manufactured in the United States of America
♾ Printed on acid-free paper

2002   2001   2000   1999   4   3   2   1

A CIP catalogue record for this book is available from the British Library.

Library of Congress Cataloging-in-Publication Data

Brehm, John, 1960–
    Working, Shirking, and sabotage : bureaucratic response to a
    democratic public / John Brehm and Scott Gates.
        p.   cm.
    Includes bibliographical references and index.
    ISBN 0-472-10764-X (alk. paper)
    1. Government productivity—United States.   2. Supervision of
employees.   3. United States—Officials and employees—Professional
ethics.   4. State governments—Officials and employees—Professional
ethics—United States.   5. Local officials and employees—
Professional ethics—United States.   6. Bureaucracy—United States.
7. Democracy—United States. I. Gates, Scott. II. Title.
JK768.4.B74   1997
353.001′02—dc20   96-43487
                                                                  CIP

ISBN 0-472-08612-X (pbk. : alk. paper)

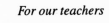

For our teachers

Contents

Preface

We began this project coming from different theoretical orientations, but with a common intuition: that a great deal of contemporary research, and a greater quantity of political rhetoric, made mean-spirited assumptions about public servants in local, state, and federal bureaucracies. How different is the academic's assumption of the leisure-maximizing subordinate from the politician's rhetoric against the lazy bureaucrat? Our intuition told us that the police officer, the social worker, the NASA engineer, the health inspector chose their jobs not for the possibility of maximizing leisure, or even for the material rewards of the job, but for the intrinsic character of the job itself.

As our research progressed, we found that our methods began to fuse, and that the intuition grounded itself in models that reflected the possibility of diverse preferences among bureaucrats, and in empirical analysis that ratified the connections between preferences and performance.

The data for our research primarily came from the Interuniversity Consortium for Political and Social Research, which bears no responsibility for our analysis and interpretations. The specific data sets we employ in this project were: the 1979 Federal Employee Attitude Survey (ICPSR 7804); the 1983 Federal Employee Attitude Survey (6304); the 1992 Survey of Federal Government Employees (9983); Attitudes and Perceptions of Police Officers in Boston, Chicago, and Washington, DC, 1966 (9087); Patterns of Behavior in Police and Citizen Transactions, Boston, Chicago, and Washington, DC, 1966 (9086); Police Services Study, Phase II, 1977, Rochester, St. Louis, and St. Petersburg (8605); Police Use of Force 1991–92 (6274); and Politics of Public Utility Regulation in the United States, 1980 (8080). We also thank Daniel Hudgins and the Durham County Department of Social Services for their assistance in collecting the data for the social worker chapter. (Data for the social worker chapter is available from the authors on request.)

We have many people to thank for their insights on aspects of this manuscript. In particular, we want to thank John Aldrich, Jim Batista, Bill Bianco, Dan Carpenter, Jay Hamilton, Jeff Hill, and Matt Holland for their willingness to comment on the manuscript in entirety or in part. Much of this manuscript appeared originally in the form of conference papers, and we thank Paul Abramson, Bob Bates, Dan Carpenter, Patty Conley, Gary Cox, Doug Dion, Evelyn Fink, Gary Goertz, William Gormley, Jim Granato, Paul Gronke, Tom Hammond, Brian Humes, John Jackson, Jonathan Katz, Paula Kearns, Gary King, Sangmook Kim, Pam Lokken, Skip Lupia, Ken Meier, Gary Miller, Wendy Rahn, Jeff Riedinger, Brian Silver, Renée Smith, Andy Sobel, Adam Stacey, Kaare Strom, Dan Wood, and Rob Worden for their comments on those early drafts.

John Brehm thanks his research assistants, Steve Balla, Brad Gomez, Dan Lipinski, Matt Holland, and David Spence, for their help in assembling the many data sets for this project. John also expresses his deep love and appreciation to his wife, Kate, and children, Laurel, Robin, Joe, and Jeff, for their support.

Scott Gates thanks Erick Duchesne and Sara McLaughlin who helped manage his office while he spent a summer at the University of Minnesota and a year at the University of Trondheim, Norway. Special thanks are extended to Ola Listhaug who so generously provided a wonderful year in Norway.

CHAPTER 1

Bureaucracy and the Politics of Everyday Life

The performance of government bureaucrats matters in profound ways to the day-to-day lives of American citizens. Decisions by unseen bureaucrats affect the safety of our homes, the quality of our air and water, the conditions of our workplaces, the security of our shores, the education of our children, the vulnerability of our national defense, and the surety of banks and insurance. Daily, nearly every citizen in the United States comes in contact with a representative of the local, state, or federal bureaucracy in the form of a police officer, firefighter, or postal worker. Others will see case workers and social workers, soldiers, foresters, or health and safety inspectors.

Compare the frequency with which citizens come in contact with the bureaucracy to other, more widely studied, aspects of American politics. We vote in national elections every other year—but only half of those eligible vote in presidential elections, and only one-third of those eligible vote in congressional elections. Even fewer citizens vote in local elections, which may occur at most twice a year. In the morning, we read the newspaper and in the evening, we may watch the news. Many of us may join interest groups, but very few are active or share even the most tangential contact with the activities of those groups. Virtually all of us, however, see bureaucrats several times a day. Our lives at home, on the job, at schools, and at play are affected by unseen bureaucrats making multitudes of decisions.

And yet bureaucracies and bureaucrats are among the least popular aspects of American government. George Wallace derided the "pointy-headed bureaucrats riding to work on a bike in their three-piece suits with a peanut-butter sandwich in their briefcase" (White 1969). The Republican party, aided and abetted by a fictitious "Harry and Louise," successfully blocked health care reform in large part because the Clinton proposals would create a new bureaucracy. A quick scan of the Nexis-Lexis News Service, in October 1996, showed 39 mentions of the word "bureaucracy" in polling data, of which 28 of those mentions were in a strictly negative context. Or consider a recent survey by Market Strategies (March 10, 1993) that found that over 54 percent of their sample rated bureaucrats poorly on "making government work for you." Even some of the most conspicuously prominent scholarly work on bureaucracy (e.g., Downs 1967, Niskanen 1971, Goodsell 1985, Wilson 1989) begins with an apology or concern for the poisonous connotation of the words.

Bureaucrats make a lot of choices that vitally influence our daily lives. Perhaps the reason that bureaucracies and bureaucrats are so unpopular takes root in the combination of the amount of discretion that individual bureaucrats have over so many facets of our lives with the appearance that bureaucrats are unaccountable through democratic procedures.

Who controls bureaucrats' choices to waive a traffic ticket, to extend a welfare mother's eligibility, to devote overtime to completing a report, to play computer games at the office for hours on end, to physically threaten or abuse a motorist, or to ignore an abusive parent's harsh treatment of a child? The accountability of unelected bureaucrats in a democracy depends on an answer to this question: who, or what, controls the choices bureaucrats make to work, to shirk, or to sabotage public policy? Our book offers one answer: bureaucratic accountability depends most of all on the preferences of individual bureaucrats. Fortunately for us, those preferences are overwhelmingly consistent with the jobs the American democracy sets for them to do.

Without a doubt, it is entirely appropriate that scholars of a democratic society express considerable concern about the accountability, responsibility, and responsiveness of unelected bureaucrats to democratic publics. Democratic elections facilitate some degree of control over the performance of elected officials, but elected officials do not implement or administer the aspects of the performance of government that affect its citizens directly. Save for some vehicle of democratic control over the decisions of bureaucrats, we cannot have democratic *government,* only democratic *elections.*

Issues of bureaucratic accountability have been with us for some time. Practically every president of the twentieth century has in one way or another sought to achieve control over the federal bureaucracy. Theodore Roosevelt convened a committee led by Charles Hallem Keep (his secretary of state) to seek ways to improve government efficiency. Taft had his Commission on Economy and Efficiency, Coolidge his Loyal Order of Woodpeckers, FDR had the Brownlow Committee. Truman, Eisenhower, Nixon, Ford, Carter, Reagan, and Clinton each organized his own separate committees or otherwise aimed to rein in the size of the federal bureaucracy. None has successfully "reinvented government."

Our central premise is that to understand issues of control and oversight *over* an organization (*inter*organizational control), one must understand issues of compliance *within* an organization (*intra*organizational control). Neither Congress nor the President control the administration of policy, if those who implement policy have such wide discretion that they cannot be affected by superiors.

We begin with two theoretical chapters that analyze the incentives, constraints, and choices of individual bureaucrats. The six chapters that follow are devoted to empirical analyses of these issues in federal, state, and local government. This book makes several contributions. We find that supervisors are severely limited in their abilities to influence subordinate behavior. Yet, despite such constrained oversight, bureaucrats for the most part are hard workers, motivated principally by what we will call "functional" preferences, the extent to which bureaucrats feel rewarded by performing their job duties well. Finally, this book provides an understanding of how bureaucracy responds to a democratic public, arguing that the most important means of control is through the norm of professionalism.

We are hardly alone in our study of the problem of democratic control over unelected bureaucrats. Questions of control over bureaucracy attract considerable attention from scholars working in a diverse set of fields. Political scientists and economists contribute to our understanding by turning our focus to the institutions and procedures that render bureaucratic decisions accountable to elected officials. The enterprise has been part theoretical and part empirical.

In order to understand the importance of learning who, or what, controls the performance of individual bureaucrats, we want to draw attention to what is missing in this extensive scholarship. We turn first to the contributions from the theory of organizations and public administration, and then to those from the formal theory of the firm. The relevant literatures are gargantuan. Our purpose here is to extract what we find to be the central theoretical insights and empirical results, in order to explain why new research must examine the behavior of individual bureaucrats with the tools of contemporary economics. We see four points that emerge across this sprawling intellectual terrain:

- The extent of elected officials' control *over* unelected bureaucrats depends on supervision and monitoring *within* an organization.
- Bureaucrats make political decisions in the implementation of policy, decisions which are affected by their own policy preferences.
- Despite significant efforts to constrain bureaucratic choices, bureaucrats possess significant degrees of discretion.
- There are four potential sources of influence over a bureaucrat's choices to work, shirk, or sabotage: the bureaucrat's own preferences, peer bureaucrats, supervisors, and the bureaucrat's clients.

We turn to the first of the two significant scholarly approaches, in public administration and the theory of organizations. Our treatment is historical, proceeding from the early days of scientific management, to the human relations school, to more recent work focusing on bureaucratic discretion.

Public Administration and the Theory of Organizations

Woodrow Wilson argued in an 1887 essay that public administration constitutes a professional field and a worthy subject of scholarly analysis. As Wilson
put it,

> Administration is the most obvious part of government; it is government
> in action; it is the executive, the operative, the most visible side of govern-
> ment, and is of course as old as government itself. (198)

Underlying his views of the "science of administration" was the belief that
governmental bureaucracy could and should lie "outside the sphere of *politics*" (210). That is, Wilson advocated a bureaucracy independent of the narrow interests of elected officials, while "public opinion shall play the part of
authoritative critic" (214).

These two themes of Wilson's essay—the need for professional administration and the need for a bureaucracy accountable to the public—are echoed
over a hundred years later. In the midst of widespread civil service reform in
late-nineteenth-century America, Wilson called for a professional, independent, but broadly accountable bureaucracy. While scholars today dispense
with Wilson's notion of a policy-neutral bureaucracy, these two issues remain
salient and fundamental. Are bureaucrats accountable? Are bureaucrats responsive? What role does professionalism play? Who ultimately controls the
choices bureaucrats make? From the very beginning of study of administration, one paramount concern has been interorganizational control: the extent
to which the institutions of democracy are able to control administrative decisions.

One of Wilson's most important points—that politics and administration
are separate enterprises—was more systematically detailed in Frank Goodnow's *Politics and Administration* (1900). Goodnow distinguished between
elective government, where democracy debated political questions involving
"the will of the state," and the professional government, which exercised all
the duties of government outside of the legislature and the judiciary, "execut-
ing the will of the state" (17).

Across the Atlantic, similar scholarly argument for the distinction between
politics and administration blossomed. In the unification of Germany in the
late nineteenth century and nearly concomitant establishment of the first European welfare state, Max Weber feared the spread of "dilettantism" by amateur
politicians. Instead, Weber argued forcefully for career bureaucrats who would
follow explicit rules, strict career paths, limited jurisdictions, and clear hierarchies. For Weber, rationally specified organization was the means to ensure
efficient administration accountable to its superiors.

The arguments from Wilson, Goodnow, and Weber intending to separate the business of government from the politics of government were not idle. In the wake of the Progressive Movement, the beginnings of an expanded role for federal government, and the Pendleton Act creating a professional civil service, the meaning of the distinction between politics and administration is an argument for neutral execution of policy, unfettered by corrupt political machines and the patronage system. Professional bureaucracies could act more responsibly than bureaucracies under the control of political machines, and they could make decisions about the implementation of policy more on the basis of the merits of the case than on the political advantages of the advocates. Bureaucratic discretion enables the possibility of professional, responsible behavior.

The Scientific Management School

Business also turned to principles of rational organization and execution. The beginnings of organization theory sprouted not long after Wilson called for professional public administration, in a series of works focusing on issues of management. In particular, Frederick Taylor, Henri Fayol, and Luther Gulick, over a span of three decades, contributed to what is now thought of as a "scientific management" school. Their unit of analysis was principally the firm, not the public bureaucracy,[1] but there are many important echoes between the original scholarship and more contemporary applications. As will be the case with both the approaches of organization theory and economics of the firm, the unit of analysis crosses back and forth from the private to the public sector. As we will show, one of the central problems in the extant literature may be in thinking about public sector employees as if they were motivated by the same things or constrained to the same set of choices as private sector employees. This question, in turn, then has implications for bureaucratic accountability. Efforts to control the actions of public bureaucrats have often drawn from studies and experiences in the private sector.

Taylor (1911) coined the term *scientific management* to refer to a set of principles for redesigning more efficient industries. There was no "plan" or "device" that Taylor would willingly label as "scientific management," but instead a series of loose maxims. First among these was the need for better study and measurement of the inefficiencies of the workplace. The most "scientific" element of scientific management became its most visible stereotype in the form of time and motion specialists (Palmer 1985). The second of the principles was to manage the selection and training of workers such that they would be "able to do a better and still better class of work than ever before" (74). The third was to institute better coordination of the skills of the workforce through

---

1. Gulick is the exception here. Much of his work and career focused on reforming public bureaucracy.

both incentives and strict rules. In later scholarship, the focus on the recruiting of the workers would become a concern over "adverse selection," while the development of appropriate incentives and rules would parallel concerns over "moral hazard."[2]

Although Taylor may be credited as the father of scientific management, subsequent arguments by Henri Fayol and Luther Gulick were instrumental in the development of schools of management. Fayol (1949, 1916) outlined some fourteen different principles of management invoking clear chains of command, responsibility, remuneration, and incentives. Gulick (1937) is perhaps most famous for coining the acronym "POSDCORB" to denote Planning, Organizing, Staffing, Directing, Co-Ordinating, Reporting, and Budgeting. By the end of the 1930s and until the mid-1940s, the scholarship of organizations and firms emphasized strict principles and rules for guiding employers and employees.

Although the scientific management school turned its explicit scrutiny to the management of firms, there are several important indications that public bureaucracies would be examined under similar lenses. Published posthumously (1922), Weber's abstraction of the characteristics of the "ideal-type" bureaucracy outlined a series of principles that continue to be useful in identifying the traits of bureaucracy, among them that bureaucracies consist of appointed officials with well-defined jurisdictions, operating under clear rules, within hierarchies of supervision. Taylor and Gulick were also often asked to address issues of public sector management with obvious implications of developing an efficient and productive governmental bureaucracy.

Scientific management approaches engendered significant opposition from nascent union activity, particularly in the private sector (Palmer 1985). Although Taylor himself went to great pains to describe his philosophy of management as one which listened to workers, its implementation was harsh. With the growth of labor unions in the 1930s, the prospect of management by command withered. While this approach lost favor at this time, some of the general principles are still seen today. We still hear echoes of scientific management in the calls for efficient and productive government. In turn, these principles still have implications when thinking about control and oversight of the bureaucracy. In fact, the ideas of the extent of a supervisor's ability to observe subordinate behavior, the problems that supervisors may face in selecting their employees, and the appropriate means for structuring incentives speak directly to ideas that appear decades later in the economics of the firm. One poten-

---

2. Adverse selection and moral hazard problems both describe situations of asymmetric information. Adverse selection focuses on a principal not knowing the ability of an agent, a hidden information problem. Moral hazard, on the other hand, stresses hidden action, an inability to know an agent's effort.

tial source of intraorganizational control—as both the scientific management school and the later principal–agent approaches attest—will be the supervisor and the supervisory chain of command.

The Human Relations School of Management

Supervisors are only one of the potential influences over subordinate discretion. The subordinate's own preferences about performance matter, too. As Mary Parker Follett (1926) put it, "the shrewd common sense of many a business executive has shown him that the issuing of orders is surrounded by many difficulties; that to demand an unquestioning obedience to orders not approved, not perhaps even understood, is bad business policy" (150). Scientific management bred skeptics, scholars of management who called for more cooperative views of the workplace.

Foremost of these scholars was Chester Barnard. Barnard's *The Functions of the Executive* (1938) described all organizations as cooperative, even to the extent that the coercive power of management was a "fiction." All supervisory power in organizations was cooperative, in that subordinates had to accept the authority of supervisors as legitimate. The practical effect of Barnard's urging was to spawn the so-called human relations school of management. Instead of time and motion analysis, management science turned to ways to consider boosting employee morale. Yet for all the activity devoted towards human relations management from the 1930s through the 1960s, scholars could only martial the weakest evidence demonstrating a connection between morale and greater productivity and efficiency.[3] Expressed in the terms we have been using so far in this chapter, Barnard denied the possibility of intraorganizational control through the coercive power of management. Even in the workplace, subordinates maintain variable "zones of acceptance," where choices about allocation of effort depend in part upon the preferences of the subordinate.

The seeds of similar debates about the control of bureaucracies sprouted at much the same time. If control over bureaucracy couldn't be obtained through coercive management, then through what means could it be? One of the most prominent debates in public administration occurred nearly contemporaneously with Barnard's arguments about the "fiction" of the coercive power of management, addressing the question of interorganizational control. Carl Friedrich (1941) contended that the responsibility of administration could best be guaranteed by professionalism, norms and standards for bureaucrats' performance, enforced internally. Modern government required administrators to perform increasingly specialized tasks, with greater levels of expertise.

---

3. See Perrow (1972), chapter 3, for an extensive review.

Inexpert legislators, lacking specialized information about the tasks of government, were ill equipped to oversee the decisions of bureaucrats. Herman Finer (1941) quickly retorted that legislative controls were the only means to ensure responsible performance by bureaucrats, since without external controls, internal controls inexorably led to consolidation of corrupt power. Put in the terms that we have been using throughout this chapter, Friedrich argued that intraorganizational control offered the best means for assuring the responsible performance of bureaucracy, whereas Finer insisted that bureaucracies had to be responsive to external, or interorganizational, control.

One aspect of Barnard's work that had a particularly lasting effect upon later scholarship was his skepticism about the rational aspects of scientific management. Two common features characterize the early (before Barnard) theorizing about organizations: a strong tendency to develop rules for administration, and an ultimate belief in the ability of rational individuals to make comprehensive decisions. Herbert Simon and his many colleagues challenged both. In his enormously influential essay "The Proverbs of Administration" (1946), Simon contended that each of the central recommendations of the scientific management approaches was not only in contradiction with another of the central recommendations, but potentially internally contradictory as well. The four nominal "principles" were that one could increase the efficiency of administration by increasing specialization; structuring determinate hierarchies of authority; limiting the span of control for any single position in the hierarchy; and grouping subordinates by one of "purpose, process, clientele or place" (53). At the same time that one increases specialization by clientele (say, with a public health plan assigned to particular public schools), one decreases specialization by function (by requiring the nurses in each school to be capable of diagnosing across multiple illnesses). For each level of additional specialization, superiors must delegate authority to subordinates.[4]

The second significant challenge from Simon and colleagues was the argument that the level of rationality required by the scientific management approaches exceeded what humans could or would do. Simon argued that instead of a comprehensive sweep of the alternatives and a deliberative assessment of their utility, human decision makers would adopt more limited rules for decision making in the form of "bounded rationality" through such mechanisms as "satisficing." Simon's work became enormously influential in the theory of organizations, turning scholarship away from thinking about how to construct rational organizations and toward the decision making of individual members

4. Hammond (1990) provides a spirited defense of Gulick, Simon's principal target in the article. Hammond contends that Simon builds many straw targets from Gulick's principles, and that Gulick was far more aware of conflicting pressures in organizational design than Simon acknowledged.

of the organization. Steadily, organization theorists rejected key elements of "procedural rationality": whether individuals comprehensively assessed the alternatives (Simon's satisficing argument); whether an organization's "goal" could be described as any more explicit than an "aspiration" (Cyert and March 1963); whether individuals would make disproportionately lopsided evaluations of risk or gain (Kahneman and Tversky 1979); and whether decisions themselves were more than mere loose couplings of "problems" and "solutions" (Cohen, March, and Olsen 1972). Simon's encouragement of a focus on the mechanics of individual decision making significantly affected empirical research on organizations as well. Observational research pointed to exceptional levels of discretion for individual members of the bureaucracy. Such delegation of authority has obvious implications for determining to what degree and how governmental bureaucracy is accountable.

Bureaucratic Discretion

Simon's arguments about administrative behavior, although relaxing the informational and cognitive constraints of individuals within bureaucracy, fundamentally still implied a professional, neutral system of government. Beliefs about the separation of politics from administration weakened considerably in the postwar years.

Just two years after Simon published *Administrative Behavior,* Norton Long's article "Power and Administration" (1949) demanded that scholars heed the importance of power and the resources to obtain it within administrations. Administrations were always political, and "attempts to solve administrative problems in isolation from the structure of power and purpose in the polity are bound to prove illusory" (226). Administrators need resources in order to implement policies. To secure these resources they must communicate policy ideas to legislators and promote policy among the public.

Scholars not only found that bureaucrats had policy preferences and needs for resources to secure implementation, but bureaucrats' preferences might lead them to significantly alter their behavior from what their superiors in the bureaucratic hierarchy might prefer them to do. Herbert Kaufman's *The Forest Ranger* (1960) might be marked as the beginning of a series of important books on the importance of bureaucratic discretion. Forest rangers are members of the federal bureaucracy, as agents of the United States Forest Service, a bureau of the Department of Agriculture. At the time of Kaufman's study, forest rangers were perhaps unique in the degree to which the Forest Service bureaucracy was so dispersed and decentralized. Their job required juggling the preferences of multiple constituencies: ranchers who wanted to graze their cattle on federal lands, timber industries that harvested trees, miners who extracted ore, conservationists who wanted to maintain ecosystems, and members of the general public who sought recreation. The forest rangers' decisions happened away from the scrutiny of the central Washington hierarchy of the Forest Service. The "tendencies to fragmentation" were powerful and pervasive.

Yet forest rangers and the Forest Service exhibited a remarkable degree of cohesiveness and a striking accomplishment of their central purposes. Instead of the ordinary tools of management, Kaufman suggests that success comes as the result of strong selection criteria, pressures to conform among fellow rangers, and improved communications between and among the central offices and the rangers in the field. While, after several reforms in the Forest Service, there is now less of a tendency toward extreme decentralization, the pattern of bureaucratic discretion and the factors that lead to broad conformity persist. Indeed, in our analysis presented in subsequent chapters these factors are identified as important to a variety of governmental bureaucracies.

Hugh Heclo's *A Government of Strangers* (1977) yields a less optimistic picture of the potential for central control, whatever the mechanism. The conflict between career civil servants and political executives undermines many presidents' ambitions to retrain and redirect the activities of the federal bureaucracy. Civil servants have not only extensive protections from political influence over their careers, but also many more subtle advantages. Civil servants, by virtue of their extended tenure, are better informed about who has what preferences, what regulations and bills are in the pipeline, where the key resources and individuals reside. The result can be that the political executives "go native" and adopt the mission, perhaps even the preferences, of the careerists. Successful management is possible, but only when

> they learn that political leadership in the Washington bureaucracy is not a task for martinets or presiding officers. For those both tough and sensitive enough, it is a job of managing a pluralistic, changing consensus with limited strategic resources. (233)

Michael Lipsky's *Street Level Bureaucracy* (1980) urged scholars to attend to the significant policy-making capacities of bureaucrats on the front lines. Teachers, police officers, social workers, judges, health workers, and so forth constitute what Lipsky termed "street-level bureaucrats": "Public service workers who interact directly with citizens in the course of their jobs, and who have substantial discretion in the execution of their work. . ." (3).

Beyond the difficulties of monitoring, the challenge for control of the behavior of the street-level bureaucrat is that many of the public service workers are protected by civil service codes preventing managers from wielding benefits or dispensing sanctions. There are formal sanctions, which are costly to managers and workers alike, but these are rarely used. This has important implications for the central question of our book: given this level of discretion, to whom are bureaucrats accountable?

Martha Feldman's *Order Without Design* (1989) looked at the behavior of policy analysts working for the Department of Energy. The task of the policy analysts was to write policy memos which ultimately would never be read.

> Yet, at the same time, I saw these analysts working hard to produce the information they claimed would be ignored. They worked late nights and weekends. They poured energy into deliberations and negotiations with analysts in other offices. They spent hours gathering information and analyzing it. They became angry when their contributions to a report were overlooked by those in charge of producing the report. (1)

The seemingly irrational behavior on the part of the analysts—working such long and strenuous hours for nonexistent material rewards—is one of the central puzzles for her book. One result is quite clear: memo-writing bureaucracies *must* prepare memos even though there is a high probability that they will not come to immediate use. These bureaus work like a library; if someone had to write the memo every time that a policymaker required policy information the delays would be enormous. Not only do these policy analysts have exceptional discretion in writing their memos, they exercise it in the only way that the bureau could function—motivated by nonpecuniary rewards.

James Q. Wilson's *Bureaucracy* (1989) stands alone in its comprehensiveness. Wilson's book sweeps its analysis over multiple bureaus, multiple levels of government, varied potential sources of institutional control, and competing standards for performance, sending many messages to scholars of bureaucracy. One is an explicit rejection of the idea of "top-down" management of bureaucracy, a message shared by this book. Supervisors at all levels of public bureaucracies face constraints not dreamed of by managers in private firms. Production in public bureaucracies nearly always differs from production in private firms, not just in the form of the goods produced (which is not always material, and may often be a public good), but in the competing standards for what comprises "efficient" production.

A second message is that bureaucracies are best defined by "tasks," the things that bureaucrats learn to do, rather than abstract, often internally contradictory goals. It is difficult to provide much precision behind an organizational goal such as to "promote the long-range security and interests of the United States" (32), the goal of the State Department. But bureaucrats in the State Department do many things, and these tasks are shaped by a process of trial and error in a sometimes competitive environment. "People matter, but organization matters also, and tasks matter most of all" (173).

Two implications of the bureaucratic discretion school stand out. First, it is largely meaningless to think of agencies as organizations under centralized control. The bureaucrats studied by Kaufman, Heclo, Lipsky, Feldman, and Wilson exercise wide latitude over policy. Discretion comes into play throughout the many stages of the policy-making process. One locus of discretion over policy is at the implementation level. Congressional policy-making is only the beginning of the implementation of policy, where significant specification and choices about allocation of resources will remain to be developed by bureaucrats. Indeed, part of the process of delegation must be not just delegation of the enforcement or implementation of specific statutory guidelines, but development of those guidelines themselves. A second locus of discretion over policy is at the application or enforcement stage. The law may be quite unambiguous, but application of the law still involves bureaucratic discretion. Many of our readers must have been the beneficiaries of police discretion over minor traffic violations (and some of us may have wished we were). Social workers must determine in the field whether their clients continue to remain eligible for benefits under income or health guidelines. Fundamentally, interorganizational control over a bureaucracy depends on the extent to which superiors within that bureaucracy maintain intraorganizational control.

The second implication is that it is also largely meaningless to think of bureaucracies as unitary actors with homogeneous preferences. To the extent that bureaucrats hold heterogeneous preferences among themselves and wield significant degrees of discretion about how to achieve those preferences, agencies will never behave as a cohesive unit. This has extremely important implications for understanding bureaucratic accountability. To understand issues of accountability, responsiveness, oversight, and control, we must focus our analysis on individual bureaucrats rather than aggregated bureaus.

But this first tradition of bureaucratic theory and research (public administration and organization theory) also leaves many unresolved issues. Simon's arguments against comprehensive rational choice as the model of bureaucratic behavior opened Pandora's box. We have no consensus about the nature of bureaucratic choice. As organization theorists dispense with element after element of the rational choice approach, no competing paradigm or approach stands in its place.[5] Agreement on a common currency for modeling bureaucratic behavior not only facilitates comparison of theoretical models, it may virtually be a requirement for empirical evaluation of those models.

The limited rationality arguments by Simon and subsequent organization theorists set up at least one straw target. While "rational behavior" of the time

---

5. Simon's arguments for a conception of bounded rationality, or subsequent attempts at formulating "nonrational" or "cybernetic" models of behavior (e.g., Steinbruner 1974), might be considered to represent alternative paradigms for models of organizations. But evidence of a consistent shift in conceptions of the organization was nonexistent even in the heyday of such models in the late 1970s (Kinder and Weiss 1979).

of Simon's original work on bounded rationality may have implied needs for full information and careful calculation, rational choice modeling in the subsequent years need not make such strong demands. In fact, the most important recent research in the economic theory of the firm explicitly notes that the supervisors (or principals) and subordinates (or agents) have asymmetric possession of information. Agents know their own abilities and preferences, and they conceal this information from principals. It is to this second literature, the economics of the firm and other rational choice models, that we now turn to examine our central question: who or what controls the choices made by bureaucrats?

Economics of the Firm and Other Rational Choice Models

Economists may have arrived late in the literature exploring bureaucratic accountability but had considerable impact and insight once they did. Five works are especially relevant: Anthony Downs's *Inside Bureaucracy* (1967), Armen Alchian and Harold Demsetz's "Production, Information Costs, and Economic Organization" (1972), William Niskanen's *Bureaucracy and Representative Government* (1971), Oliver Williamson's *Markets and Hierarchies* (1975, 1983), and the broader body of principal–agent literature.[6]

Downs's *Inside Bureaucracy* (1967) is a sprawling theoretical enterprise exploring multiple facets of how bureaucracies work. For purposes of understanding how democracies might control bureaucracies, two major contributions stand out: that bureaucratic officials may have widely varying preferences, and that a bureaucracy's failure to accomplish specific formal goals arises from those varying preferences. Downs describes five bureaucratic types. Two of the types behave in a purely self-interested way: *climbers* maximizing their own power and prestige, and *conservers* aspiring only to maintain their current power and prestige. Three of the types mix their own self-interested motives with "altruistic loyalty to larger values" (88): *zealots* who are loyal to particular narrow policies, *advocates* who are loyal to broader policies or organizations, and *statesmen* who are loyal to society as a whole. Diverging preferences, along with differential information and differential perceptions of reality and uncertainty, are reasons for conflict within bureaus.

Because the preferences of bureaucrats are so varied, and because bureaucracies must delegate discretion to officials further down the hierarchy, the performance of subordinate officials will not be precisely what the supervisor intends. The result is a "leakage of authority" (134). One of the consequences of the leakage of authority is that

---

6. We make reference to others who fall under these five groupings below.

in any large, multi-level bureau, a very significant portion of all the activity being carried out is completely unrelated to the bureau's formal goals, or even to the goals of its topmost officials. (136)

Downs's contributions to the study of bureaucracies are significant, but the work leaves new questions. If self-interested preferences of bureaucrats lead to bureaucratic inefficiency and an inability to control, why not simply hire the appropriate mix of "mixed-motive" bureaucrats (zealots, advocates, statesmen)? If self-interested action dominates the pool of potential bureaucrats, why do we have bureaucracies that achieve any policy goals at all? In turn, how do the preference orientations of individual bureaucrats affect their responsiveness to supervision, or to other political actors or factors?

Alchian and Demsetz's article "Production, Information Costs, and Economic Organization" (1972) offers an answer to the first question but it compounds the second.[7] Alchian and Demsetz consider the firm, not bureaucracies per se, but their findings are significant. Their insight was that firms have internal markets for labor and cannot simply expect action from subordinates by command:

It is common to see the firm characterized by the power to settle issues by fiat, by authority, or by disciplinary action superior to that available in the conventional market. This is delusion. The firm does not own all its inputs. It has no power of fiat, no authority, no disciplinary action any different in the slightest degree from ordinary market contracting between any two people. (777)

They also note that the utility function of any subordinate will be composed of both higher income (pecuniary goals) and leisure (any nonpecuniary goals).[8] Since the subordinates' "relaxation cannot be detected perfectly at zero cost" (780), there will always be some shirking. Firms must then ponder the relative

---

7. Ronald Coase's economic analysis of property rights precipitated the economic theory of the firm and played an explicit role in shaping Alchian and Demsetz's argument. Coase's (1937) article established the importance of transaction costs in understanding the emergence of the firm, although the primary focus of that article was on the role of the firm in the market. The conclusion to that article raised the problem of internal organization with respect to the difference between "agents" and "servants," wherein an agent maintains a degree of freedom in carrying out employment. Alchian and Demsetz, in many important ways, begin from this observation in their explicit concern for the design of internal labor contracts.

8. Note here that policy goals may then be part of the subordinates' utility function. Downs's mixed-motive officials acquire utility by accomplishing policy objectives. For purposes of the mathematics of the firm, we will argue that confounding different nonpecuniary goals as a single form of "leisure" leads to serious mistakes in understanding bureaucratic behavior.

gains in efficiency under different remuneration schemes. Since every subordinate derives some utility from shirking, it is impossible to staff a firm, or a bureaucracy, solely with policy-driven automatons.

Every limit on the disciplinary power and monitoring capabilities of the supervisor in the firm holds, and doubly so, for the supervisor in a public bureaucracy. For one, subordinate bureaucrats typically have far more strenuous protections against supervisory discipline than do private employees. Beginning with the Pendleton Act of 1883 and subsequent reforms in 1908 and 1923, civil servants in the federal bureaucracy earn tenure and are outside of direct political control. For another, bureaucracies' policy accomplishments may be harder to monitor than production within a firm. It is difficult (not impossible) to come up with a public bureaucracy's equivalent to piece rates in the firm.[9]

William Niskanen's *Bureaucracy and Representative Government* (1971) provided the first positive theory of supply by bureaucracies. In the language and focus of economics, Niskanen asks "What budget and output behavior should be expected of bureaus under different conditions?" (9). If one thinks about bureaucracies as providing services or goods on the basis of a publicly funded budget, then it is entirely appropriate to ask about the relationship between what citizens pay (the budget) and what they receive from bureaucracies.

Niskanen's bureaucrats are primarily motivated by budget.

> Among the several variables that may enter the bureaucrat's utility function are the following: salary, perquisites of the office, public recognition, power, patronage, output of the bureau, ease of making changes, and ease of managing the bureau. All of these variables except the last two, I contend, are a positive monotonic function of the total *budget* of the bureau during the bureaucrat's tenure in office. (38)

Save for competition between bureaus to provide services, bureaucracies are monopoly suppliers prone to oversupply of output. Bureaucracies, in league with high-demand committees, capture Congress, compelling Congress to dispense essentially anything that the bureaucrats want.[10] Clearly, the implication is a runaway bureaucracy unaccountable to the broader public.

Two different groups of scholars challenge Niskanen. One group ques-

---

9. An example of an equivalent to piece rates illustrates the monitoring difficulties. One could pay police officers by the number of tickets they write. But remunerating police officers by the ticket sets up incentives for officers to overenforce the law. On the other hand, some municipalities use private parking meter services who pay piece rate. There is nothing that inherently precludes a public bureaucracy from adopting this practice.

10. Migué and Bélanger (1974) focus on the discretionary aspects of the budget as bureaucrats want to maximize their discretionary abilities. Niskanen (1975) concedes this point.

tions the reasonability of the budget-maximizing assumption. Subordinate bureaucrats typically exercise little control over their own budgets. At best, agency chiefs argue for incremental increases in budgets, and are severely constrained as maximizers (Aberbach et al. 1981). Further, in describing the day-to-day policy choices by bureaucrats, nonpecuniary returns may matter more and are not constrained in the same way by budgets (Campbell and Naulls 1991). Blais and Dion (1991) conclude that there is evidence for budget-boosting activity, but individual bureaucrats are not budget-maximizers per se.

A second group of scholars questions the extent to which bureaucracies dominate congressional decisions. Miller and Moe (1983) persuasively demonstrate that Congress has the ability to organize the budgetary process in a number of ways. They present a model demonstrating that bureaucratic organization does not necessarily lead to oversupply.[11] In a seminal paper, Mc-Cubbins and Schwartz (1984) argue that oversight committees construct "fire alarms" that enable interest groups and active citizens to monitor the activities of bureaucratic agencies. Congressional committees have both ex ante controls (such as the Administrative Procedures Act, notice and comment rule making, or even the appointments process) and ex post sanctions (such as budgetary executions).[12]

Economics also contributed to our understanding of organizations through the body of work focusing on transaction costs. In particular, Oliver Williamson (1975, 1983) provides a very important elaboration of the problems of internal and external market uncertainty. Many insights from Williamson's book on the firm extend to the public bureaucracy. Williamson noted that the idiosyncrasies of different tasks within a producing firm lead to internal labor transaction costs. Different tasks involve idiosyncrasies where the subordinate who is familiar with those idiosyncrasies becomes more productive than the subordinate who is not. Operating machinery, for example, leads a worker to become familiar with the symptoms of the machine overheating or beginning to show signs of wear. One can easily imagine similar task idiosyncrasies in public bureaucracies: regulators who understand the ways in which polluting firms disguise their transmissions of toxins, police officers who have a sense of when community tensions are peaking, or social workers who are personally familiar with the work records of their clients.

Task idiosyncrasies cause informational asymmetries not only with respect to the employer and employee, but also between employees. Supervi-

---

11. See Bendor, Taylor, and Van Gaalen (1985, 1987) for a more thorough extension of this conflict between Congress and the bureaucracy through the use of two-sided asymmetric information games.

12. For more on the issue of oversight and regulation see Fiorina (1981), Hill (1985), Mc-Cubbins, Noll, and Weingast (1987, 1989), Aberbach (1990), as well as Lupia and McCubbins (1992).

sors, due to their limited familiarity with these task idiosyncrasies and their limited time, cannot always know when subordinates are productive and when they are shirking. Furthermore, subordinates may not always share information about task idiosyncrasies, since this special knowledge is what separates their performance from the pool of outside, reserve labor. Task idiosyncrasies produce a distinction between perfunctory and consummate cooperation, where perfunctory cooperation simply means performing at a minimally acceptable level, and consummate cooperation means that the subordinate exploits his or her knowledge of the task idiosyncrasies to maximize his or her productivity.

Williamson forcefully argues that contractual schemes cannot ensure more than perfunctory cooperation. Instead, Willliamson argues for rewarding cooperation by use of internal incentives separate from collective wage bargaining, specifically, the use of internal promotion. These tools may not be readily malleable to the supervisor in a public bureaucracy. As we will show in chapter 4, supervisors in public bureaucracies are highly constrained in their abilities to use internal ratings and internal promotions.

Two concepts originating in the insurance industry now play a central role in a growing body of scholarly work on organizational compliance. These are the ideas of moral hazard (hidden actions) and adverse selection (hidden information). These two types of asymmetric information play a fundamental role in principal–agent relationships. The central problem analyzed in such models is that a principal is unable to monitor the agent's actions and information. Subordinate effort is difficult to monitor; interdependence of workers in a team can make it nearly impossible to identify who is responsible for what, or random factors that affect production can obscure an individual's effort. Similarly, in conveying information to a principal, an agent may have an incentive to misrepresent or disguise his or her report. Principal–agent models often are oriented toward designing an incentive mechanism that will lead to hard work or honest conveyance of information.[13]

Holmström (1982) demonstrates, however, that an incentive scheme that could effectively induce all to work and none to shirk would be too expensive; such a budget-balancing incentive system is impossible. Groves (1985) similarly demonstrates that there is no budget-balancing revenue-sharing scheme that can effectively induce agents to honestly and accurately report information to the principal.

Several solutions have been offered to solve these two problems. Bianco

---

13. The first application of these ideas to organizations is hard to pinpoint. Many people were working on similar problems concurrently. Ross (1973) and Mitnick (1973) discuss the role of moral hazard in organizations. Hurwicz (1973) in the meantime was modeling incentive-compatibility problems, while Groves (1973) and Groves and Ledyard (1977) were developing our understanding of incentive compatibility mechanisms (first as it applied to public goods). Arrow (1985) provides a nice review of the application of these concepts to organizations.

and Bates (1990) focus on the role of managers as leaders to induce compliance among agents in an environment with repeated contact between principals and agents. Compliance and conformity among subordinates varies with the capabilities of the leader in this model. Kreps (1990) also looks at developing an enforceable contract designed to overcome the problems described by Holmström and Groves. Kreps demonstrates in his Trust–Honor game that under iterative conditions, there are too many equilibria in the game played between a principal and an agent to provide any guide for choosing between different outcomes.[14] Kreps turns to the concept of the focal point to get around the ambiguity of multiple equilibria. From a game theoretic perspective, organizational culture offers a set of principles for dealing with unforeseen contingencies and establishes a code of conduct between supervisors (principals) and subordinates (agents). Miller (1992) extends this analysis by specifically examining organizational cultures and conventions. "It is this psychological network of reinforcing expectations that make one perfectly feasible outcome (e.g., cooperation) occur instead of another perfectly feasible outcome (e.g., non-cooperation)" (207). Different organizational cultures lead to a variety of relationships between subordinates and supervisors, which in turn produce "functional" or "dysfunctional organizational sociologies."

First Kreps's and then Miller's work on the Trust–Honor game demonstrates how some of the key concepts developed in the first body of literature on organization theory can be analyzed with the rigor that characterizes the second body of literature. We begin to see how the two literatures can be linked. Yet, several insights evident in the first literature remain unaddressed by the second. While Kreps and Miller help us understand how moral hazard and adverse selection problems are overcome through the establishment of a "productive organizational culture," they do not inform us of the specific costs of supervision. Principal–agent models analyze the role of such organizational constraints as budget, but do not address costs and constraints that directly affect individual supervisors. Such restrictions limit the appropriateness of such models for understanding the effectiveness of supervision, particularly in the public sector where there are no residuals to distribute.[15]

Political scientists and economists now devote considerable efforts into deducing the effects of various modes of interorganizational control, most often as the ability of Congress to constrain the performance of bureaucratic agencies. A recent book by Kiewiet and McCubbins (1991) presents four ma-

---

14. The plethora of equilibria is shown in the Folk Theorem.

15. By residuals we mean residual returns which can be defined as whatever is left over after all revenues have been collected and all expenses and other contractual obligations have been paid (Milgrom and Roberts 1992: 291). Given this definition it is quite evident that the notion of a residual cannot be effectively applied to a governmental bureaucracy.

jor classes of approaches to solving problems of agency oversight. Congress could design contracts (such as systems of compensation) such that agents are motivated to behave in a way consistent with the principals' interest. Congress could develop selection and screening mechanisms in an attempt to mitigate adverse selection problems. Principals might install monitoring and reporting requirements, either through "police patrols" regularly auditing the performance of bureaucracies, or through "fire alarms" wherein aggrieved clients notify the principals of inappropriate behavior by the agents. Principals might establish institutional checks, requiring a second agent to sign off on the performance of another agent. Each of these methods deals with the coercive powers of supervisors within a bureaucracy, in the form of concerns over hiring and firing (selection), design of compensation (contracts), methods for identifying subordinates' performance (monitoring and institutional checks), or attempts to constrain individual choices (institutional checks). What looks to be a problem of interorganizational control—how Congress relates to agencies—is at base an intraorganizational control problem.

We know that supervisors in public bureaucracies are highly constrained. Two constraints are imposed by the fact of delegation: supervisors cannot know their subordinates' true preferences and abilities (adverse selection), nor can they observe all of the subordinates' actions (moral hazard). Johnson and Libecap (1994) convincingly demonstrate that supervisors at the federal level are further constrained by civil service laws limiting not only the supervisors' ability to sanction inadequate performance, but also to reward superior performance.[16] Most works regarding bureaucratic oversight focus on overcoming moral hazard problems, leading to an emphasis on supervision and oversight.[17] Our book will demonstrate, however, that adverse selection problems are much more important.

Few principal–agent models account for the variation in a single subordinate's disposition to work or shirk within a single organization. Subordinate payoffs are not linked to the production of particular outputs, but rather by a general incentive scheme. By focusing on such universal incentive systems, these models are unable to account for the positive efforts of policy-oriented bureaucrats, social workers with guiding agendas, police officers who honestly prefer to enforce the law, and professors who like to teach. The third problem is related to the second; subordinates can respond to organizational rules in a multitude of ways when producing bureaucratic output. Defection and compliance can take on a variety of forms, ranging from "go slow" to sabotage to even

---

16. The strictures of civil service laws came to dominate supervision in the federal bureaucracy, in their argument, due to the growth of federal employees as an interest group.

17. Calvert, McCubbins, and Weingast (1989) is one of the exceptions where incomplete information (or adverse selection problems) are the focus.

working to the rule to such an extent that it works against the intended policy. We will demonstrate that supervisors face additional constraints, and that the constraints we identify are much more imposing limitations on the ability of supervisors to coerce performance from subordinates.

Furthermore, these economic approaches (with the exception of Downs) proceed from the assumption that agents and principals differ in preferences. The differences may be in the magnitude of the budget, a desire for different policy goals, or in maximizing leisure, but as Kiewiet and McCubbins put it,

> There is almost always some conflict between the interests of those who delegate authority (principals) and the agents to whom they delegate it. Agents behave opportunistically, pursuing their own interests subject only to the constraints imposed by their relationship with the principal. The opportunism that generates agency losses is a ubiquitous feature of the human experience. It crops up whenever workers are hired, committees are appointed, property is rented, or money is loaned. The message that we are all reckless agents of a Divine Principal is at the very heart of Judeo-Christian theology. (5)

An assumption of divergent preferences, even when cloaked in theological robes, constitutes neither a demonstration of the presence of those differing preferences, nor proof that those preferences are consequential. We will demonstrate that the very best explanation for why some bureaucrats work and others don't is that many bureaucrats share the principal's preferences.

Integrating Two Literatures

At the end of the two literatures' treatment of the problem of bureaucratic control, we are left with many puzzles. What do bureaucrats maximize? Is it leisure, budget, pecuniary rewards, or policy goals? How do bureaucrats maximize? Who influences bureaucrats' choices? Is it the supervisor, the fellow bureaucrat, the clientele, political leaders, or the bureaucratic environment? How do these actors influence bureaucrats? Is it by wielding sanctions and rewards, appointments, budgetary control, or by constricting the flow of information? What role does professionalism play?

By uniting these two disparate approaches to the study of bureaucracy we can begin to answer these questions. We explicitly attempt to integrate aspects of the public administration and organization theory approach with the economics of the firm and general rational choice perspectives. Our book directly relates the insights of these two literatures to the specific domain of the behavior of individual bureaucrats. By combining formal theoretical techniques with statistical and computer modeling, we aim to provide a theoretical and empirical understanding of bureaucracy.

Our book argues that we can go a long way toward integrating the two theoretical perspectives and toward understanding the problem of bureaucratic control by answering a deceptively simple question: *Who, or what, controls the policy choices of bureaucrats?* It is deceptively simple, because what one means by "bureaucrats," "control," and "who" or "what" can mean many different things.

The dominant image of a "bureaucrat" is a paper pusher (when most are not), residing in Washington or the state capital (when most do not). "Bureaucrats" include police officers, firemen, social workers, forest rangers, game wardens, and a variety of other civil servants who do not fit the stereotype. These are the people who carry out and deliver governmental policy, the "street-level bureaucrats," to borrow Lipsky's term (1980).

Bureaucrats can choose from a variety of policy output decisions, which we label "working," "shirking," and "sabotage." Some bureaucrats devote extraordinary effort toward accomplishing policy ("work"), where others may expend as much effort deliberately undermining the policy objectives of their superiors ("sabotage"). Other bureaucrats may be directing effort towards non-policy goals ("shirking"). In all three instances, the central concern is whether bureaucrats are producing policy as intended by the public.

Control implies some influence by an individual or a set of factors which influences how a bureaucrat chooses to act on a specific policy. Bureaucrats respond to at least four different types of individuals. Management science, and its application by political scientists, suggest that the "whom" refers to the bureaucrat's supervisors at the agency. Bureaucrats also respond to their own initiatives and purposes. (And whether those purposes include a sense of the mission of the organization significantly affects the performance of the agency.) Bureaucrats respond to one another. And bureaucrats respond directly to the public, the "customers" or "clients" they serve.

At the aggregate level, Moe (1982, 1985), Wood (1988, 1991), and Wood and Waterman (1991, 1993, 1994) demonstrate that bureaucratic agencies can be responsive to political principals, whether construed as the Congress or the presidency. How do we reconcile aggregate responsiveness with a literature emphasizing discretion for individual agents, and constraints upon individual supervisors? Our argument in this book is that the basic unit of analysis in the problem of supervision in public bureaucracies is the individual bureaucrat and his or her relationship to potential actors. We will demonstrate that the means by which democratic publics gain responsiveness from agents, and hence agencies, depends upon factors outside traditional conceptions of coercive authority underlying applications of the economics of the firm to public bureaucracies.

Working, Shirking, and Sabotage

In order to address the question *Who, or what, controls the policy choices of bureaucrats?* our book follows in two main sections. First, we develop models that explicitly capture divergent preferences of bureaucrats and their varying responses with respect to a supervisor's administration of sanctions or rewards.

In chapter 2, we develop an "enhanced principal agency" model specifying the relationship between a single supervisor and her bureaucratic agent. The agent divides her efforts at work among three possible forms of activity: working, or devoting energy in order to accomplish the policy goals of the principal; shirking, which may be either leisure-shirking or politically motivated shirking; and sabotage, devoting time at work in order to undermine the policy goals of the principal. The principal faces a constrained optimization problem: how to allocate her resources so as to gain the most from her subordinate.

Our book will not consider all aspects of the supervisor's job. Long ago, Barnard (1938) argued that supervision is a combination of potential functions. Supervisors provide (1) a system of communications, (2) promote securing of essential efforts, and (3) formulate and define purpose (217). The coercive, or administrative,[18] aspect of supervision reflects a supervisor who rewards good workers and punishes inadequate performers. Administrative supervision is, itself, only one means for the first two functions (coordination and persuasion are alternatives). Supervisors can also act as "educators," in helping subordinates to identify more efficient ways to accomplish what is in both of their interests. Supervisors may also provide support, trying to reduce demands on their performance from outsiders, or to boost morale. This book solely considers the "administrative" aspect of supervision, because administrative supervision is the only form that is directly consistent with both principal–agency approaches and the arguments from organization theory.

We measure performance in terms of effort. Our choice to measure performance by effort allows us to skirt some questions of ambiguity of noncompliance. In both the theoretical and empirical sections of this book, we assume that the principal prefers work from the subordinate, and not shirking or sabotage. Our analysis does not directly consider the principal who prefers that a subordinate shirk or sabotage.

---

18. We borrow the terms "administrative," "education," and "support" as modes of supervision from Kadushin (1976).

In chapter 3, we relax several assumptions in the enhanced principal agency approach, turning to the social psychology of organizational compliance in order to develop a model of intersubordinate learning. Political organizations in general and bureaucracies in particular are fundamentally organizations where multiple actors at approximately the same level learn how to respond to policy demands. We turn to two specific heuristics for intersubordinate learning, maintaining behavioral consistency and learning from "like others" under uncertainty. We demonstrate that these heuristics are grounded in both of the traditions of this chapter, in classical theory of organizations and in contemporary economic rationality.

These two theoretical chapters lead to a series of propositions about why subordinate bureaucrats behave the way they do, and who influences them. Our purpose in these theoretical chapters is to set the stage for an empirical study of organizational behavior. In the subsequent six chapters, we unify data on local, state, and federal employees over four different decades of data collection on a common unit of analysis: the behavior of individual bureaucrats.

In chapter 4, we examine attitudes in the federal bureaucracy towards work, accountability, and professionalism. We demonstrate in this chapter that attitudes about professionalism tend to come more from fellow subordinates than from supervisors on the job. Our data in this chapter comes from three different samples of over one hundred thousand respondents in total spanning over three dozen different agencies. There are common threads unifying the diverse work across these different agencies, conditions of a common organizational culture.

Chapter 5 extends the analysis of chapter 4 by examining the factors influencing the level of working and shirking by federal bureaucrats. As Weber argued nearly a century ago, strong conditions of professionalism reduce the threat of subordinate shirking and sabotage. What has but a scant effect on the incidence of shirking in the federal bureaucracy are the particular efforts of supervisors. We again draw on the massive surveys of federal employees in order to demonstrate these claims.

Chapter 6 draws upon our own data on the attitudes and behavior of social workers and case workers in North Carolina. The tasks of social workers and case workers are enormously varied, and often not merely uncomfortable but potentially hazardous. In this chapter, we examine what it is about the activities of supervisors, fellow subordinates, and their "customers" that affects the policy choices of social workers.

Chapter 7 turns to the quintessential "street-level" bureaucrat, the local police officer. Police officers are among the bureaucrats we see on a (nearly) daily basis. In this chapter, we examine the responsiveness of police officers in multiple cities (Chicago, Washington, Boston, St. Louis, Rochester, St.

Petersburg, and Baltimore) under two different dimensions of response: the amount of time that the officer spends shirking and the rapidity of the officer's response to citizen requests for service.

In chapter 8 we take up a form of policy sabotage that has engendered enormous amounts of recent scrutiny by citizens, policy makers, and the press: the incidence of police brutality. After the savage beatings of Rodney King in Los Angeles and Malice Green in Detroit, what many of us may have thought as a problem of an earlier, more divisive era is no longer obviously behind us. Some forms of brutality are physical, as in the use of unnecessary force. Other forms of brutality are nonphysical but may have the effect of subverting the civil rights of suspects: unnecessary searches, ridicule, and threats of violence. In this chapter, we again examine the police officers of multiple cities and decades, examining how professionalism may limit the incidence of policy sabotage.

In chapter 9, we examine a level of bureaucracy that is typically out of reach for the normal citizen, state utility regulators. State utility regulators have to juggle competing claims from industries, unions, interest groups, and citizen activists for appropriate rates and safeguards for those who cannot pay for services. Here, we turn our examination to the perceptions by the utility regulators of the degree to which different groups are influential in the regulators' decisions. This chapter argues for an alternative mechanism for democratic control in the form of citizen and interest group intervention in bureaucratic decisions.

Finally, in chapter 10, we return to questions of accountability of bureaucracies. The theoretical and empirical analysis of the preceding chapters leads to mounting skepticism that bureaucracies can be under the control of their supervisors. If the first link in the chain of command fails, how is control of the behavior of bureaucracies through elected officials even possible? In our concluding chapter, we argue that there are two different mechanisms for successful democratic control: recruitment and direct citizen activity. To understand the foundations of these two mechanisms, we turn to the theoretical aspect of our enterprise.

CHAPTER 2

Why Supervision Fails to Induce Compliance

Hierarchical control is an old problem stalking many domains.[1] How might presidential administrations or congressional oversight committees prod activity from recalcitrant bureaucrats? How do supervisors make and enforce rules successfully? What determines whether a production unit produces efficiently? How do workers learn standard operating procedures? These questions are related by virtue of the decisions by subordinates to work or to shirk, and by a supervisor to make and enforce an order. Recent work illuminates the work/shirk dichotomy and the nature of the supervision game[2] but we believe this literature stops short, leading to an overemphasis of the role of the supervisor and an underemphasis of the capacities of the subordinates. In this chapter we present a model of hierarchical supervision that takes into account varying preferences and responses by subordinates toward supervision, demonstrating circumstances where supervision fails to induce compliance, between a single supervisor and her subordinates.[3]

The central problem examined in the model presented here is that a principal is unable to monitor an agent's information and actions: She cannot reliably ascertain the intelligence, aptitude, values, and beliefs of the would-be employees (adverse selection) and she cannot readily determine that the agent's activities are in her interest (moral hazard). (Throughout this book, when we refer to the abstract "supervisor" or "subordinate," we designate the supervisor (the principal) with feminine pronouns and the subordinate (the agent) with male pronouns. This provides an easy way to clearly differentiate the two actors. It also allows us to avoid the clumsy he/she pronoun.) These models assume that the principal knows what she wants; the problem is getting it. Most principal–agent models focus on devising a feasible incentive scheme in order to induce

---

1. An earlier version of this chapter appeared in *The Journal of Theoretical Politics* 6(3):323–43 (1994).

2. There has been much work along these lines, but we point to two works by political scientists, Bianco and Bates (1990) and Miller (1992).

3. An extension to our treatment here would be to regard the supervisor as a subordinate to her supervisor. The pairwise comparison of supervisor and subordinate clearly antecedes the nested comparison.

the agent to act in the interests of the principal. Since the principal operates under incomplete information, the task of designing such a scheme (or contract) is complicated. The heart of principal–agent models, thus, involves the setting of a wage for an agent without knowing the agent's effort (moral hazard) or ability (adverse selection). We maintain this focus on the issues of moral hazard and adverse selection, in fact we examine both problems in the model presented in this chapter, but we focus on a wider set of motivations than material rewards and punishments.

Works by Miller (1992) and Bianco and Bates (1989) further our understanding of these two problems in many ways. One of the key contributions to our understanding of effective supervision is that a leader may initiate and sustain cooperation by targeting rewards and punishments. This game-theoretic approach permits Bianco and Bates to conclude "the benefits of having a leader must lie in the leader's ability to help followers initiate, not sustain, cooperation" (142). Miller's (1992) extension of Kreps's (1990) Trust–Honor game provides valuable insights into the role organizational culture plays in establishing a code of conduct between supervisors and subordinates.

Nonetheless, we think that even these expanded views of supervision are critically limited. First, the costs and characteristics of supervision surely affect production. Bianco and Bates move well beyond prior principal–agency approaches by distinguishing among the many constraints facing supervisors. The leaders in Bianco and Bates's model come with one of two capacities: a leader who is able to observe every play by the subordinate (an "enhanced" leader), or one who is only able to observe the group (a "limited" leader). This addition of variation in observability of subordinate action is helpful in understanding a supervisor's problem, but cannot help in understanding the effects of other physical constraints on the supervisor's work (such as time or budget) or personal constraints on the supervisor's judgment (such as the ability to distinguish productive from nonproductive work). In this chapter, we offer an approach that takes the costs of supervision and the gradations of supervisory capability into account.

Second, these principal–agency approaches depend on a clarity of actions available to subordinates, typically limited to a work/shirk dichotomy or a one-dimensional scale ranging from complete compliance to complete defection. However, there are many potential responses by a workforce to a disliked rule, from sabotage to "go slow." The range of subordinates' responses to a rule belies the appropriateness of a dichotomy or a one-dimensional scale of work. In fact, one form of defection is complete compliance: working to the rule becomes a form of defection when it removes flexibility.

Third, none of these models accounts for variation in the subordinates' disposition to work or to shirk. They uniformly assume that subordinates prefer to shirk unless bribed by side-payments or residuals to work.[4] Payoffs are tied to maximizing production regardless of what is being produced. Because previous models never explicitly link subordinate payoffs to the production of particular outputs, the capacity to understand the effort of subordinates who like their jobs or have goals favoring production is lost. Unless we acknowledge that some agents may prefer to work, we cannot conceptualize such problems as the efforts of policy-oriented bureaucrats, social workers with guiding agendas, police officers who honestly prefer to enforce the law, or professors who like to teach. To understand what motivates workers we must move beyond simple reward–punishment incentive schemes.[5] We present a model that relaxes such assumptions.

Our new model is grounded in an earlier literature, drawing inspiration from conflicts in early organization theory. The principal–agency models contribute significantly to our understanding of hierarchical control. But the principal–agency tradition forgets work from the early part of the century in both the "efficiency movement" (or scientific management) and "human relations" schools of organization theory. By integrating these literatures (more completely described in the introduction), we can begin to answer the question: *Who, or what, controls the policy choices of bureaucrats?*

Our project unifies the principal–agent and organization theory traditions by formalizing ideas about the constraints of supervisors (from the scientific management school) and the preferences of subordinates (from the human relations school). We offer a new view of supervision, relaxing three assumptions of the aforementioned principal–agent models: (1) supervision demands costly, hence constrained, resources, (2) defection and compliance take on a variety of forms, and (3) subordinates' preferences vary across policies. This model is an enhanced principal–agent game emphasizing the choice of actions available to agents as they produce output and the constraints limiting a supervisor's authority over bureaucrats (the agents). With this chapter we conclude that effective supervision depends on the characteristics of subordinates, not on the characteristics of supervision.

---

4. The notion of residuals is difficult to apply to public bureaucracies as there often is nothing "left-over" to distribute.

5. An extensive set of work has built up arguing that incentives alone fail to alter long-term behavior. See, for example, Freedman et al. (1992), Kohn et al. (1993), Locke et al. (1968), and Pittman et al. (1982).

An Enhanced Principal–Agent Model of Bureaucratic Management

The "Perils of Pauline" might picture the saboteur as a mustachioed man with a detonator, but the term "sabotage" has more pedestrian origins. *Sabots* were the clogs that French weavers would toss into the mechanized looms during industrial crises. Later, among the IWW, sabotage was expressed as the "conscientious withdrawal of efficiency" (Veblen 1921, 1963: 38–39). Indeed, sabotage involves a variety of such maneuvers including delay, hindrance, bungling, and obstruction. Such tactics induce others to devote more work toward the production of a particular output for it to be produced; thus an individual spending time and energy on sabotage activity can be viewed to be engaged in negative work. Utilizing such a definition, it is apparent that sabotage is multifarious and not limited to violent actions. Sabotage is a phenomenon that is evident in a wide variety of environments playing a special role within a variety of organizations ranging from the industrial work place to governmental bureaucracy. Veblen's focus on the "conscientious withdrawal of efficiency" helps us understand supervision by drawing attention to the agents' varying responses and incentives. We, in turn, want to emphasize the importance of why and how agents respond to supervision.

The following model resembles prior principal–agent models, but it differs in several key respects. Principal–agent models tend to emphasize the development of an incentive scheme that induces an agent to work rather than to shirk. Supporting this theme is the central assumption that agents derive positive utility from shirking and negative utility from working. More particularly, such models assume agents' utility is a function of their effort and their income from working. Formally, an agent's utility is defined as:

$$U(I,a) = f(a)V(I) - G(a) \tag{2.1}$$

where $U(I,a)$ is a von Neumann–Morgenstern utility function which depends on both the agent's action, a, and remuneration from the principal I that is additively separable into the utility derived from income $V(I)$ and the disutility of effort $G(a)$. V is assumed to be continuously differentiable, strictly increasing, and concave (Grossman and Hart, 1983).

Following in line with our third criticism of principal–agent models presented above, the enhanced principal–agent (EPA) model makes a different set of assumptions regarding agents' utility functions. While most principal–agent models assume a universal disutility of work, the EPA model assumes that the utility of work for individual agents varies across tasks. Under the EPA model, an agent is capable of valuing working on one task while loathing any effort devoted to another. In this way, agents alter their effort according to their utility for what they are producing. The EPA model thus recasts agents' efforts toward the production of output. Accordingly, this model assumes that a broader set of incentives influences agent behavior than simply the flow of residuals. In this way we reflect to some degree the research that contends that incentives alone fail to provide lasting changes in behavior (Locke et al. 1968; Freedman et al. 1992). For each of these reasons, our model incorporates the political or mission orientations of bureaucratic agents to account for behavior not explained by other principal–agent models.[6]

Reflecting our first criticism of the prior principal–agency literature, this model of bureaucratic supervision also focuses on the factors that constrain the behavior of individuals within a bureaucracy rather than the agency as a whole: the limited amounts of work that an individual can allocate across policy outputs. We assume that work is a function of both time and effort. Work serves as a constraint since both time and effort are limited inputs and work is a function of both effort and time, such that $w_{iwb} = f(t_{iwb}, q_{iwb})$; where $t_{iwb} = $ time input on a particular policy, I, by bureaucrat, b, and $q_{iwb} = $ effort input on i by b. It is evident how time constrains all individuals and always limits the amount of work that an individual can devote to a task. Effort, on the other hand, is an expandable but finite input. While there may be terrific variability in the amount of effort devoted to different tasks, there is a limit to how much energy one can expend. Because both of these inputs are limited, so is work, which, in turn, constrains supervisors. The treatment of a work constraint in this analysis is similar to that used in household economics, which incorporates both time and budgetary constraints.[7] The constraints imposed by limited availability of work for supervisors serve as one of the foundations for this model of bureaucratic management. These allocations of time and effort, in turn, shape the types of policy produced by an organization. In this way, the model departs from most of the principal–agent literature, where the accumulation and distribution of residuals play a central role in the analysis (e.g., Holmström 1979, 1982; Bianco and Bates 1990; Alchian and Demsetz 1972). In this model, the choices of agents depend on the underlying psychological attitudes toward such factors as wages, perquisites of office, power, and disposition toward particular policies.

By incorporating political factors into this utility-maximizing framework,

---

6. This game also differs from the specific characteristics of production-by-teams models. A production-by-teams model involves a group of agents that independently allocates levels of effort to produce a single output for the entire group (Holmström 1982; Miller 1987; Bianco and Bates 1990). Such team effort also is one rationale for why individual effort cannot be observed. In this enhanced game, production is assumed to be separable between individual agents, overcoming the free-rider problems associated with production by teams.

7. As developed by Becker (1965), household economics assumes that consumers face a home production possibility frontier and a market wage budget line. A consumer can produce goods at home by exchanging time for goods that could be purchased from an earned wage.

the number of choices available to an individual subordinate bureaucrat regarding the production of policy outputs expands beyond a work/shirk dichotomy. In this manner, we address our second criticism of most principal–agent models. For purposes of simplicity, we define the set of alternative actions from which a subordinate bureaucrat chooses to include:

1. Work, producing output from a variety of policy output tasks (or the production of positive output);

2. Leisure-shirking, not working because you do not feel like working;

3. Dissent-shirking, not working because one is opposed to a particular policy output;

4. Sabotage, or the production of negative output.[8]

Leisure-shirking and dissent-shirking are differentiated in this analysis not to draw out conclusions about different types of shirking, but to emphasize the linkage between subordinate choice and the production of particular policy output. Shirking because one does not feel like working (leisure-shirking), while a form of defection, is not a variety of strategic organizational dissent; it is not motivated by principle or politics. Dissent-shirking, on the other hand, stems directly from an organization member's opposition to some policy. Not working thus serves as silent protest.[9] Dissent-shirking is a common expression of protest over the production of disliked output. Yet, it is probably safe to say that most shirking stems from a simple desire not to work very hard (leisure-shirking). Similarly, while no one would say that sabotage occurs more frequently than working positively, it is not an unknown activity. While strategic dissent is not a regularly occurring event (most workers want to efficiently produce output),[10] it is a significant phenomenon that organizations must address. Varieties of nonvoiced dissent abound, including the AFDC caseworker who decides to postpone ending a woman's eligibility until the dependent woman has an alternative source of income as well as the development officer who spends his time helping organize local opposition to his own project. Both public and private sector organizations regularly develop

---

8. The consideration of negative output requires that bureaucratic production functions be transformed. Individuals in the following model are not seen to maximize utility with respect to output, but with regard to input, where work is treated as a primary constraint.

9. See Farrell and Rusbult (1981), Rusbult, Zembrodt, and Gunn (1982), Farrell (1983) for examples of the systematic study of organizational dissent.   These works trace their roots to Hirschman's *Exit, Voice, and Loyalty* (1970), and extend his analysis to exit, voice, loyalty, and neglect (EVLN), where neglect involves spending less time and effort on work (shirking).

10. See Gates and Worden (1989) and subsequent chapters of this book.

mechanisms to deal with aspects of strategic dissent, attempting to prevent it from happening before it becomes a problem. Moreover, supervisors directly deal with the possibilities of dissent as they allocate work and supervise their subordinates.

These four choices provide a wide range of alternative actions available to a subordinate bureaucrat with respect to the production of a policy output. A subordinate, thus, selects from one of these four alternative sets of action for each policy. Across a set of policies, a bureaucrat selects an amount of time to shirk and allocates the remaining time to the other two nonshirking choices across a set of policies. By choosing to produce output, the bureaucrat serves the organization through the production of positive output. A choice of either leisure-shirking or dissent-shirking will bring an individual's output of a particular policy toward zero.[11] Sabotage, by definition, creates a condition in which other bureaucrats must devote more time to the production of a given output for it to be produced; thus for the individual it is negative output. It is for this reason that sabotage is treated as a discrete choice, fundamentally different from shirking.

The sabotage of policy is an often overlooked but significant phenomenon affecting bureaucratic management and policy implementation. It is not uncommon to hear of bureaucratic subordinates who have successfully prevented a particular policy from being implemented; yet few scholars have included sabotage in their analysis.[12] Economists and some political scientists have addressed the problems of shirking, but the politically motivated act of attempting to wreck a policy or to prevent policy reform has been ignored. By focusing on subordinate motives, activities such as dissent-shirking and sabotage become more evident. It should be further noted that subordinate bureaucrats' decisions do not occur in a vacuum. Particular policy outputs are considered in the context of general policy. An individual bureaucrat's disposition toward a general policy will influence his or her decision regarding a particular policy output. This is an important point of emphasis: the amount of work input by a bureaucrat varies from policy to policy; subordinates do not choose pure strategies.

Policies can be viewed as bundles of particular policy outputs, where the sum of particular bureaucratic outputs constitutes a general policy orientation for the organization. Since it is rather common to find several policy sets to be competing for support within an organization, individuals will form factions

---

11. Shirking alone, then, may prevent a policy from being implemented; sabotage may not be necessary.

12. Lazear (1989, 1995) addresses a different kind of sabotage where one member of a production team engages in a costly action which adversely affects the output of another while competing for organizational rewards.

as they align themselves behind general policy sets. In this manner, individual bureaucrats' decisions regarding particular policy outputs affect the implementation of policy for the organization as a whole. In other words, bureaucrats' decisions about how they allocate work across a set of tasks directly affects the production of policy.

The following formal presentation of this model provides greater insight into the problems of supervision and compliance in a bureaucratic setting and its role in the implementation of policy. Before presenting this model and overview, we tell a stylized story of the strategic interaction that takes place between a bureaucrat and a supervisor. Our story begins with a supervisor who must decide who is going to do what. In other words, the supervisor decides which subordinates will work on what policies. The supervisor has a set of policy production goals which she will try to best attain by matching the "best" person for each task, where every subordinate is given several assignments (or tasks). After a set of tasks is assigned to a subordinate, the bureaucrat must decide how to allocate his time for each task. We limit the bureaucrat's choice to three general categories, *working, shirking,* and *sabotage* After a subordinate has made a choice as how to allocate his time on a particular task, the supervisor must decide how to respond so as to best accomplish her goals regarding policy production. Unfortunately for the supervisor, she has limited time to monitor and supervise subordinates, as well as to produce policy directly. Taking these time constraints into account the supervisor must decide which subordinates will be more likely to respond to her supervision so as to get the most out of her subordinates. Bureaucrats then respond differentially to supervision. The next time the supervisor decides who does what, she takes into account how the subordinate decided to use his time on different types of policy tasks and how amenable he was to supervision. A more formal overview of the enhanced principal agent (EPA) game is presented below and a more detailed elaboration follows.

A Summary of the EPA Game

Players: supervisor (s) and subordinate (b).
Information: asymmetric, incomplete, and uncertain

Actions and Events:

Round 1:

1. Supervisor allocates tasks across subordinates (several tasks per subordinate).

2. Subordinate decides how to allocate work across tasks: working, shirking, and sabotage.

3. Supervisor decides how to allocate supervisory resources across subordinates.

4. Subordinate responds (or does not respond) to supervision.

Round 2:

5. Supervisor allocates tasks across subordinates—this time with some information revealed from the subordinate's actions taken in the previous round.

Stage 1: Task Assignment

The problem facing the supervisor, s, is to allocate a set of tasks to all subordinates in her charge so as to maximize the production of output she likes best. Assume that there are n subordinate agents, b. She, s, must figure out a way to distribute all policy output tasks, x_{ib}, to all subordinates, such that each subordinate has several tasks to produce a set of policy outputs, where the time and effort that a supervisor desires to be allocated toward each policy output, w^*_{iWb}, sums to some total desired work allocation for all tasks for each subordinate, such that $\sum w^*_{iWb} = W^*_b$.[13] At this initial stage of the game, tasks are allocated with asymmetric information. The supervisor does not know the predispositions of different subordinates towards different policy outputs. This is the problem of adverse selection; the supervisor must make an allocation decision without complete information about what type of subordinate she faces. In the second round of the game some information regarding subordinates' types will be revealed through their actions. Every subsequent round will reveal more and more information about agents' types.

---

13. w^*_{iWb} is the amount of work a supervisor would like to see allocated toward the production of a particular policy output by a bureaucrat. W^*_b is the total work allocation by a bureaucrat across policies. As discussed above, work is a function of time and effort.

Stage 2: The Subordinate's Problem—Policy Production

The decision to dissent is considered here in the context of a subordinate deciding how to allocate his work across a set of assigned tasks. Obviously, choosing to work hard on an output does not constitute dissent. Similarly, shirking merely to avoid work is not dissent either. Principled dissent springs from a moral, political, or ethical opposition to a particular policy. A subordinate who disagrees with a particular policy and engages in dissent will choose not to work on tasks that produce such output. Given a choice not to work on a particular task, a dissident decides whether to merely not work (dissent-shirk) or to work actively to prevent a policy from being implemented (sabotage). In the context of policy production, the set of alternative actions from which a subordinate (b) chooses at time (i) includes:

1. Work, w_{iWb};

2. Leisure-shirking, w_{iLb};

3. Dissent-shirking, w_{iDb};[14] and

4. Sabotage, w_{iSb}.

The generation of policy can be expressed in terms of a production function.[15] The production function for each policy good, x_{ib}, is defined as:

$$x_{ib} = f_{ib}(w_{iWb}, w_{iSb}, s_b, k_b, \theta_{ib}) \tag{2.2}$$

where s_b = the supervisory time subordinate b receives from a supervisor s; k_b = the capital input available to b; w_{iSb} and w_{iWb} are sabotage and working, as defined above; and θ_{ib}, a random state of nature. This random state of nature, θ, prevents a supervisor from knowing whether lower rates of production stem from the actions of the subordinate (shirking or sabotage) or from events beyond the control of the agent.[16] In other words, the amount of output produced depends on work, capital, and supervisory inputs as well as broad environmental factors which are treated as random events of nature.

---

14. Leisure-shirking and dissent-shirking are differentiated in this analysis to distinguish dissent from other forms of defection.

15. By using a production function, we account for the inputs that go into producing public policy. This approach is quite distinct from most principal–agent models.

16. The hidden action problem is fundamentally compounded by this environmental uncertainty (θ). Principals cannot know whether low productivity stems from the actions of agents (work allocations by bureaucrats) or stochastic environmental factors outside of the agent's control. In an iterated game, principals' expectations can take a prior probability distribution, $f(\theta)$, over the random states of nature. We, however, do not explicitly model this updating here.

This model focuses on limited amounts of work that an individual can allocate across policy outputs. Work is assumed to be a function of both time and effort.[17] We also assume that the more work spent on productive output yields more output, such that: $\partial x_{ib}/\partial w_{iWb} > 0$. On the other hand, the more work spent on sabotage results in less output being produced, such that: $\partial x_{ib}/\partial w_{iSb} < 0$. In effect it is negative work. More shirking (leisure and dissent) is assumed to lead to no increase in the production of a particular policy output, (i), by a subordinate, (b). Shirking, therefore, does not formally enter the production function.

These decisions are all subject to supervision, to capital stock, and to a work constraint (since both time and energy are limited). The utility function of a subordinate bureaucrat (b) appears as follows:

$$U_b = u_b[x_{ib}, w_{iLb}, w_{iDb}, (-p_{ib})] \tag{2.3}$$

where U_b = a subordinate's utility function; x_{ib} = the quantity of output i produced by subordinate b; w_{iLb} and w_{iDb} are leisure- and dissent-shirking, as defined above; and $(-p_{ib})$ is the subordinate's disutility associated with the punishment levied for defection, which is conditional upon the supervisor detecting defection and choosing to punish the dissident. That is, subordinates receive negative utility for working for disliked policies or against liked policies, and positive utility for working for policies they like or against policies they dislike, while taking the risk of punishment into account. Appendix A (Models) presents the subordinate's constrained optimization problem in detail.

This stage of the EPA game highlights how moral hazard affects this game. While stage 1 highlights adverse selection (incomplete information about agents' types), incomplete information about agents' actions (moral hazard) is evident in the inability of the supervisor to determine whether or not an agent's low output is a product of work inputs or random events of nature, θ_{ib}. Even if supervisors detect defection, they still cannot determine whether the subordinate has intentionally shirked or sabotaged. Compounding this uncertainty (as demonstrated in the next section), supervisors may not be able to adequately monitor all subordinates, because of supervisory input constraints.

---

17. Work serves as a constraint since both time and effort are limited inputs and work is a function of both effort and time, such that $w_{iWb} = f(t_{iWb}, q_{iWb})$; where t_{iWb} = time input working on a particular policy, i, by subordinate, b, and q_{iWb} = effort input working on i by b. Sabotage also requires a time and effort commitment, such that: $w_{iSb} = f(t_{iSb}, q_{iSb})$.

Stage 3: The Supervision Problem and Stage 4: Subordinates' Responses

The supervisor's problem is to convince subordinates to allocate their work in a manner desired by a bureaucratic supervisor. In this section, we examine this relationship by looking at supervision and subordinates' allocation of work in the production of public policy.

As with the subordinate, the bureaucratic supervisor allocates her work across a set of policies. Supervisory effort and time, in turn, must be distributed over a set of subordinates responsible for the implementation of particular policy outputs. In this way, the EPA model more explicitly accounts for monitoring than typical principal–agent models do. Such models assume that a supervisor may not be able to distinguish compliance from defection, but the actual task of monitoring is not modeled.[18] As with subordinates, the supervisor's utility varies across different policies and her allocation of time producing policy and monitoring subordinates reflects this. The objective function for the supervisor is maximized with respect to a production and work constraint seen below in Appendix A (Models).

A supervisor's utility function is defined by a number of factors, including: the quantity of policy output produced directly by the supervisor and by subordinates, administrative supervision imposed on the supervisor, the capital input available to the supervisor, the total amount of work time available to a supervisor for each policy, and all manners of allocating work on a policy by a supervisor (including the amount of work spent leisure-shirking, the amount of work spent dissent-shirking, the amount of work spent producing negative output, and the amount of work spent producing and supervising the production of output). Note that the work/time constraint for the supervisor includes her own policy production plus the amount of work that goes into supervising subordinates. (This is presented formally in Appendix A.) In this manner, supervisors both directly and indirectly produce policy output. Since the amount of work available to a supervisor is limited, supervision is limited. In this manner the supervisor selects a level of output desired and makes her choices accordingly.

To better understand bureaucratic management, we still need to determine the optimal amount of time a supervisor should spend supervising a bureaucrat. To help illustrate this relationship, we assume the marginal effect of supervision on subordinate work inputs is a function of how amenable a subordinate is to supervision (γ_{bs}) and the difference between the amount of work input by the subordinate (w_{iWb}) and the amount of work input desired by the supervisor (w_{iWb}^{*}), such that:

---

18. Arrow points to this problem of vagueness of monitoring as something not adequately addressed by the principal-agent literature (1985, 1986).

$$\frac{\partial w_{iWb}}{\partial s_b} = \gamma(w_{iWb} - w_{iWb}^*) \tag{2.4}$$

where γ = a constant indicating how amenable subordinate b is to supervision. This value is assumed to be constant for an individual regarding a particular policy; degrees of amenability, however, vary across individuals and policies. In other words, γ determines how responsive a subordinate is to supervision. Some individuals are highly responsive (large γ), others recalcitrant (small γ). By explicitly incorporating amenability, this model differs from most principal–agent models which typically assume more uniform compliance or defection on the part of bureaucratic subordinates. The other two terms are defined as follows: w_{iWb} = the amount of work spent on a particular policy by bureaucrat b; and w_{iWb}^* = the amount of work spent on i by b desired by s. This is illustrated below in figure 2.1, which can also be expressed as:

$$w_{iWb}(s_b) = w_{iWb}(0) - (w_{iWb}^* - w_{iWb}(0))(1 - e^{-\gamma s_b}). \tag{2.5}$$

This simplifies to:

$$w_{iWb}(s_b) = w_{iWb}^* - (w_{iWb}^* - w_{iWb}(0))e^{-\gamma s_b} \tag{2.6}$$

where $w_{iWb}(0)$ = unsupervised work spent by b on i. In other words, it is the amount of work that a bureaucrat would spend producing a particular policy if left unsupervised. It is assumed that $w_{iWb}^* > w_{iWb}(0)$ for any i.

From this diagram and equation, the diminishing marginal returns of supervision become evident. Greater and greater amounts of supervision (s_b) lead to smaller and smaller marginal increases in the amount of work input by the subordinate (w_{iWb}) which asymptotically approaches the amount desired by the supervisor (w_{iWb}^*). We assume that compliance involves producing output as desired by the supervisor. It also becomes apparent that the predisposition of the subordinate plays an important role in this game. The subordinate's predisposition affects both the initial unsupervised allocation of work $(w_{iWb}(0))$ and subordinate amenability to supervision (γ).[19]

Figure 2.1, shows a significant difference between the amount of work initially allocated by a subordinate, $w_{iWb}(0)$, and the amount of work desired by a supervisor, w_{iWb}^*. If a bureaucrat is responsive to supervision (a large γ), the

---

19. Amenability only takes the responsiveness of the subordinate into account. We do not attempt to determine which methods of supervision most successfully induce subordinate compliance. See chapter 3 of this book as well as Brehm and Gates (1990) which explicitly examines how variation in three aspects of supervision (punishment, tolerance for defection, and observability) affects subordinate compliance.

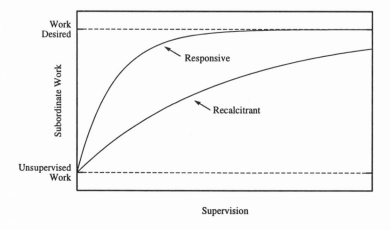

Fig. 2.1. Subordinate amenability to supervision

bureaucrat will quickly shift his work allocation close to the work level desired by the supervisor ($w_{iW_b}^*$). If the bureaucrat is recalcitrant and not amenable to supervision (a low γ), larger amounts of supervisory time must be invested before the bureaucrat's work allocation will start to come close to that desired by the supervisor. We assume that supervision always leads to more production. In a situation where there is little difference between a subordinate's initial work allocation and that desired by the supervisor, amenability to supervision is not as relevant. We do not diagram this, but it would mean pushing $w_{iW_b}(0)$ and $w_{iW_b}^*$ close to each other. This analysis extends beyond most principal–agent models in that supervision and amenability to supervision are explicitly modeled.

A principal's decision regarding supervision will depend on how she values the production of a particular policy. One particularly interesting situation occurs if the marginal utility for a supervisor of producing a good (x_{is}) minus the marginal utility of work to produce that good is less than zero, reflecting a possible corner solution to the problem. Under such conditions, a supervisor derives greater utility from her work input than from the production of a policy output. Since time spent supervising subordinate bureaucrats ($w_{iW_b}(s_b)$) is one component of a supervisor's total time investment (W_{is}), a supervisor should not put any time into supervising activity under such conditions. In this case:

$$\frac{\partial U_s}{\partial x_{is}} - \frac{\partial W_{is}}{\partial x_{is}} < 0. \tag{2.7}$$

If the supervisor does decide to supervise the production of a particular output, she must then decide to whom authority should be delegated. This decision depends on the marginal conditions.[20] Subordinate bureaucrats whose supervision falls under the conditions of equation 2.7, where the costs of work outweigh the benefits of output, are left unsupervised. This first condition occurs under three different situations. First, an unsupervised subordinate whose allocation of work $(w_{iWb}(0))$ approaches the work allocation desired by the supervisor (w^*_{iWb}) is not profitably supervised. Allocating additional supervisory resources (s_b) leads to little gain in the production of output (x_{ib}). The second way this condition emerges involves a situation where a subordinate is unresponsive to supervision; in other words, the subordinate possesses a low γ, such that additional supervisory resources would lead to little additional output of a policy. The third situation takes place when the supervisor places low value on a particular policy; in this case, the supervisor's marginal utility for a particular policy output is lower than the marginal value of any work (W_{is}) needed to produce it. In each of these situations, subordinates are left unsupervised. This is significant. Supervisory resources constitute all the mechanisms by which supervisors motivate subordinates. These marginal conditions indicate the situations where no supervision is allocated.

An alternative condition exists when the benefits of a policy output (x_{ib}) outweigh the costs of work. Under these conditions, subordinates are supervised. This condition occurs under two other situations. When a subordinate's γ is high and there is a big difference between $w_{iWb}(0)$ and w^*_{iWb}, additional supervision (s_b) leads to additional output (x_{ib}). Also, under conditions where a supervisor places a high value on the production of a policy, she may find it worthwhile to invest inordinate amounts of supervisory time; this may occur in light of sabotage. In this case:

$$\frac{\partial U_s}{\partial x_{is}} - \frac{\partial W_{is}}{\partial x_{is}} > 0. \tag{2.8}$$

Given the constraints on a supervisor's resources, the supervisor has five general options summarized as follows: (1) bureaucrats who produce desirable benefits without supervision are left alone; (2) subordinates unresponsive to supervision are left alone; (3) supervisors allocate little work to produce output that they do not value; (4) bureaucrats who improve production under supervision and are responsive to a shift in the amount of supervision time allocated receive the most supervision; and (5) if the marginal utility of eliminating the

---

20. These marginal conditions implicitly incorporate a supervisor's tolerance for defection and the willingness to allocate supervision. See Brehm and Gates (1990) and chapter 3 of this book for more explicit modeling of tolerance.

production of negative output (sabotage) is greater than the marginal utility of the time spent supervising, a supervisor will take action against the saboteur. Thus, situations 1–3 fall under the conditions of equation 2.7, while situations 4 and 5 come under the domain of the conditions for equation 2.8.

One should keep in mind that these results differ from those of the principal–agent literature. By recasting the focus of the principal–agent framework so that agents alter their effort across different outputs, different results are obtained. By varying the responsiveness of subordinates and limiting supervisory resources, the conditions where supervision fails to induce compliance become apparent. Getting the incentive structure "right" may not be enough. This is where the results of the EPA model differs so substantially from most principal–agent models. These comparative static solutions correspond to the equilibria for iterated versions of this game as well. These results are seen below.

Round 2: The Task Assignment Problem Iterated

The closed form solutions seen in one round of the EPA game are evident in iterated versions of this game as well. Appendix A identifies all the equilibria for this game. Adverse selection as well as moral hazard continue to play a role in Round 2 and subsequent rounds. Recall that moral hazard involves an agent taking action unknown to the principal. Adverse selection involves a principal trying to allocate tasks to subordinates without knowing their type (whether high γ or low γ). In the Task Assignment Problem, a supervisor must delegate assignments to various subordinates. With iteration, subordinate predispositions (agents' types) are sometimes revealed to the supervisor. The supervisor, in turn, delegates tasks to the agents most positively predisposed towards those assignments that maximize the supervisor's utility. Any time new rules or policies are implemented, the task assignment game begins again at Round 1. Iteration reveals more and more information to supervisors. If a separating equilibrium holds (where a subordinate's type is revealed through actions), then as the game is played, supervisors will face smaller and smaller degrees of adverse selection.[21] This, in turn, could lead to a reduction in problems (or benefits) of moral hazard. On the other hand, if a pooling equilibrium holds (where a subordinate's actions do not reveal any information regarding type), no additional information comes to the supervisor as the game proceeds. Given the sheer number of subordinates and tasks, x_{ib}, supervisors will always face some degree of adverse selection. Moreover, moral hazard will enforce the

---

21. Further research might examine how supervisors utilize recruitment, training, selection criteria, and task definition as mechanisms to address issues of adverse selection. As presented here, this model (as most principal–agent models) is limited to the command aspects of hierarchy.

adverse selection problem as long as nature (θ_{ib}) plays a role in determining outcomes. Since moral hazard works to maintain a level of uncertainty about subordinates' actions, supervisors will face uncertainty about subordinate predispositions.

Many equilibria result in little or no supervision. The specifics of these marginal relationships are specified in Appendix A. They are also further specified in terms of subordinate responsiveness given in equation 2.6. More specifically, we identify these equilibria in terms of the difference between the time allocation desired by the supervisor ($w^*_{iW_b}$) and the amount of work initially allocated by the subordinate ($w_{iW_b}(0)$) and in terms of the subordinate's type, γ.

As long as the conditions of moral hazard and adverse selection hold, subordinates will possess the capability of preventing policies from being implemented through the use of nonvoiced dissent (namely dissent-shirking and sabotage). Under conditions where large numbers of subordinates politically resist producing particular policies, it is unlikely that these policy outputs will be produced. By directly examining subordinate motives and choices as well as supervisor constraints, the enhanced principal–agent game of bureaucratic management provides a framework for better understanding recalcitrance. The Task Assignment Problem, in this way, serves to focus attention on organizational dissent.

Moreover, this enhanced principal–agent model provides a framework for understanding some of the choices supervisors make to attain subordinate compliance. Given constraints on supervisory resources, supervisors must choose to efficiently allocate their time (and other supervisory resources) in such a manner to maximize the production of a particular set of policy outputs. Supervisors allocate their resources (especially time) across subordinates and policies to achieve this end. As different subordinates are more amenable to supervision, some policies inherently cost supervisors less in terms of supervisory resources than other policies. Some outputs can be produced with little supervision, especially when their production can be easily verified or enumerated post hoc. As a result, supervisors not only tailor their allocation of resources across subordinates to maximize the production of certain outputs, but certain policies are chosen simply because they may be "cheap" to supervise.

The implications of this game are significant. Given that supervisors often do not have adequate time for supervision and that bureaucrats will occasionally shirk or even engage in sabotage, we can expect to see problems for any organization that expects to produce all intended output. Under conditions in which large numbers of bureaucrats politically resist producing particular policies, it is unlikely that these policy outputs will be produced. As long as there are constraints on supervisory time, bureaucrats will possess the capability of preventing policies from being implemented. By directly examining sub-ordinate motives and choices as well as supervisor constraints, the enhanced principal–agent game of bureaucratic management provides a framework for better understanding recalcitrance. Most of these differences stem from assum-ing that people have different utilities for different tasks and that supervisors face time constraints. It is a particularly useful framework for understanding the problems of bureaucratic sabotage. Such a perspective allows us directly to incorporate politics into our analysis of bureaucracy.

Conclusions: Contrasting Predictions

Our enhanced principal–agent model stresses the importance of subordinate predispositions. In this final section, we review the differences in the assump-tions of the EPA game and other models of the principal–agent relationship with regard to supervision, subordination, and compliance. In particular, we examine the nature of supervision, the work–shirk dichotomy, the incentive structure, and how these assumptions lead to predictions about the likelihood of compliance by agents.

Supervision

In our enhanced principal–agent model, the capabilities of the principal play a prominent role. We portray supervision as the allocation of supervisory re-sources across subordinates. The supervisor has no certainty about whether a subordinate's action constitutes compliance or defection; she must determine which subordinates to supervise under uncertainty. Constraints on supervisory resources play an important role in this model, as does limited information. In fact, constraints such as limited time are potentially so severe that they serve to inhibit supervision even in environments of complete information. In this manner, the enhanced principal–agent supervisor resembles the Bianco and Bates (1990) enhanced supervisor with constraints. These constraints are quite significant. Because of limited supervisory resources, the enhanced principal–agent supervisor often is unable to alter the behavior of subordinates.

Evidence abounds demonstrating how coercive supervision (particularly in the form of punishment) is limited (Malcomson 1984; Lazear and Rosen 1981; Lazear 1995). Other studies contend that performance plays a far more limited role (in both the private and public sectors) than seniority and tenure do; salary rewards tend not to reflect performance (Hashimoto and Raisian 1985; Johnson and Libecap 1989, 1994). Civil service rules, designed to eliminate capricious activity, play a particularly significant role in constrain-ing supervision. Even if these rules do not explicitly ban certain sanctions or rewards, the time and energy required to fill out all the forms to justify special treatment of an employee effectively rules out such activities, especially when supervisory resources are otherwise constrained.

Rules which constrain supervision further affect the activities of supervisors. Supervision entails both monitoring and sanctioning subordinates. Supervisory resources are used to determine what subordinates are doing as well as to sanction or reward. Constrained supervisory resources, in turn, limit both monitoring and sanctioning. Moreover, the act of monitoring itself often constitutes a punishment; frequent and close scrutiny that comes with monitoring is certainly disliked by most workers. Rules restricting rewards (in particular, special monetary rewards) may make limited monitoring ("backing off") a reward to a good employee. Under such conditions, the problems of a one-dimensional monitoring and sanctioning decision variable to induce subordinate compliance is evident. By incorporating constrained supervisory resources into the EPA model, the relevance and importance of the structure of sanctions becomes apparent. Nevertheless, these factors only come into play depending on the characteristics of subordinates. In other words, limits to supervision become most evident when a subordinate's work allocation differs considerably from that of the supervisor and when a subordinate is relatively unresponsive to supervision.

The goal of principals is to maximize "production" (or compliance, or adherence to the law), but supervisors earn different rewards. The enhanced principal–agent supervisor does not value all output equally. A supervisor allocates time and effort preponderantly toward those policies she favors.[22] We explicitly model this as the supervisor's marginal utility associated with the output of a particular policy. The enhanced principal–agent supervisor places great weight on the particular policies being produced. In this manner we explicitly incorporate the political dimensions of bureaucratic supervision.

Subordination

Another key difference between the models lies in the range of alternative actions for the subordinates and in the subordinates' incentives. The assumption that subordinates necessarily prefer shirking over working is unnecessarily simplistic. We offer in our model richer assumptions about the preference structures of subordinates. Workers will prefer *producing* some outputs over other outputs; they don't necessarily seek to shirk at every opportunity. As we show in later chapters, public sector bureaucrats and other governmental offi-

---

22. In fact, the enhanced principal–agent model of supervision even allows for supervisors to sabotage policy output or at least to ignore subordinate recalcitrance when they view a policy output disfavorably. However we do not develop this aspect of the model here.

cials such as police officers and social workers enjoy their jobs, stressful and dangerous though they may be.[23]

The point to emphasize is that unlike other principal–agent models, our model directly ties subordinate utility to a particular policy. For our model, the intrinsic payoffs to a subordinate for compliance mean more than simply redistributing residuals; to understand subordinate behavior one must examine subordinate dispositions.

In the enhanced principal–agent model, subordinates shirk or work depending on their attitudes toward the policy. If the subordinate dislikes the policy for political reasons (i.e., wants a discontinuation of the policy), his incentives are quite different from the subordinate who is merely lazy. This more sophisticated assumption about subordinate preferences significantly alters the results of the enhanced principal–agent model. The central assumption of this model is that subordinates are concerned about what they are producing (particularly bureaucrats producing policy output). The marginal conditions of the model indicate that such sentiment affects productivity across different kinds of output.

Compliance

In prior principal–agency models, one sees compliance from the subordinates if the supervisor's punishment poses a credible threat. In our model, one sees compliance when subordinate predispositions favor the policy.

If the reader is surprised by our finding that the capacities of supervisors have little effect on subordinate compliance, that reader should note wide empirical confirmation in public administration of our more formalized findings. In surveys of Israeli banking organizations, Adler (1983) finds that only those subordinates low in self-esteem are influenced by supervisor's coercive power. In observations of subordinate–supervisory relations in seven different public and private organizations in northern India, Ansari (1990) finds that those supervisors who rely solely upon reward and coercion are more autocratic and less likely to attain cooperation from subordinates. Bachman, Bowers, and Marcus (1968) find in their surveys of salesmen, professors, insurance agents, factory workers, and utility company workers that the least effective bases of power (in terms of inducing subordinate performance) were reward and coercion, while the most effective is expert persuasion. Rahim and Buntzman (1989), in a survey of university students and their supervisors, observe that the supervisors' coercive authority is far less effective in inducing compliance from the students than expert or referent authority. Freedman et al. (1992) found that as incentives to workers increased, they viewed the activity

---

23. See Brehm and Gates (1993a) and Gates and Worden (1989).

for which they received the bonus more negatively. Perhaps most persuasive of all, Kanter (1977) in her studies of power in corporations finds that the least powerful are most likely to resort to coercion, leading to a vicious cycle: ". . . powerless authority figures who use coercive tactics provoke resistance and aggression, which prompts them to become even more coercive, controlling and behaviorally restrictive" (190).

There is no such consensus of empirical confirmation in the recent work on the congressional control of the bureaucracy, a literature which may be more familiar to political scientists. Here, the convention is to regard Congress (or a specific oversight committee) as the principal and a bureaucratic agency as the agent. Weingast and Moran (1983) demonstrate congressional dominance by way of the sensitivity of the FTC to changes in the composition of relevant oversight committees; Muris (1986) claims that the composition of the FTC changed concurrently. McCubbins, Noll, and Weingast (1990) identify OSHA and the former AEC as agencies under congressional dominance. Mashaw (1990) points to the extraordinary discretion possessed by the FCC, FPC, and SSA over the areas most sensitive to constituency interests, despite repeated attempts by Congress to structure these very agencies. Why the lack of consensus? Moe (1984, 1990) argues for the need to better integrate the contributions of principal–agency theory with behaviorally oriented organization theory in the Simon–March tradition. We believe that our model is an effort in that direction: to think more about the preferences and capacities of bureaucratic subordinates. Congress does not "dominate" when agents are unresponsive to reward or sanction, are already producing at levels compatible with Congress's demands, or when the agency produces "goods" that yield little return to congresspersons' constituents. We explore this issue of organizational oversight in later chapters of this book as we turn from oversight *within* an organization to oversight *over* an organization (e.g., bureaucratic oversight). In order to understand *inter*organizational forms of oversight, we argue, one needs to understand *intra*organizational oversight. Both types of oversight ought to be considered together.

One sees compliance in the enhanced principal–agent model if the subordinates prefer the policy. Supervision, in general, does not affect the subordinates' decisions. This model leaves room for recalcitrance even in the face of direct supervision. This is evident when the marginal costs of work exceed the marginal benefits of a policy being produced.[24] Problems of supervision, however, are particularly evident where supervisors face extreme time constraints over a large set of subordinates.

In our model, we make the constraints of effective supervision even more

---

24. This is seen in equation 8 where: $\frac{\partial U_s}{\partial x_{is}} - \frac{\partial W_{is}}{\partial x_{is}} < 0$.

apparent: neither the frequency nor the severity of punishment affects the decision by the agents to comply or to defect. The final efficiency of a policy depends much less upon the severity or frequency of "punishment" by the supervisor than upon subordinates' preexisting dispositions. While we do not make the claim that supervisors are never able to induce compliance, we show that compliance depends more on the subordinates' than upon the supervisor's attributes. The next chapter further examines this issue.

CHAPTER 3

Foundations of Organizational Compliance

Political scientists often view democratic accountability in a bureaucracy as depending on whether political superiors are able to persuade their subordinates to comply with specific requests for the implementation of policy. In chapter 2, we demonstrated that a supervisor's expectations about performance vitally depend upon the preferences of her subordinates. Supervision does not "induce" compliance if the subordinates would have complied anyway, if subordinates are unresponsive to supervision, or if the cost of eliminating sabotage is greater than the cost of the sabotage itself. In this chapter, we focus on how the psychological foundations of compliance affect the subordinates' amenability to supervision, in particular, how the behavior of fellow subordinates leads to the emergence of standard operating procedures.

The problem of understanding why one individual would comply with a request from another extends across diverse domains. Compliance is a routine factor in political organizations: army officers expect subordinate soldiers to follow orders, party whips seek the complying votes of members of their own party in the legislature, political systems expect citizens to obey laws. Compliance requests are rife in nonpolitical settings: salespeople seek agreements from prospective clients, interviewers seek the cooperation of prospective respondents to their surveys, and parents expect compliance from their children (and vice versa).

"Compliance" is a broad category of human behavior, and recent social psychological work identifies some surprising and subtle factors that cause an individual to heed the requests of others. Coupled with an extended scholarship in the related area of "persuasion,"[1] there is considerable fruit for scholars of bureaucratic behavior.

Principal–agency theory provides a clear basis for conceptualizing the importance of monitoring subordinates' actions and creating effective incentives to induce compliance. The value of the psychological research on compliance

---

1. The distinction between persuasion and compliance as research areas is somewhat hazy, but conventionally one refers to a request to perform a specific task as a "compliance" request, whereas an attempt to affect the attitudes of another is "persuasion."

suggests that the forces influencing compliance extend beyond the presence of rewards and punishment for workplace behavior, or the constraints on the supervisor's ability to observe subordinate behavior.

To attain a more comprehensive understanding of organizational compliance, we need to look beyond incentive structures alone. Bureaucracies have histories, where workers are constrained by their decisions and behavior of the past. And bureaucracies have cultures, where workers learn from one another about appropriate behavior.

Specifically, in the social psychology of compliance and persuasion, one convenient distinction falls between "central" and "peripheral" routes to persuasion (Petty and Cacioppo 1986). Under the central route to persuasion, the subject elaborates upon and deliberates the intrinsic aspects of a message's subjective credibility. In a compliance setting, where the principal asks the agent to perform some task, the agent weighs the costs and benefits associated with the activity. The central route to persuasion is ripe for the explicit manipulations of observation, reward, and punishment implied in agency theory. Under the peripheral route to persuasion, the subject does not deliberate on the message, but instead focuses on simple heuristics which are extrinsic to the communication. Examples of such a heuristic would include the police officer who gauges the extent to which use of force is appropriate by the behavior of officers around him, or the inspector who continues to file the same report, even if conditions at the facility have changed. By examining the peripheral paths to persuasion, we move beyond the typical domain of agency theories.

To attain a more complete understanding of the nature of supervision and bureaucratic compliance we shift our focus away from the "central" role played by supervisors (principals) toward more "peripheral" routes to compliance. In particular, we examine how under conditions of uncertainty, individuals learn from others and look for "social proof" for their own actions. Agents interact with one another through networks. Such learning within an organization leads to a more dynamic conceptualization of how standard operating procedures evolve. We also stress the importance of agent predisposition, where commitment and principles play a particularly significant role.

This distinction between central and peripheral persuasion matters in several respects. First, to the extent that subordinate behavior is governed more by peripheral than central persuasion, then rewards and punishments become inefficient—perhaps futile—means for bureaucratic control. Second, peripheral persuasion is fundamentally short-term, but with long-term consequences for bureaucratic responsiveness. Third, the peripheral routes to persuasion suggest that bureaucrats respond to requests that fall outside of hierarchical chains of command, and they do this in systematic and understandable ways.

The purposes of this chapter are threefold. First, we identify the elements of the social psychology of persuasion which we believe will be most informative for the problem of bureaucratic compliance. Second, we incorporate these elements into an extension of the model we develop in the previous chapter. Finally, we derive some propositions from this new model about who, and what, shapes the choices by individual bureaucrats to work, shirk, or sabotage.

Central and Peripheral Routes to Persuasion

One puzzle pestering the extensive research in compliance and persuasion is that individuals do not always appear to be affected by communications which appear to be objectively credible and of significant importance for the would-be recipient. Recipients of the message demonstrate a remarkable ability to "counterargue."

Why is it that bureaucrats sometimes fail to obey the requests from their superiors? The traditional principal–agency approach would look toward the bureaucrats' expectations of sanctions for failure to comply or conversely at the rewards for compliance. Bureaucrats might reasonably expect sanctions to be onerous. For instance, military reprisals for failure to obey the chain of command can be fierce and certain. Elsewhere, firing a noncompliant worker can also serve as an effective deterrent. But there are times when subordinates seem quite resistant to sanctions. The psychology of persuasion and compliance offers some answers.

Petty and Cacioppo (1986) argue that recipients of persuasive messages might handle the message in one of two distinct ways. In the "central" route to persuasion, the recipient of the message evaluates the subjective credibility of the messenger, and incorporates the new information in a deliberated evaluation of "what's in it for me?" In order for the recipient to process the communication under the central route, the recipient has to be both motivated and able to cognate the message. The central route to persuasion is what we implicitly invoke in traditional agency models: the agent considers whether defecting or complying is within his interest, and he proceeds accordingly. Principals might manipulate the stream of rewards and punishments, or structure systems of supervision, in order to encourage compliance by agents who are deliberating over the consequences of defecting or complying.

If the recipient is either unable or not motivated to cognate the message, the recipient handles the message by a "peripheral" route to persuasion. Whether the recipient accepts the request depends on the presence of alternative persuasion cues under the "peripheral" route. Such alternative cues might include the behavior of others, the recipient's past record with respect to similar communications, the recipient's perception of the availability of other communications, and so forth.

It is surely not too great a stretch to hazard that every one of us has been in a position where we have asked ourselves why we agreed to some compliance request, knowing full well that it wasn't in our immediate interest. We find ourselves persuaded by features of the request situation that may strike us as more "extrinsic" than intrinsic to the particular request—features of the requester, the circumstances of the request, our own moods may all encourage us to do things that we may not objectively consider to be significant. For example, when a pleasant, attractive salesperson persuades us to purchase an automobile (or stereo component, or article of clothing) because there's only one left on the lot, and it won't last long, we have been persuaded on grounds of the scarcity of the object or perhaps the attractiveness of the requester, but probably not the object's intrinsic worth.

We should take note of two significant points about such cues. First, all of these cues are heuristics, shortcuts, for perfectly rational decisions. On the whole, following such cues as paying heed to what others are doing, striving to maintain a sense of consistency, reciprocating requests from others, obeying symbols of authority, or maximizing ranges of choice serve us reasonably well in circumstances when it is not worth the effort to make a separate deliberated decision each time. One could explicitly model such decisions by taking the costs of decision making into account. The peripheral route to persuasion is not an "irrational" or "nonrational" decision process—it is simply one where we are reliant on rules we have previously established for our behavior. Behavior under the peripheral route might be undeliberated, but it is not devoid of rationality.[2]

Second, persuasion by the peripheral route is strictly short-term. Since the recipient is not cognating the new information, the recipient makes no long term storage in memory of any attitude or opinion change. In fact, by Petty and Cacioppo's original model, one would ordinarily not expect that the recipient could be persuaded by a peripheral route to do anything that was not already consistent with prior behavior or attitudes.

Cialdini's (1984) book develops six different categories of such peripheral routes to persuasion, of which two elements of the peripheral route to persuasion pertain to bureaucratic compliance. Put yourself in the position of a bureaucrat who has received a request from his supervisor: What are the heuristics that you might draw upon? An immediate shortcut is to ask "What have I done in the past?" (*consistency*). A desire to maintain consistent behavior is a standard feature of compliance behavior. Standard Operating Procedures (SOPs) prevail in bureaucracies, some of which emerge not from specific implementations within the rules, but from bureaucracies' regular handling of routine circumstances.

---

2. In this respect peripheral routes to persuasion are different from Elster's norm-based decision making which stems from means- rather than goal-oriented behavior (Elster 1989).

A second shortcut might be to ask "What are others like myself doing?" (*social proof*). In a state of uncertainty about whether it is appropriate to comply or defect, a bureaucrat might look toward fellow bureaucrats in order to identify the consequences of defection. Imitation is a very simple and direct information shortcut for conditions when rules are ambiguous.

In the remainder of this section, we will try to accomplish two separate tasks when reviewing both of these peripheral cues. We will identify that the cues, although heuristics, are merely short-hand forms for sensible, although nondeliberated, decisions. One could, in fact, view the cues as ways of acting rationally in the presence of limited information. Second, we will demonstrate that both of these cues are persistent features of what we already know about bureaucratic behavior.

Commitment, Consistency, and the Emergence of SOPs

A persistent feature of compliance behavior is a powerful desire to maintain behavioral consistency. At one level, the desire for behavioral consistency is an extension of a well-documented desire for cognitive consistency in general. The arguments on the importance of consistency can be traced back to Heider (1946, 1958), Festinger (1957), and others, who argue that a desire to maintain a consistent state of attitudes is a central motivator for reception of persuasive messages in general. Under Heider's scheme, individuals seek to maintain cognitive balance between positive and negative valence attitudes toward some object and another individual. If one is, say, positively predisposed toward the other individual (e.g., her spouse), but both disagree about attitudes toward some other object (e.g., whether or not to purchase a new car), then the individual is in a state of imbalance. That person experiences a strong desire to modify attitudes toward the object or the other. Festinger and colleagues expanded on the idea in the now famous concept of "cognitive dissonance." People do not like to maintain contradictory attitudes toward others or objects. Although the concept of cognitive dissonance in particular and consistency theory in general have been controversial,[3] considerable scholarship in psychology is able to demonstrate that attitudes and cognitions may change when one's behavior conflicts with one's sense of self-integrity (Leippe and Eisenstadt 1994; Steele 1988; Tesser and Cornell; Cooper and Fazio 1984; Eagly and Chaiken 1993).

The desire to maintain *behavioral* consistency is even more potent than the equivalent need to maintain cognitive consistency (Eagly and Chaiken 1993; Baumeister and Tice 1984; Kiesler 1971). Behavioral consistency implies a

---

3. Rival explanations for dissonance-reducing behavior include self-perception (e.g., Bem 1967), impression management (Tedeschi 1981), and self-presentation (Steele and Liu 1983).

publicly observable commitment to a prior behavior. Instead of maintaining merely privately held (and therefore invisibly altered) conceptions, behavioral consistency involves one's reputation and self-image. From diverse research, we know that those who have made a public commitment to performing an act are much more likely to perform that same act in the future.

Within bureaucracies, there is even greater pressure for bureaucrats to maintain consistent behavior. At perhaps the most basic definition of what bureaucracies do, bureaucracies enact and apply rules for handling diverse inputs. Rules enter into at least four elements of Weber's (1947) classic definition of bureaucracy as "rational legal authority": bounding organizational functions, specifying spheres of competence, principle of hierarchy, and regulating conduct of an office (331–32). Or, consider more contemporary scholarship on bureaucracies. Gary Miller defines bureaucracy in terms of hierarchical social intuitions where "hierarchies are political settings in which people continually struggle to achieve the potential made possible by specialization and cooperation" (1992: 237–38). Hierarchy, specialization, and rules define bureaucracy as a special social institution.

Beyond the consistency imposed on bureaucrats by official rules, bureaucrats generate for themselves standard operating procedures and routines. Wilson's (1989) account of the practices of the armed services found:

> Popular accounts of service in the peacetime army or navy are replete with stories about rules and procedures. ("If it moves, salute it; if it doesn't move, pick it up; if it is too big to pick up, paint it.") As we shall see in a later chapter, in recent decades the U.S. Army has devoted much of its peacetime efforts to elevating SOPs to the level of grand tactics by trying and then discarding various war-fighting doctrines. But when war breaks out, SOPs break down. The reason is obvious: outcomes suddenly become visible. Staying alive, taking real estate and killing the enemy are such important outcomes that the only SOPs which continue to have much force are those that contribute directly to producing those outcomes. At least that is almost true. Some SOPs, such as those that seem central to the mission of the organization, continue to exert and influence even though they are actually getting in the way of producing good outcomes. (164)

We have literally decades of research in organizational behavior on the emergence of routines, how routines break down, and how bureaucracies perpetuate SOPs (see March and Simon 1958; Merton 1957; Selznick 1957). There are powerful psychological, organizational, and political reasons for bureaucrats to maintain consistent behavior.

Maintaining consistent behavior also makes perfect sense as a general heuristic. When faced with what appear to be similar choices, consequences, and preferences, it is probably more rational for an individual to replicate his or her first decision than to reanalyze the value of the choice (as long as the first decision fared well for the individual). Independent of psychological weight to appear consistent, independent of the consequences for an organization of appearing arbitrary or inequitable, it is probably not worth the time or effort for a bureaucrat to consider each choice anew.

Consequently, one of the first peripheral cues influencing a bureaucrat's decision to comply with his supervisor's request must be "what did I do in the past?" It is a "peripheral" or "nondeliberated" cue since the bureaucrat does not elaborate on the ramifications of the choice, but replicates a prior choice.

What are the consequences of consistency as a peripheral cue? Standard operating procedures of a bureaucracy reinforce the individual patterns of consistent behavior. The rules and regulations that define bureaucracy also provide efficiency (in reducing the costs of decision making) and policy consistency (by limiting bureaucratic discretion). Nevertheless, even without standard operating procedures to fall back on, individuals tend to follow their own patterns of behavior. Such behavioral consistency can lead to compliance or noncompliance; the determining factor is whether or not the pattern of previously established behavior fits with the superior's request.

Learning from "Like Others"

A second important peripheral cue that is relevant to understanding bureaucratic compliance is "social proof," or using individuals like oneself as cue givers about appropriate action. People who are in a state of uncertainty about what behaviors are appropriate look toward others who, on some dimensions, share common characteristics with themselves.

The importance of social proof as an explanation for compliance is another insight established in the 1950s. Asch (1951) placed three subjects in a room with an "experimenter." The experimenter would draw three lines of unequal length on a blackboard, and ask the three to state which line was the longest. In fact, two of the "subjects" were confederates of Asch, who were instructed to follow a particular pattern of reporting which line was the longest. Initially, the two confederates would report that the true longest line was longest. After a short time, the two confederates would begin falsely reporting which line was longest. The true subject always went into a state of stress. Many of the subjects rubbed their eyes or fidgeted in the chair. A large fraction of the subjects waited until the two confederates would make their reports about which line was longest and then also falsely report.

Milgram's famous (1969) experiments demonstrated the appalling degree to which subjects would obey the commands of an authority figure dressed as a scientist to administer "shocks" to a supposed subject. The "shocks" and the scientist were false, and the supposed "subject" was in fact a confederate acting out a state of great pain, but the experiments themselves demonstrated that subjects were willing to "punish" others at supposedly near-lethal doses of electricity.

Among the few occasions when the obedience to authority would fail was when Milgram included two shock-givers, one of whom was a confederate. If the second shock-giver began to resist administering the "shocks," the true subject would likewise resist. The subject of the experiment resisted authority only when receiving the support of another "subordinate."

These experiments are compelling demonstrations of the degree to which individuals look toward others to sustain the appropriateness of their choices. These experiments are also directly—and hauntingly—applicable to bureaucratic organizations. Both experimenters were, in part, interested in the effects of military-style organizations on individual free will. Their findings suggested that conformity in organizations swamped individual choice. The social psychological evidence of the pervasive nature of "social proof" as a stamp on appropriate behavior is extensive.[4]

Organizational behavior has its own terminology for the extent to which members of an organization learn from one another: "corporate culture." Kreps conceptualizes corporate culture as that which prescribes "how things are done, and how they are meant to be done" (1984: 5). Corporate or organizational culture is a set of principles for dealing with unforeseen contingencies that are communicated to subordinates, who monitor its application, and to superiors, so as to establish some consistency among different individuals exercising authority. In this way, "it gives hierarchical inferiors an idea ex ante how the organization will 'react' to circumstances as they arise—in a very strong sense, it gives identity to the organization" (Kreps 1984).

Miller (1992) extends Kreps's analysis of corporate culture by examining the roles played by cultural norms and conventions in organizations. For Miller organizational culture provides a mechanism through which players develop expectations between superiors and subordinates. "It is this psychological network of mutually reinforcing expectations that makes one perfectly feasible outcome (e.g., cooperation) occur instead of another perfectly feasible out-

---

4. For work on the importance of social information in organizations, see Salancik and Pfeffer 1978; Griffin et al., 1987; Weiss and Nowicki 1981; Weiss and Shaw 1979; and Schnake and Dumler 1987. Further work relevant to the general problem of social proof includes Festinger, Riecken and Schachter 1956; Fuller and Sheehy-Skeffington 1974; Janis 1972; Bierhoff and Bierhoff-Alfermann 1976; Bandura et al. 1977; Giola and Manz 1985; Hogarth, Michaud, and Mery 1980.

come (e.g., noncooperation)" (Miller 1992: 207). Such expectations about the behavior of others can lead to extremely different relationships between subordinates and supervisors or workers and management, which in turn, produce functional or dysfunctional organizational sociologies.

Contemporary economics offers a very similar rationale behind conformity in the study of "informational cascades" and "herd behavior." Scharfstein and Stein (1990) model managers making investment decisions by mimicking the investment decisions of other managers. They find that such imitative behavior is most likely under circumstances where managers have to "share the blame" for failures, or where the external labor market restricts opportunities to exit the firm. Bikhchandani, Hirshleifer, and Welch (1992) argue that it can be optimal for an individual to follow the behavior of those who precede him or her, ignoring his or her own information. Lee (1993) further demonstrates that the informational cascades are optimal when there is a one-to-one mapping between the actions of individuals and their posterior preferences. In a similar vein, Jones (1984) provides an economic perspective on conformity in the workplace, analyzing how subordinates interact with one another. Jones develops twin models of conformity featuring internalization and tradition in a utility maximizing decision environment. All of these models treat conformity as a product of communication, or sharing of information, and not as a result of sanctions on deviants, payoffs for conformity, or (except for Jones) internal preferences for conformity. Individuals behave like the individuals around them, because the behavior of others serves as the best information about maximizing utility.

In a variety of ways, these models provide an explanation for the wide diversity of organizational cultures as well as their persistence. Such models demonstrate how rational actor economic models can be integrated with psychologically- or sociologically-based models of decision making. In turn, models which integrate these perspectives give us insight into a wide variety of factors shaping compliance in a bureaucracy.

The structure of organizational cultures can have tremendous consequences for the prospects of attaining compliance. Conformity that stems from organizational culture can either induce or impede compliance with superiors. Bureaucratic supervisors will experience considerable difficulty in implementing policies that run counter to organizational norms. On the other hand, compliance will be very high in those cases where the organizational culture reinforces the superior's requests.

Modeling Intersubordinate Learning

In this second model, we require that bureaucrats *learn* how to respond to a policy.[5] For the reader who is uncomfortable interpreting models expressed in formal algebraic terms, we encourage the reader to develop an understanding of the verbal story of the model, and perhaps to skip ahead to the next section (Results of the Simulation).

Verbally, the imitation model works as follows. Subordinates confront each new policy by asking two questions. The first question is "How do I feel about the policy?" As we first developed in the enhanced principal agent (EPA) model, subordinates can feel both positively and negatively toward a new policy. We assume that the subordinates' feelings about a policy remain unchanged. The second question is "What do I do about the policy?" Also like the EPA model, subordinates respond with working (devote energy to accomplish a policy), shirking (devote no energy), or sabotage (devote energy to undermine the policy). The utility to the subordinates is a product of the two, such that the subordinate acquires positive utility either by working for desirable policy or by working against undesirable policy. We assume that the supervisor prefers that subordinates work as hard as possible and that the supervisor is allowed to administer penalties to subordinates that she considers to be working at an unacceptable level. Once we subtract any penalties administered by the supervisor, the subordinates then examine the utility of others' choices and adopt the response of the subordinate that appears to be doing the best under the new policy. We let this cycle of subordinate performance, supervisor's punishment, and subordinate imitation repeat until the responses to policy remain fixed.

Formally, we assert that a bureaucrat b may adapt the amount of work w_{br} at each iteration r. Each bureaucrat b maximizes his utility by evaluating the utility obtained by himself for his amount of work against the utility obtained by the other bureaucrats for their amounts of work. In other words, the bureaucrats learn from each other on the basis of imitation, the simplest form of social proof. Our model incorporates "consistency" by requiring that each bureaucrat adopt the responses of another only if the apparent utility of that other's response exceeds his own, current, utility.

---

5. In this model, like the second part of the first model, the plays and responses of bureaucrats and supervisors are iterated. The iterated nature of this model raises the question of the applicability of alternate work, especially the iterated prisoner's dilemma as a model of public goods problems (e.g., Axelrod 1984). While the model itself does not conform to the payoff structure of the prisoner's dilemma (only when the subordinates prefer to shirk does the preferred outcome for subordinates differ from that of the supervisor), the strategy of the supervisor resembles Tit-for-Tat. We hesitate to draw any implications about the relative ineffectiveness of the supervisor in this model to the general usefulness of Tit-for-Tat.

Like the enhanced principal–agent model, bureaucrats have a range of responses to policy, which we take to mean the particular elements of a public policy program (such as the details of a welfare policy), rather than internal organizational policies intended to control the behavior of bureaucrats. Some responses may work against the policy, some responses might work toward a policy. Among a set of m bureaucrats, we define the work of bureaucrat b toward a policy at a given iteration r as w_{br}. When a policy is first implemented among a set of bureaucrats, the bureaucrat's work is distributed normally with mean μ_w and variance σ_w^2:

$$w_{b0} \sim N(\mu_w, \sigma_w^2). \tag{3.1}$$

(When we operationalize this model, we truncate the distribution of work (w_b) and desirability (d_b) to the bounds -1 to 1.) If $w_{br} < 0$, the bureaucrat b is working against a policy (*sabotage*). If $w_{br} > 0$, the bureaucrat b is working in favor of a policy (*work*). Complete shirking occurs when $w_{br} = 0$. (For now, we set aside the distinction between leisure and political shirking.) We opt for a normal distribution that is eventually truncated because it permits us to describe in compact terms a wide range of potential scenarios. Not only are we able to capture the average initial response to a policy (μ_w), but also we are able to capture settings where there is anything from no diversity at all in initial reactions to those where there is wide diversity.

In the enhanced principal–agent model, we defined the utility to bureaucrat b as a production function (U_b) of a bureaucrat's work allocation toward a set of policy outputs, such that:

$$U_b = u_b(x_{ib}, w_{iLb}, w_{iDb}, s_b). \tag{3.2}$$

In this model, we operationalize the production function such that the utility to bureaucrat b is the product of the work that a bureaucrat puts toward a policy (w_{br}) and the desirability of that policy to the bureaucrat (d_b), less any punishment levied by the supervisor (p_b):

$$U_{br} = u_b(w_{br}, d_b, p_b) = w_{br}d_b - p_b. \tag{3.3}$$

And, in the notation of the EPA model, such that[6]

$$U_{br} = U_b = u_b(x_{ib}, w_{iLb}, w_{iDb}, s_b). \tag{3.4}$$

---

6. Note that this model implies costless work and provides one reason why we would expect behavior under this model to run toward extremes.

Further, the desirability of the policy to bureaucrat b (d_b) is distributed normally with mean μ_d and variance σ_d^2:

$$d_b \sim N(\mu_d, \sigma_d^2). \tag{3.5}$$

In other words, a bureaucrat b receives positive utility (U_{br}) at iteration r for either working against a policy she dislikes $(w_{br}, d_b < 0)$ or working for a policy she likes $(w_{br}, d_b > 0)$. The bureaucrat receives negative utility for working for a policy she dislikes $(w_{br} > 0, d_b < 0)$, or working against a policy she likes $(w_{br} < 0, d_b > 0)$. Note that the desirability of a policy (d_b) does not change, whereas the bureaucrat's efforts with respect to the policy may change. The use of the two parameters in the normal distribution also allows us to capture settings where there is consensus about the desirability of policy (low σ_d^2) to those settings where there is little agreement about the policy (high σ_d^2). The punishment (p_b) that a bureaucrat b receives from a supervisor is contingent on whether the supervisor observes b, the tolerance of the supervisor, and the sanction the supervisor applies to the bureaucrat; this parameter is defined explicitly below.

As in the enhanced principal–agent model, we define the utility to the supervisor as a function of the subordinate's responses. In this case, we will let the supervisor's utility at iteration r be the mean of the subordinates' responses:

$$U_s = u_s(w_{br}) = \text{Mean}(w_{br}). \tag{3.6}$$

This means that we always assume that a supervisor always prefers her subordinates to work. Under some conceivable settings, supervisors might prefer the opposite (as in an administration where the EPA or OSHA supervisor stands against increased regulation of industry).

Imitation enters into this model via connections among fellow bureaucrats. In addition to their individual utilities (as a product of their work and attitudes toward policy), the bureaucrats are connected to each other with varying probabilities of contact. We assume that an $m \times m$ matrix of observability O describes the probability that a bureaucrat will see the response and utility for another bureaucrat. Specifically, O_{ij} is the probability that bureaucrat i sees bureaucrat j. We assume that these probabilities are distributed normally with mean μ_O and variance σ_O^2 (but truncated to 0–1 bounds). We define a related matrix O^* as an $m \times m$ matrix of 1's and 0's recording whether bureaucrat i actually sees bureaucrat j (1 denotes seen, 0 denotes unseen).

Likewise, we assume that the supervisor's ability to observe bureaucrats also varies. The vector S_b $(m \times 1)$ describes the probability that the supervisor sees bureaucrat *b*. This vector is distributed normally with mean μ_S and variance σ_S^2, truncated to 0–1 bounds. The related matrix S^* records whether the supervisor actually *sees* the bureaucrats.

Once we move from a model with a single subordinate to a model with multiple subordinates, we not only introduce problems of cross-subordinate influence, we also implicitly invoke problems of ambiguous performance standards and enforcement by the supervisor. In many organizational settings, a supervisor might be able to identify the workers from the shirkers with ease. In a production line setting, the foreman is probably relatively well-equipped to identify which workers are completing tasks at an appropriate rate and which are not.

But in political settings, supervision across multiple subordinates becomes murkier. Consider one of the examples we will use later in this book: the amount of time that a police officer spends shirking, or "actively not looking for work." Merely by driving around in the patrol car, police officers provide some measure of deterrence. Officers also express something of a firehouse attitude, where they regard the time that they are not actively handling a complaint as time that they should spend in a state of alert readiness. What should the supervisor declare as the appropriate amount of time to be driving around in the patrol car?

Two variations of our model permit two distinct methods by which the supervisor might discriminate between acceptable and unacceptable performance. One method is for the supervisor to punish defectors whose performance stands out from the others. This method, which we refer to as "relative punishment," obviously has the potential to exaggerate the effects of conformity. An old saying from the Soviet bureaucracy probably puts it best: "The nail that sticks up gets hammered down." An alternative method is for the supervisor to establish some fixed standard of acceptable behavior. Anyone who performs below that standard is punished. We refer to this method as the "fixed standards" method.[7]

Under the "relative punishment" method, supervisors punish defectors, provided that the defection is beyond some threshold of tolerance *and* the supervisor detects the defection. We assume that supervisors cannot necessarily identify the optimum efficiency of a policy, but that supervisors are able to see the range of work from bureaucrats. (In this model, supervisors *are* able to see the net output from the *m* bureaucrats, even if individual bureaucrats' behavior

---

7. A further variation of this model, consistent with much of what we know happens in organizations, would permit coworkers to punish defections by fellow bureaucrats. This variation should surely increase the conformity among the bureaucrats, strengthening the robustness of the conclusions we report below.

is invisible.) Bureaucrat b receives a punishment $p_b = P$ from a supervisor if and only if:

$$w_{br} < \text{Mean}(w_{br}) - (T \times \text{Std. Dev.}(w_{br})) \text{ and } S_b^* = 1 \tag{3.7}$$

where T is the rate of toleration of variation in response and P is the sanction applied to defectors. That is, the supervisor punishes b if the work from b is T standard deviations below the mean. T may be negative, in which case the supervisor punishes even those bureaucrats who perform at rates *above* the mean for the m bureaucrats. We may also vary the level of sanction (P).

Under the "fixed standards" method, bureaucrat b receives punishment $p_b = P$ from a supervisor if and only if:

$$w_{br} < S \text{ and } S_b^* = 1 \tag{3.8}$$

where S is the standard set by the supervisor, and falls in the range -1 to 1. When S is close to 1, the supervisor is relatively intolerant of shirking. When S is close to -1, the supervisor lets all behaviors pass.

Bianco and Bates (1990) argue for a distinction between a "limited" and an "enhanced" leader, where the leader distributes residuals within a team production setting. The "enhanced" leader is able to observe the contribution of every member of the group, while the "limited" leader only observes the net output. A further variation of the punishment scheme in our model is an extension of the "fixed standards" approach: we allow an omniscient supervisor that is able to observe the work of every subordinate. Under the "omniscient supervisor" method, bureaucrat b receives a punishment $p_b = P$ from a supervisor if and only if:

$$w_{br} < S. \tag{3.9}$$

After bureaucrats act out their initial responses (w_{b0}), supervisors assess performance and punish defectors. After the supervisor punishes the defectors, the bureaucrats engage in a search to improve their utility from their response to a policy. Bureaucrats maximize U_b, but they can only choose from a set of responses at that iteration (w_{br}). Bureaucrat i adopts the response of the bureaucrat who achieves the highest utility, among the set of bureaucrats that bureaucrat i sees:

$$\text{Choose } w_j \text{ iff } u_j = \max(u|O_{ij}^* = 1). \tag{3.10}$$

That is, bureaucrat i imitates bureaucrat j if bureaucrat j obtained the maximum utility visible to bureaucrat i. If there are no bureaucrats visible to i, then bureaucrat i retains his response from that iteration. Further, bureaucrat i always sees himself, so that he never adopts the performance of a bureaucrat faring worse than himself.

We note that there are some significant differences between our imitation model and the models of herd behavior or informational cascades. Unlike Jones's (1984) model of conformity, individuals in our model do not maintain a preference for conforming. Unlike the model developed by Bikhchandani, Hirshleifer, and Welch (1992), or Lee's (1993) extension, individuals in our model act simultaneously, not sequentially. Also unlike the latter models, the information pool (the set of responses to policy) remains fixed, without innovations in information.

As we discussed earlier in the chapter, we should expect the bureaucrats to converge to a "standard operating procedure." From the formal theory tradition, we expect to see the emergence of an equilibrium of work. From the organization theory tradition, we expect bureaucracies to develop routines. (And, as the reader will see below, the work of subordinates converges very rapidly.) Formally, we designate a "standard operating procedure" (w_{bf}) as a response that does not vary in future iterations:

$$w_{bf} \equiv w_{br} = w_{br'} \quad \forall \, r' > r. \tag{3.11}$$

What influences the final distribution of w_{bf}? We might proceed, as we do in the enhanced principal–agent model, to identify the marginal effect of supervision, tolerance (T) and sanction (P) on the supervisor's outcome:

$$\frac{\partial U_{sf}}{\partial T} = \frac{\partial}{\partial T} \text{Mean}(w_{bf}). \tag{3.12}$$

However, we believe that a closed form solution to this model is unattainable. In addition to the scalars for tolerance (T) and sanction (P), the adaptation of the bureaucrats is nonlinear and contingent on four discrete sets: the available set of responses to a policy (w_{b0}, responses at first iteration), disposition toward a policy (d_b), and connections among bureaucrats (O_{ij}) and supervisors (S_b). Learning is not continuous. We do not assert that a closed form solution is impossible, only that we are unable to produce one.

Our model is obviously a complex one. But instead of removing aspects of our model that we consider to be vital so that we might arrive at closed form solutions, we advocate the use of computer simulation in order to produce a statistical solution. In addition to the advantages of permitting a higher level of complexity, computer simulations allow several unique advantages. We can

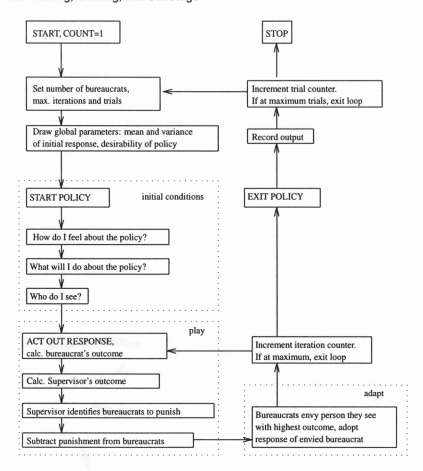

Fig. 3.1. Flowchart for imitation model

vary the initial conditions of the model, and replicate the model over an arbitrary number of settings. We can run each round of a replication for arbitrary duration, allowing us to have arbitrarily tight standard errors for our estimates. Appendix A (Models) provides a full description of the methods we use in conducting the simulation. A flow chart of the simulation of the Imitation model appears in figure 3.1.

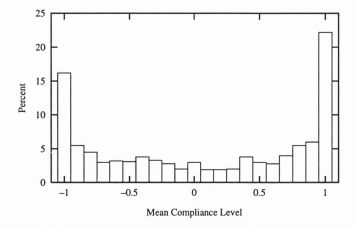

Fig. 3.2. Histogram of mean compliance level, imitation simulation, punishment by fixed standard

Results of the Simulation

There are six possible variations of our model that we simulate here, with three enforcement methods (relative punishment, fixed standards, omniscient and fixed) by two ranges of disposition (random initial predispositions and positive predispositions). The chief dependent variable of interest is the supervisor's utility, the mean of the bureaucrats' final responses (w_{bf}).

The six simulations generate one of two archetypal histograms of the supervisor's utility. One of these forms appears in figure 3.2, which reflects the "fixed standard" mode of enforcement and where the subordinates' predispositions toward the policy vary from -1 to $+1$. The histogram displays the distribution of the supervisor's utility (which we model as the mean compliance level in equation 3.6) at the final iteration for each of the 1,000 replications. This simulation produces rapidly converging responses which hug one of two extremes (-1 or $+1$). (Although not shown here, there is little deviation among the workforce. After only ten iterations of punishment and adaptation, the modal standard deviation of the bureaucrat's response is zero.)

In fact, histograms of the bureaucrats' response to policy under the "relative punishment" and "omniscient supervisor" methods are virtually identical to the histogram from the "fixed standards" approach. (And the reader will shortly see some confirmation of the striking robustness of the results of the model in the statistical estimates below, which are nearly identical across the variations.)

Figure 3.3 demonstrates the other archetypal form of bureaucrats' response under the imitation model. This histogram depicts the final compliance of the subordinates when the subordinates are positively predisposed to the policy and where the supervisor enforces from a fixed standard. Here, the histogram is sharply skewed toward working (+1), but there is still a tail that extends all the way toward complete sabotage (−1). The presence of the tail in this histogram leads to our first substantive conclusion from the model: learning by imitation can lead agents to behave in ways which are contrary to their initial preferences.

Why is it that these subordinates, who actually favor the policy in question, can sometimes be in a position where they are undermining the policy? The answer stems from the mechanics of the model. Subordinates begin with the same repertoire of responses to policy that exists throughout the model. There are no innovations to the set of responses. If positively predisposed subordinates begin with a repertoire of responses to policy which only include varying degrees of sabotage, the subordinates learning by imitation will always be undermining policy and can only improve to the extent that they minimize the level of sabotage. Although the result is an immediate consequence of the structure of the model, we think that it resonates with real circumstances. Well-intentioned people may not understand that there are positive ways to improve upon policy. Although the subordinates may be making the best of a bad situation, it is still a bad situation.

Again, the figure for the positively predisposed subordinates in the "fixed standards" approach is virtually identical to equivalent histograms for the "relative punishment" and "omniscient supervisor" approaches.

That the process converges toward extremes is hardly a surprise: the simulated bureaucrats learn what to do from the people who either possess strong feelings about the policy, respond strongly to the policy, or both. What is surprising are the factors that account for the positive or negative sign on the final response: the mean feeling about the policy and the mean response to the policy appear to affect the sign of the final efficiency, whereas the severity of punishment, the supervisor's rate of observation and the tolerance rate do not appear to affect the sign.

Our method for assessing the effects of the different factors on the imitation model is to apply maximum likelihood techniques utilizing an appropriate distribution. One of the more common distributions we will use in this book is the *beta distribution*. It is exceptionally well-suited for models where the dependent variable is bounded, but where the distribution itself varies significantly in shape across different contexts, or across different representations of the dependent variable. Further discussion of the beta distribution appears in Appendix B (Distributions).

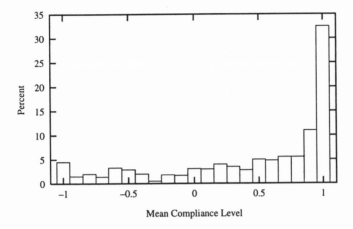

Fig. 3.3. Histogram of mean compliance level, imitation simulation, punishment by fixed standard, positive predisposition

From the organization theory tradition, we would expect the magnitude and frequency of punishment to affect both compliance and defection. Additionally, this tradition should also lead us to expect that the supervisor's capacity to induce compliance should also depend on the supervisor's probability of seeing any given bureaucrat. From the logic of this imitative model, we should expect the mean of the bureaucrats' feelings about the policy and initial reactions to the policy to affect both compliance and defection. (Since the bureaucrats learn from each other, and only from the set of reactions and feelings present at the outset, the initial state of both parameters should affect the final outcome.) The variation among the bureaucrats' sense of what to do about the policy should also affect the extent to which the bureaucrat is drawn to the extremes: the more variation in the response to the policy, the more likely that the set of bureaucrats will be able to pick an extreme response. The degree of connectivity among the bureaucrats should also tend to encourage policies to drift to the extremes: the more highly connected the workforce is, the more likely that there will be little variation among the bureaucrats at the final outcome. All of these predictions bear forth, save the prediction that punishment rates and tolerance matter.

We report the beta coefficients for each of the six principal variations of the imitation model in Appendix C (Estimates) in table C.1. For purposes of interpreting the effects of the coefficients, we direct the reader to table 3.1. Interpreting maximum likelihood coefficients can be cumbersome, and so for the main discussion in each chapter, we will focus on three different techniques.

First, the statistical significance of beta model coefficients is directly interpretable, although usually of less interest than the substantive significance. In the present case, since we have arbitrary control over the precision of the estimates (by adding more replications), the lack of statistical significance for a coefficient means that it has essentially no effect on the compliance of the subordinates. In addition to our calculations of the effect of the variables, table 3.1 also displays one of three symbols denoting the nature of statistical significance of the estimates. The left-triangle ($\triangleleft$) indicates that the shirking parameter is statistically significant at $p < .05$, but not the working parameter; in other words, the effect of the variable is on shirking, but not on working. The right-triangle ($\triangleright$) means that the working parameter is statistically significant, but not the shirking parameter. The bowtie ($\bowtie$) indicates that both the working and shirking parameters are statistically distinguishable from zero with $p < .05$.

Second, we can interpret the substantive effects of changes in the variables

TABLE 3.1. Estimated Effects of Supervision and Bureaucrats' Attitudes on Compliance

	Random Initial Predispositions		
	Relative Punishment	Fixed Standards	Omniscient and Fixed
Mean desirability (d_b)	.38 $\bowtie$	.35 $\bowtie$	.26 $\bowtie$
Mean initial response (μ_w)	.36 $\bowtie$	.33 $\bowtie$	.24 $\bowtie$
Std. dev. (initial response) (σ_w)	.03 $\bowtie$	.00 $\bowtie$	.04 $\bowtie$
Connectivity	−.10 $\bowtie$	−.06 $\bowtie$	.03 $\triangleright$
Tolerance (T)	.08 $\triangleleft$		
Standard		.03	.09 $\triangleleft$
Sanction (P)	.09	.02	.06 $\triangleleft$
Probability supervisor observes	−.06	−.11	

	Positive Initial Predispositions		
	Relative Punishment	Fixed Standards	Omniscient and Fixed
Mean desirability (d_b)	.30 $\bowtie$	.35 $\bowtie$	.17 $\triangleleft$
Mean initial response (μ_w)	.29 $\bowtie$	.40 $\bowtie$	.20 $\bowtie$
Std. dev. (initial response) (σ_w)	.25 $\bowtie$	.24 $\bowtie$	.14 $\triangleright$
Connectivity	.05	.01	.03 $\triangleright$
Tolerance (T)	.03		
Standard		.04	.05
Sanction (P)	.08	.01 $\triangleleft$	−.03 $\triangleleft$
Probability supervisor observes	−.07	−.01	

Note: Estimates are first differences computed on the basis of Maximum Likelihood estimates for the model of the beta distribution. Cells are estimated change in level of working (scale from 0–1) due to a shift of the variable from the mean to the maximum, holding all other variables at their mean. $\triangleleft$ means shirking parameter significant at $p < .05$, $\triangleright$ means working parameter significant at $p < .05$, and $\bowtie$ means both parameters significant at $p < .05$. $N = 1,000$.

with the "first differences" approach. This approach computes a base line value for the dependent variable by evaluating the coefficients at the mean for all variables. Then one computes an alternative value for the dependent variable by evaluating, one by one, the function for each independent variable held at its maximum, while holding the others at the mean. The first difference is the difference between the maximum effect of a variable and the baseline. Since our dependent variable here is scaled in terms of percentage of work, the first differences can be read as the percentage increase (or decrease) in work when one shifts a variable from its mean to its maximum, holding all others at the mean.

A third technique, which we will use sparingly in the present chapter, compares maximum and minimum effects of a variable, holding all the other variables at the mean. By doing so, we can graph the probability density function (PDF) for the variables under different scenarios, a kind of "smoothed-out" histogram.

For example, the mean desirability of the policy consistently is among the strongest effects upon subordinate performance, throughout the six variations. In the "relative punishment–random initial predispositions" variation, a shift from a policy of average desirability to one of maximum desirability accounted for a 38% increase in subordinate compliance. This is surely no great surprise: the more popular a policy is, the more likely that the subordinates will work in favor of the policy. The $\bowtie$ symbol denotes that the effect of desirability of policy can be seen both as discouraging defection and as encouraging cooperation. (A further examination of the actual coefficients suggests some asymmetry across the two extremes: the effect of desirable policy is always greater against sabotage than it is for work.)

Figure 3.4 portrays the effect of the minimum, average, and maximum levels of the desirability of a policy, holding all the other variables at their means, with coefficients drawn from the "fixed standards" model with "random initial predispositions." The desirability of policy has an asymmetric effect in this model. When policy is undesirable to most of the bureaucracy (at the minimum level of desirability), the bureaucracy uniformly engages in sabotage: the density function is sharply skewed to the left. When policy is highly desirable to most of the bureaucracy, it can lead to both widespread compliance and defection: the density function is U-shaped, with the larger tail of the U at the positive, or compliance, end. Desirability of policy is not sufficient to guarantee compliance, although undesirable policy tends to lead to defection in this imitation model.

As the graphical approach illustrates, the most significant factor in guaranteeing compliance is the repertoire of initial responses. The coefficients for the effect of the mean initial response follow a consistent pattern across all six

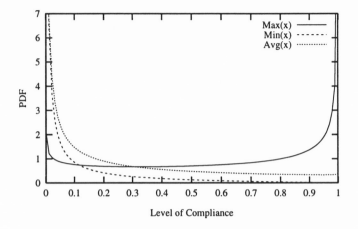

Fig. 3.4. Estimated effect of initial predispositions on compliance

of the variations of the simulation: the effect of a change in the mean initial response from average to maximum produces an increase in cooperation from the subordinates on the order of 20–40 percent, a figure on par with that for the effect of the desirability of the policy. Like the effect of the desirability of the policy, the direction of initial response affects both shirking and working (every effect has a ⋈ symbol).[8]

Figure 3.5 demonstrates the estimated density function for the effect of the minimum, average, and maximum levels for initial response to policy on compliance. Here, the pattern is symmetric and distinct. When the mean initial reaction is sharply negative, then the bureaucracy uniformly engages in sabotage. When the mean initial reaction is sharply positive, the bureaucracy uniformly engages in work. When the mean initial reaction is neutral, sabotage and work are equally probable. In comparison to the effects of the desirability of policy, the effect of the initial response is sufficient to drive the final compliance of the bureaucracy in the simulation.

The variability of that repertoire of initial responses matters also. As the standard deviation of the initial responses increases, the extremes (either sabotage or work) become more probable. The effect of changes in the variability

8. Perusing the actual coefficients leads to further interpretations: under the "random initial predispositions" variations, the effects of ν and ω are roughly equal (although ν is always greater in absolute value than ω). For the three "positive initial predispositions" variations, the effect of ν is substantially greater than the effect of ω. In other words, the more favorable the initial reaction from the bureaucracy, the substantially less likely that bureaucracy is to engage in sabotage. Further, the effect of positive initial responses to policy is much stronger in discouraging sabotage than it is in encouraging work.

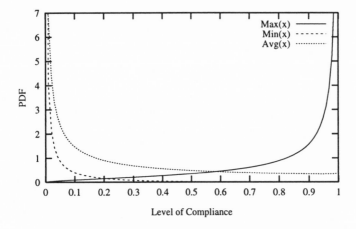

Fig. 3.5. Estimated effect of initial response on compliance

of the repertoire of initial responses is substantively slight under the random initial predispositions: even though both shirking and working coefficients are statistically significant, a change from average to maximum variability leads to at most a 4 percent increase in working. Not so for the effects of variability under the positive initial predispositions setting: a change from average to maximum variability could lead to as much as a 25 percent increase in work. Why the difference? When predispositions may be either positive or negative, wider variability in initial repertoire of responses leads to either extreme equally, depending on the distribution of those predispositions. When predispositions are positive, then an increase in the variability of the initial response means that the subordinates have a greater chance of locating a fellow subordinate working at a high level. The implication is tantalizing: diversity of abilities (initial responses) among subordinates can be a positive boon for the supervisor, provided the subordinates are positively predisposed to the policy. (Of course, subordinates who uniformly prefer the policy and uniformly work their hardest to sustain the policy will yield the best outcome for the supervisor.) Diversity of abilities yields nothing for the supervisor when the distribution of predispositions is as likely to be unfavorable as favorable.

The connectivity of the network of subordinates has a similar although less pronounced effect. The connectivity of the network ranged from zero (which meant that all subordinates acted in isolation) to a maximum of eight (which meant that every subordinate was in contact with a minimum of eight other subordinates).[9] As the network becomes more dense, and subordinates

---

9. Directed graphs and other elements of graph theory make up a peripheral issue in this sim-

have more information to draw on, the extremes become more likely. The substantive effect is usually small. (The one exception appears to be under conditions of relative punishment in the random initial predispositions, where a more densely strung network of subordinates tends to depress work.)

The degree to which a supervisor permitted defection mattered some, but substantially less than the attributes of the bureaucrats. Tolerance (the number of deviations acceptable under relative punishment) affected the level of sabotage but not the level of work, and only slightly so, and only for the "random initial predispositions" variation. In contrast, the mean initial response by subordinates was eight times more important than the supervisor's tolerance in determining the final response. The standard (the cutoff point delineating acceptable and unacceptable performance in the "fixed standards" approach) had an approximately equivalent effect in three out of the four relevant variations. Increasing the level of the standard decreased the chances for sabotage, but did not appreciably affect the chances for work.

Sanctions mattered only in one of the six variations: when the leader was omniscient, and when subordinates possessed (potentially negative) random initial reactions to the policy. When subordinates were already positively predisposed to policy, the level of sanctions had no effect at all, no matter what the system of detection might be. In the lone case where the level of sanction did matter (omniscient supervisors), its effect was asymmetric: it discouraged sabotage, but did not significantly enhance cooperation (i.e., pushed the subordinate compliance to the middle of the range).

Notice that the mean observability of the subordinates to the supervisor had no effect at all on the final compliance of the bureaucracy. In neither the "relative punishment" nor "fixed standards" methods, and for neither the random nor positive predispositions scenarios, does either the shirking or working coefficient for observability achieve any level of statistical significance. This

---

ulation. While the simulation does collect a few graph-theory–based variables, these variables do not turn out to explain a whole lot. One exception is the concept of connectivity or the number of nodes (in this case bureaucrats) one would need to remove to break the communications network into distinct partitions of nodes. (In an unconnected graph, some bureaucrats cannot communicate with other bureaucrats, even via a third set of bureaucrats.) If connectivity is one, then the communication network is connected; in this case, the bureaucrats tend to settle on a single response. If the graph is unconnected, then the bureaucrats settle on more than one response. The diversity of the final response reflects the connectedness of the communications network. Connectivity greater than one has some significance in graph theory, but it seems to result only in faster convergence to a single response. In effect, higher connectivity means a greater likelihood that any bureaucrat will see another. This is slightly surprising, since we originally expected that circuits in the network would tend to increase the instability of the final response. (A circuit exists if communications from bureaucrat i can travel through some other bureaucrats until it reaches back to bureaucrat i.) Connectivity greater than 1 means that a circuit connects all the bureaucrats. See Brualdi (1977) for more information about connectivity in networks.

stands in marked contrast to Bianco and Bates' result, where they found that the "enhanced" leader was able to induce cooperation better than the "limited" leader. We note that under the Bianco and Bates model the task of the leader is to distribute the residuals in a team-production setting, and the interest of the subordinates is to maximize team-production while minimizing their own efforts (free-riding, if possible). Our model is not a team-production setting, and the utility to the subordinates is strictly a product of the individual's performance (and any punishments levied). Furthermore, since punishment is such a weak tool for the supervisor under the imitation model, greater or lesser degrees of observability are unlikely to matter.

In other words, the variables that matter in our imitation model of bureaucratic compliance are those that are associated with the bureaucrats, not with the supervisor. The repertoire of initial responses mattered enormously: final compliance depended mostly on the set of initial reactions by subordinates. The desirability of that policy to subordinates mattered, although it was only sufficient to lead to sabotage, not to lead to work. And the more interconnected the subordinates were, with more variability in the range of initial responses, the more likely that the imitation model led toward extremes. By contrast, the degree of discretion (either tolerance or standard) mattered very little, although some, and the level of sanction mattered in only one out of the six variations. The observability of the subordinates mattered not a whit.

The results of the imitation model are extraordinarily stable with respect to a large number of modifications (not reported in the present tables). We vary the maximum possible punishment to as high as 100 times the maximum possible utility with no effect on the importance of punishment in the final outcome for the supervisor. We allow supervisors to fire defecting subordinates, replacing the defecting subordinate with another draw from the pool (i.e., another subordinate with the same underlying distribution of reactions to policy and desirability of the policy), again with no effect. We permit subordinates the capacity to remember the best outcome they had received, so that subordinates never fare worse on subsequent iterations, also with no effect to the importance of punishment or tolerance.

Propositions for Compliance of Networks of Subordinates

The imitation model we develop in this chapter leads to several specific propositions for the degree to which bureaucracies will comply with political supervisors.

The more individual bureaucrats look to fellow bureaucrats for information about appropriate behavior, the more likely it is that the bureaucrats will be in a state of conformity. The imitation model in this chapter specifically models the effects of looking toward "like others." We found that imitation proved to be an extremely efficient learning process, in the sense of rapid convergence toward an SOP. Our model produced convergence to one or two SOPs in the network within ten iterations, and usually much faster.

Our derivations of the reasons for the emergence of SOPs differ from some prior reasonings. It is possible that SOPs result as the product of top-down management directives about the way members of an organization should handle differing inputs (e.g., Simon 1945, 102–3). It is also possible that SOPs result from management decisions to expel deviants or misfits (e.g., Kaufman 1975). Or it is possible that markets select out organizations with inconsistent behavior (e.g., Kaufman 1985, Nelson and Winter 1982). Under our model, SOPs emerge as equilibrium responses to policy, the result of an informational search among subordinates. We prefer our model, since it describes the emergence of conformity as a consequence of choices by those acting out the SOPs, rather than choices imposed externally by hierarchy or market. Models that externalize the source of conformity trivialize the role of subordinates, while at the same time they assume capitulation by those subordinates to the external factors.

An important aspect of the mode of conformity we are able to produce in our imitation model is that conformity is strictly due to information, rather than coercion, intersubordinate bribery, or a preference for conformity. Subordinates converge to a single SOP because, initially, some subordinate was able to fare better than the others for his choice of response to the policy, and, subsequently, because other subordinates also acquired better utility from the performance. Subordinates exchange two things, and these only: information about their response to a particular policy and the utility they receive from their response.

Unlike the informational cascade models of some recent popularity in economics (Bikhchandani, Hirshleifer, Welch 1992; Welch 1992; Lee 1993), the actors in our model will always fare at least as well as they started. Lee (1993) demonstrates that the informational cascade model developed by Bikhchandani, Hirshleifer, and Welch (1992) has a positive probability that the actors will imitate actions that are counter to their preferences and interests, and worse than alternative actions in the set. Under our model, the bureaucrats never retain a response to policy if they had acted out another response to policy which yielded higher utility. (It is possible that in the short run a bureaucrat will choose a suboptimal response, but in a subsequent iteration, the bureaucrat will reject that response in favor of earlier responses that fared better.) In fact, with only modest probabilities of contact with others, the bureaucrats always choose the response from the repertoire of responses that yields the best outcome. Although the mechanics of the imitation model may seem nonrational, the model generates optimal outcomes for the bureaucrats under relatively weak conditions.

Our model also informs us about what should increase the chances that social proof would be a useful heuristic for a bureaucrat. Among these, *the greater the sense of uncertainty a bureaucrat feels about appropriate behavior, the more likely that bureaucrat will look toward others, which in turn leads to greater conformity.* This proposition may be slightly counterintuitive, in that one might have expected individuals who are uncertain about appropriate behavior might vary significantly in the kinds of behavior they adopt. In our subsequent analysis, the level of conformity in response to policy is most pronounced among those bureaucrats who are in the most uncertain of environments: police officers and social workers. Instead of finding widespread diversity in treatments of an uncertain environment, we will demonstrate convergent and consistent behavior.

Relatedly, *the greater the frequency of contact among subordinates, the greater degree of conformity we would expect to see in their behavior.* The mechanism that produces conformity is information, when subordinates are uncertain. The greater the contact among subordinates, the greater the information the subordinates have about one another's performance. Hence, we expect that the performance of bureaucracies varies more by offices and precincts in the level of compliance with political supervisors, and less by the specific tasks assigned to each bureaucracy.

As we observed in chapter 2 in the interactions between a single subordinate and his supervisor, the performance of subordinates is foremost the product of the preferences of the subordinates. *Whether or not a bureaucracy, in general, tends to comply with political supervisors depends primarily on the policy predispositions of the bureaucrats.* We found that the mean level of the desirability of a policy across the workforce mattered most to the final compliance level of that workforce. In fact, we also found that individuals could be induced to work hard for rules they disliked, or work hard against rules they liked, provided that they were learning by imitation and that there was wide variance in the subordinates' initial response to policy.

Simply to say that subordinate preferences with regard to policy are determinate is a strong statement for theoretic approaches, yet it provides multiple levels of ambiguity in empirical applications. As we will detail in the subsequent chapters, subordinates might derive utility from their performance in many ways. Subordinates might receive pecuniary, or material, benefits from their performance on the job. One's paycheck, job security, and benefits are the pecuniary rewards one receives from the job. Subordinates might also garner utility from their performance on the job. We will show police officers who enjoy their jobs because they believe they help to prevent crime, social workers who prize their jobs because they help to bring people off welfare or protect children, and utility regulators who say that the elderly should not be cut off from the electric grid simply because they are unable to pay their bills. Why these bureaucrats choose to make more work for themselves is directly related to their preferences for the job. We will also demonstrate that solidary benefits, or the rewards one receives from the camaraderie and recognition of ones' peers, are real, and that they affect how subordinates respond.

An additional result is that *learning by imitation might lead to extremism, not to middle-of-the-road behavior.* In this imitation model, individual bureaucrats derived utility on the basis of a function which combined desirability of a policy with level of effort toward the policy. Individuals could maximize their utility only by behaving in an extreme way (working or sabotaging to the maximum and minimum of the range of the repertoire of initial responses to the policy).

The most common manifestation of subordinate performance we will show in this book will not only be conformist, but it will also favor high levels of productivity and superior performance. As our models demonstrate, when subordinates maintain preferences that favor supervisors' policy, then we expect that performance will be skewed in favor of working, rather than shirking or sabotage. Most of the bureaucrats in this book are strong performers, no matter the level of bureaucracy, and no matter who is observing. *Learning by imitation can lead to extreme levels of compliance as well as extreme levels of noncompliance.* It may be a convention in contemporary models of the behavior of bureaucratic agents to treat the preferences of the agents as opposite to those of the supervisor. We demonstrate that there are circumstances under which a "corporate culture" within the bureaucracy can lead to exceptional levels of effort, not just shirking and sabotage.

If subordinates adopt SOPs on the basis of learning by imitation, their supervisors are but feeble influences on the ultimate compliance level of their bureaucracies. Note that supervisors in the imitation model were liberated from many constraints: no civil service laws, no ambiguity of production. We allowed supervisors to be omniscient, eliminating the hidden action aspects of principal–agency problems. We allowed supervisors to act as tyrants and to slap outrageous penalties upon their subordinates. Yet no matter how we varied the capacities of supervisors, the preferences and repertoire of subordinates determined how the subordinates performed.

Our enterprise in the six chapters to follow is to test the propositions derived from the EPA model and the imitation model on the behavior of individual bureaucrats in a diverse range of bureaucracies.

CHAPTER 4

The Preferences of Federal Bureaucrats

Our models of bureaucratic behavior depart from those of prior scholars of bureaucracy when we argue that bureaucrats prefer nonpecuniary as well as pecuniary rewards. In this first empirical chapter, we look to the descriptive information taken from a series of three massive surveys of the federal bureaucracy in 1979, 1983, and 1992. With descriptive statistics from these surveys, we make our first pass at three pivotal questions. What do bureaucrats prefer? How effective are the coercive aspects of supervision at encouraging better performance? How hard do bureaucrats work?

By pecuniary rewards, one might mean pay, promotions, job security, perquisites, or leisure. Any incentive which the principal offers to the agent as a condition of employment could be considered to be a pecuniary reward. Recall from chapter 1 that two of the more significant forms of pecuniary rewards featured in the scholarship on bureaucracy include leisure time (à la Alchian and Demsetz 1972) or budget (à la Niskanen 1975). Leisure time is a relatively straightforward incentive to operationalize, but budget is less obvious in the context of individual bureaucrats who exercise no direct control over the budget. Instead, look to the things that an expanded budget might purchase: greater pay, bonuses, fewer hours, or perks.

By nonpecuniary rewards, one might look toward specific policy accomplishments, recognition from others for service, or the friendship of coworkers. Borrowing from the language on interest groups (Clark and Wilson 1961, Salisbury 1969), we distinguish between *functional* and *solidary* preferences for one's job. A functional preference is one where the subordinate acquires utility by performing the very things that he is supposed to do. A police officer who likes his job because he likes to arrest criminals or to assist lost children has a functional attachment to the job. Likewise, Environmental Protection Agency inspectors who want to reduce pollution, social workers who want to move people off of welfare, and utility regulators who want to keep continuous service are all motivated by a functional preference.

A solidary preference for one's job occurs when the subordinate acquires utility from the friendship with fellow employees. The bureaucrat who enjoys his job because of the department's softball team and the police officer who

75

likes his job because of the support from fellow officers are both expressing a solidary attachment. We take a brief detour to explain our data sources for this chapter and then turn to the three questions raised at the outset of this chapter.

Data

The data for this chapter (and the one to follow) come from a series of three surveys conducted by the Office of Personnel Management. The first two surveys fall under a common title, the "Federal Employee Attitudes" survey (ICPSR 7804, 6304); the more recent 1992 survey came under the label of "Survey of Federal Government Employees" (ICPSR 9983). These are enormous studies that cut across dozens of different agencies, ranging from the military (Office of the Secretary, Army, Navy, Air Force and Logistics) through human services (Housing and Urban Development, Health and Human Services). All of the studies are voluminous not just in terms of the number of respondents and the breadth of agencies covered but also in terms of the number of questions that are asked. Only a handful of questions are replicated on all three waves, although there are many questions with a high degree of similarity.

Our tactic in this chapter is to compare distributions of a selected subset of the questions that reflect the preferences of subordinates, the effectiveness of the supervisor in encouraging better performance, and measures of how hard the subordinate works at his or her job. Except where there appears to be useful information gained by such an approach, we will not be presenting the marginals broken down by agency. The patterns are quite uniform across the agencies, and we will be reporting the exceptions.

The first of these studies began as part of an evaluation of the 1978 Civil Service Reform Act. In 1979, the Office of Personnel Management distributed 20,000 questionnaires to a stratified random sample of federal employees. Sample selection was drawn from the Central Personnel Data File (thus a listed sample). Of those 20,000, a total of 13,862 were returned (for a completion rate of 69 percent). Because of an unequal probability of selection varying by agency, the data must be weighted by the probability of selection before tabulation (as has been done for this chapter).

The second study was intended to be an additional follow-up on the Civil Service Reform Act. The survey took place in September and October of 1983, with a sample again drawn from the Central Personnel Data File. A total of 20,152 valid cases were returned. The completion rate for this self-administered questionnaire was an astoundingly high 74 percent.

The third study, completed in early 1992, was the first survey conducted by the OPM of federal employees since the 1983 wave. Again, the sample was drawn from the Central Personnel Data File, for a total of 56,797 sample persons. The number of usable surveys returned was 30,854, for a completion rate of 54 percent.[1] We now turn to some results from these studies.

Pecuniary and Nonpecuniary Incentives

The fundamental pecuniary incentive of any organization is the base pay. The evidence here is that the federal employees across all agencies are sensitive to their level of pay, but with implications that immediately suggest that other incentives—pecuniary or otherwise—must be important in their selection of their job. Table 4.1 presents responses to three relevant questions from the most recent 1992 Survey of Federal Employees (SOFE).[2]

Satisfaction with pay levels is low. Nearly half of the respondents answered "Strongly Disagree" or "Disagree" to the question "I am satisfied with my pay." Although there is no agency in which a majority of the respondents indicated satisfaction with pay, it is also the case that of the 32 agencies covered in the 1992 SOFE, majorities were in disagreement in only 8 of those agencies (Food and Drug Administration [FDA], National Institutes of Health [NIH], Health and Human Services [HHS], Parks, Interior, Customs, Office of Personnel Management [OPM], and Veterans Affairs).

---

1. The significant variation in the nonresponse rates across the four waves is typical for academic surveys in person, and actually substantially higher than most mail questionnaires. Because no information was collected about the nonrespondents, model-based nonresponse adjustments are not possible.

2. Due to the enormous size of the samples in the three studies, virtually every difference is a statistically significant one: for instance, the margin of error in the 1992 SOFE at the 95% confidence level is plus or minus 1.1%. We will draw attention to the circumstances where one could find a majority of the respondents in agreement or disagreement.

TABLE 4.1. Employees' Reported Satisfaction with Pay, 1992 Survey of Federal Employees

Question	Strongly Disagree	Disagree	Neither Agree nor Disagree	Agree	Strongly Agree
I am satisfied with my pay.	17.9	31.9	18.3	28.3	3.6
Considering the skills and effort I put into my work, I am satisfied with my pay.	20.5	37.1	16.4	23.5	2.5
My pay is fair considering what other places in this area pay for the same kind of work.	15.1	27.7	25.7	28.8	2.6

Note: Cells are percentages weighted by probability of selection.

When one shifts the question to reflect on what the employees bring to their jobs, the level of dissatisfaction rises, and uniformly so. A solid majority (57 percent) disagrees with the statement "Considering the skills and effort I put into my work, I am satisfied with my pay." More than 50 percent disagree with the statement in every one of the 32 agencies.

The third question in the table is relevant to whether the employees could take those skills elsewhere. Overall, 42 percent of the respondents disagreed with the statement "My pay is fair considering what other places in this area pay for the same kind of work." One finds that a majority were in disagreement with the statement only in three of the agencies (Parks, HHS, and Veterans Affairs). Nonetheless, considering the high level of dissatisfaction with pay, the proportion is sizable who believe they would be more fairly compensated elsewhere.

A second handle on the preferences of subordinates is to ask what they would prefer as compensation for good work. There is strong evidence to demonstrate that the employees preferred increases in pay as a reward for good performance (table 4.2). In response to the question "To what extent would you like to receive each of the following as a reward for good performance?" employees overwhelmingly supported three of the options to a "great extent." An outstanding performance rating (80 percent), an increase in base pay (82 percent), and a cash bonus (77 percent) were favored by supermajorities (greater than two-thirds) across every agency. Of the three, the "outstanding performance rating" stands out as slightly anomalous: we will show there is a weak relationship between strong performance ratings and pay increases. The majority supporting "recognition" of some form leads one to think that the potential

TABLE 4.2. Employees' Preferences about Potential Rewards for Good Performance, 1992 Survey of Federal Employees

Question	No Extent	Some Extent	Great Extent
Recognition (e.g., verbal praise, certificate)	3	41	56
An outstanding performance rating	1	19	80
An increase in base pay	2	16	82
A cash bonus	2	21	77
Paid time off	20	43	37
A training opportunity	15	47	38
A special assignment	13	44	44

Note: Cells are percentages weighted by probability of selection, in response to the question "To what extent would you like to receive each of the following as a reward for good performance?"

connection of performance ratings to pay is part, but not all, of the story. Praise is in and of itself a reward for good performance.

If leisure-maximization means "equal pay for less work," then it should be readily apparent from table 4.2 that it is not regarded by the employees as one of the more significant rewards. "Paid time off" was the least popular of the seven alternatives. In fact, *additional* work ("a special assignment") earned greater levels of support than did time off. While the employees were clearly motivated by pecuniary returns, maximizing those returns by maximizing leisure is not demonstrated by the evidence.

Rewards such as these are infrequent. But accomplishment, security, respect, and friendship can be daily commodities. We find evidence of the mix of nonpecuniary as well as pecuniary preferences for the job from the earlier surveys. The 1979 and 1983 Federal Employees Attitude Survey (FEA) were closely intertwined with parallel questions. One of the pertinent batteries of questions asked the respondents:

> Different people want different things from their work. Here is a list of things a person could have on his/her job. How important is each of the following to you?'

The results for the batteries appear in table 4.3.

In both the 1979 and 1983 surveys, the most popular aspect of job was a nonpecuniary return: "getting a feeling of accomplishment from your job." Fully 77 percent of the respondents in 1979 and 65 percent of the respondents in 1983 felt that a feeling of accomplishment was "very important."[3] The second most popular alternative in 1979 (not asked in 1983) was a very similar option: "The chances you have to accomplish something worthwhile." Neither of these questions imply any personal financial gain to the respondents, yet both are directly related to the supervisors' requests to the subordinate. These are *functional* attachments, since the acquisition of these benefits is a direct product of performing well.

The next most popular aspect of the job is a pecuniary reward, and one that turns out to be enormously important for subsequent tables on the reasons employees accepted and retain their jobs. "The amount of job security you have" garnered nearly 59 percent in 1979 and over 61 percent in 1983, and highly uniformly across the agency. In fact, majorities supported the "very important" label in all but five of twenty agencies surveyed in 1979 and 1983 (but not the same five).

---

3. The verbal interpretation of the middle categories is cumbersome, since the questionnaire itself failed to label the midpoints. We will refer to the fourth category (between "somewhat important" and "very important") as "important," although there is no such label.

There is a further indication in the present table that the value of recognition as a reward (noted above in Table 4.2) is more than the pecuniary return of potential advancement. In every agency, more than 50 percent of the respondents felt that "the respect you receive from the people you work with" was "very important." Further, "the friendliness of the people you work with" achieved a high degree of support (a majority saying "important" or "very important" in every agency). At the same time, the chance of receiving a performance award was the least important aspect across both surveys. The importance of recognition from others, and of friendships with others, is what we identify as a *solidary* attachment to the job.

Pecuniary motives, especially job security, dominate the reasons that employees express for taking a job with the federal government (table 4.4). Respondents were asked "How important was each of the following factors in

TABLE 4.3. Employees' Assessment of Importance of Aspects of Job, 1979 and 1983 Federal Employees Attitude Surveys

Question	Not Important at All		Somewhat Important		Very Important
	1979				
The friendliness of the people you work with?	1.2	1.7	21.9	29.3	45.8
Getting a feeling of accomplishment from your job?	.3	.3	4.9	16.8	77.6
The respect you receive from the people you work with?	.6	1.0	13.3	27.4	57.6
The chances you have to accomplish something worthwhile?	.4	.7	9.0	26.3	63.7
Your chances for getting a promotion?	3.0	3.0	17.8	23.0	53.2
The amount of job security you have?	1.5	2.2	15.8	21.7	58.8
Your chances of receiving a performance award?	8.0	9.4	29.1	20.5	32.9
	1983				
Getting a feeling of accomplishment from your job?	.8	.7	11.2	22.0	65.2
The amount of job security you have?	.9	1.3	15.0	21.5	61.3
Your chances of receiving a performance award?	8.2	9.0	29.4	20.1	34.4

Note: Cells are percentages weighted by probability of selection, in response to the question "Different people want different things from their work. Here is a list of things a person could have on his/her job. How important is each of the following to you?" Question responses between "Not Important at All" and "Somewhat Important" and between "Somewhat Important" and "Very Important" were unlabeled in questionnaire.

your decision to work for the federal government?" Nearly half of the respondents in both 1979 and 1983 felt job security was "very important." Fringe benefits and salary were second and third in the average level of support. Close behind the pecuniary incentives was support for "challenging work responsibilities." Distinctly at the bottom of the list is the "opportunity for public service," where the modal category is "somewhat important."

Pecuniary motives dominate the reasons that employees express for *retaining* a job with the federal government (table 4.5). In fact, the order of support is exactly the same as the reasons for taking a job, but the marginals supporting the "very important" category are all larger. More than half of the respondents across every agency felt that salary and job security were "very important," and nearly half felt the same for fringe benefits. Challenging work responsibilities and opportunities for public service fall far down on the list.

No mistake should be made: employees express strong preferences for pecuniary rewards. At the same time, there is evidence that nonpecuniary rewards are also appreciated. Because it may be more difficult to obtain pecuniary rewards than nonpecuniary rewards, the presence of functional and solidary attachments can be enormously important for understanding subordinate performance. In table 4.6, we look to functional attachments across the three different surveys.

TABLE 4.4. Employees' Assessment of Importance of Reasons They Took a Job with the Federal Government, 1979 and 1983 Federal Employees Attitude Surveys

Question	Not Important at All		Somewhat Important		Very Important
1979					
Salary	4.2	5.1	33.5	23.7	33.5
Fringe benefits	3.8	4.7	25.6	27.1	38.9
Challenging work responsibilities	4.1	6.3	27.1	30.1	32.4
Job security	2.7	3.8	19.8	24.7	49.0
Opportunity for public service	17.8	14.8	32.2	19.2	16.1
1983					
Salary	3.8	5.6	35.0	21.7	33.9
Fringe benefits	4.7	5.8	26.8	22.9	39.9
Challenging work responsibilities	4.2	5.3	28.0	28.8	33.7
Job security	2.1	3.3	17.9	22.5	54.2
Opportunity for public service	20.2	14.3	30.9	17.3	17.4

Note: Cells are percentages weighted by probability of selection, in response to the question "There are various reasons for selecting a place of employment. How important was each of the following factors in your decision to work for the federal government?" Question responses between "Not Important at All" and "Somewhat Important" and between "Somewhat Important" and "Very Important" were unlabeled in questionnaire.

Personal accomplishment, satisfaction, and challenge of the job matter in all three surveys. Over 90 percent of the respondents in the 1979 and 1983 surveys agreed with the statement "Doing my job well gives me a feeling that I've accomplished something worthwhile." More than 90 percent of the respondents in the 1979 survey agreed with "Doing my job well makes me feel good about myself as a person." Nearly 80 percent of the respondents agreed with "I enjoy doing my work for the personal satisfaction it gives me."

The 1992 SOFE did not ask exactly equivalent questions, but majorities expressed support for functional attachments in other forms. More than 50 percent of the respondents in every agency agreed with the statements "I like making decisions that affect other people" and "My job is challenging." In one-third of the agencies, we find that more than half of their respondents agreed with "I am satisfied with the chances I have to accomplish something worthwhile."

At the same time that respondents across the three studies express strong functional attachments to their jobs, there is also a substantial proportion who agree with the statement "I often think about quitting." To be sure, over a majority in every agency but one (Treasury) disagrees with the statement, but in every agency, over twenty percent agree. More than a third agreed with the statement in Energy, HHS, Labor, OPM, and State.

Employees value pecuniary returns. Pay and cash bonuses are preferred over other forms of compensation for good performance. In contrast to non-pecuniary returns, job security and pay matter most in their reasons to take and keep a job. While employees may not be leisure maximizers, the implications of the findings in this chapter is that they would certainly approve of an expanded budget that happened to yield greater benefits for employees. At

TABLE 4.5. Employees' Assessment of Importance of Reasons to Stay Working for the Federal Government, 1983 Federal Employees Attitude Surveys

Question	Not Important at All		Somewhat Important		Very Important
Salary	1.6	2.4	19.7	24.1	52.3
Fringe benefits	2.9	4.4	19.8	23.7	49.3
Challenging work responsibilities	3.3	3.9	23.3	28.0	41.5
Job security	1.4	2.8	15.0	21.5	59.3
Opportunity for public service	18.1	13.0	31.8	17.9	19.1

Note: Cells are percentages weighted by probability of selection, in response to the question "How important is each of the following for you to stay working for the federal government?" Question responses between "Not Important at All" and "Somewhat Important" and between "Somewhat Important" and "Very Important" were unlabeled in questionnaire.

the same time, we also find that nonpecuniary returns in the form of recognition from others, accomplishing worthwhile things, serving the public interest, all have some level of desirability. In the next section, we explore the degree to which employees and their supervisors sense that employees can maximize pecuniary benefits through good performance.

Effectiveness of Supervision in Encouraging Performance

In response to widespread public concern over perceived bureaucratic inefficiency, Congress passed the Civil Service Reform Act of 1978 (CSRA). Among the linchpins of the CSRA are performance appraisals, to be completed by the immediate supervisor and to be used for potential personnel actions.

The employees regard as appropriate bases of pay the very things that a principal would prefer. Performance on the job appears to be valued by employees. When asked about their beliefs about the appropriate bases for pay (table 4.7), employees testify support for the same criteria as would be favored

TABLE 4.6. Employees' Functional Attachments to Job, 1979 and 1983 Federal Employee Attitude Surveys, 1992 Survey of Federal Employees

Question	Strongly Disagree	Disagree	Neither Agree nor Disagree	Agree	Strongly Agree
			1979		
Doing my job well gives me a feeling that I've accomplished something worthwhile.	1.4	3.6	3.3	50.8	40.9
Doing my job well makes me feel good about myself as a person.	0.6	1.2	1.9	53.8	42.5
I enjoy doing my work for the personal satisfaction it gives me.	1.6	6.2	7.7	59.3	25.2
I often think about quitting.	25.5	35.5	8.9	19.0	11.2
			1983		
Doing my job well gives me a feeling that I've accomplished something worthwhile.	1.2	3.4	4.5	47.8	43.2
			1992		
I like making decisions that affect other people.	1.6	7.7	35.1	43.0	12.6
My job is challenging.	5.1	8.9	15.5	46.4	24.1
I am satisfied with the chances I have to accomplish something worthwhile.	8.0	17.5	23.9	42.6	8.1

Note: Cells are percentages weighted by probability of selection.

by management. Overall, majorities agree that pay should be based on job-related experience, level of responsibility, difficulty of the work, quality of performance, amount of work, timeliness of work, and amount of effort. For three of these questions (level of responsibility, difficulty of the work, quality of job performance), more than fifty percent strongly agree. Furthermore, strong support for the three is uniform across all thirty-two agencies (where "only" 49 percent strongly agree to difficulty of work at the USDA and NASA).

Although there was never a majority in disagreement with any of the listed bases for pay, there were some that did not engender as strong support. Level of education garnered a majority agreeing only in four of the agencies (FDA, NIH, HHS, and Commerce). A majority supporting "job-related training" as a criterion could be found only at HHS. No agency yielded a majority supporting seniority ("length of service in the Federal Government"), nor market pressures (cost of labor in the locality).

While individual performance seems to be something that the employees

TABLE 4.7. Employees' Beliefs about Appropriate Bases for Pay, 1992 Survey of Federal Employees

Question	Strongly Disagree	Disagree	Neither Agree nor Disagree	Agree	Strongly Agree
Level of education required by the job	6.7	3.2	49.8	13.1	27.2
Job-related training	4.3	4.7	47.0	14.7	29.2
Job-related work experience	1.7	1.5	30.1	19.0	47.7
Level of responsibility	.7	.4	19.1	19.7	60.1
Difficulty of the work	1.1	.6	22.4	20.6	55.3
Quality of job performance	.6	.4	12.6	16.6	69.7
Amount of work done	3.1	2.4	39.4	19.1	36.0
Timeliness of work	2.0	1.5	32.9	21.3	42.3
Amount of effort expended on the job	4.0	3.7	36.4	17.8	38.1
Quality of your work unit's performance	15.6	7.8	39.9	13.1	23.6
Productivity of your work unit	16.8	8.3	42.5	12.9	
Overall performance of your organization or agency	28.7	11.6	39.0	8.5	12.2
The locality (regarding cost of labor) where the job is	13.9	5.2	38.8	13.6	28.4
Length of service in the federal government	17.4	6.9	41.1	12.1	22.5

Note: Cells are percentages weighted by probability of selection, in response to the question "People have different ideas about how they should be paid. How important do you think each of the following should be in determining your pay?"

consider to be a fair basis for pay, the performance of the organization or work unit does not. There were no agencies where a majority could be found agreeing with "quality of your work unit's performance," "productivity of your work unit," or "overall performance of your organization or agency." One could interpret the lack of support for organizational performance (while supporting parallel individual level performance) as some sensitivity to collective goods or team production problems.

One of the most striking changes between the 1979 and 1992 surveys happens in the employees' understanding of the performance appraisals (table 4.8). Majorities of the respondents across every one of the agencies in the 1979 and 1982 surveys agreed with the statement "There is a tendency for supervisors here to give the same performance rating regardless of how well people perform their jobs." By 1992, the majority switches to the other side (to a similar, although not identical question): 65 percent of the respondents disagreed with the statement "In my organization, management gives everyone the same performance rating." As performance appraisals became a more institutionalized feature of working in the federal bureaucracy, subordinates became more aware of variation in those ratings.[4]

---

4. Anecdotal evidence suggests that federal employees are well aware of the specific requirements for their perfomance appraisals, and make specific efforts to ensure that they perform well in those categories covered by the appraisal, perhaps to the neglect of noncovered activities.

TABLE 4.8. Flatness of Performance Ratings, 1979 and 1983 Federal Employee Attitude Surveys, 1992 Survey of Federal Employees

Question	Strongly Disagree	Disagree	Neither Agree nor Disagree	Agree	Strongly Agree
1979					
There is a tendency for supervisors here to give the same performance rating regardless of how well people perform their jobs.	3.9	27.9	13.0	36.3	18.9
1983					
There is a tendency for supervisors here to give the same performance rating regardless of how well people perform their jobs.	4.8	29.2	14.3	34.0	17.7
1992					
In my organization, management gives everyone the same performance rating.	19.3	45.6	27.0	6.7	1.5

Note: Cells are percentages weighted by probability of selection.

Even if the federal employees began to recognize variation in the performance appraisals since the 1978 CSRA, the effect of these appraisals on rewards appears to be relatively flat. Table 4.9 displays the percent agreeing and disagreeing with the effects of supervision and performance appraisals on personnel actions.

In 1979 and 1983, more than half of the respondents agreed with the statement "Performance appraisals do influence personnel actions taken in this organization." Nonetheless, fewer than half of the respondents felt that "when an employee continues to do his/her job poorly, supervisors here will take the appropriate corrective action."

In 1992, when there is a more widespread sense that performance appraisals vary than there is in the earlier studies, the sense that performance is related to compensation is weak. Just under half of the respondents agreed with the statement "I can expect to receive a pay raise or a cash award if I perform exceptionally well," although over a third disagreed with the statement. Less than one-fifth of the respondents felt that "The performance appraisal system in this agency motivates employees to perform well," and less than 40 percent of the respondents agreed that "Pay raises and cash rewards around here depend on how well you perform." The picture that emerges is that unusually high performance ratings may lead to pay raises or cash bonuses, but that usual ratings did not. Further, very few of the respondents felt that the performance appraisal system motivated better performance from employees.

Furthermore, less than a third of the respondents agreed with the statement "My supervisor deals effectively with poor performers," down from the 40 percent agreeing with a comparable statement in 1979 and 1983. No agency had a majority of respondents agreeing or disagreeing with the statements "High performers tend to stay with this organization" and "Low performers tend to leave this organization." (It is interesting to note that more disagreed with the statement that low performers tend to leave than agreed with the statement that high performers tend to stay.) Subordinates appear to have at best a sense that supervisory activity is weakly related to subordinate rewards.

The supervisors themselves feel constrained in their ability to reward employees, but they did not feel constrained in their ability to discipline poor performers (table 4.10). In both the 1979 and 1992 surveys, separate questions were asked only of supervisors. In 1979, the questions about constraints were phrased in the negative ("I do not have enough authority to. . ."), while the questions in the 1992 survey were phrased in the positive ("I have enough authority to. . ."). The two are not logically equivalent, but the parallels between the series, thirteen years apart, are important. One might expect a positivity bias in the later questions, with more supervisors willing to attribute capacities to themselves than to dissociate from those capacities.

In 1979, supervisors tended to feel that "their ability to manage [was] restricted by unnecessary rules and regulations." Almost two-thirds of the supervisors agreed "I do not have enough authority to remove people from their jobs if they perform poorly." In 1992, a less harsh form of punishment than termination, with the question phrased in a more positive light, found supervisors agreeing "I have enough authority to discipline employees if they perform

TABLE 4.9. Employees' Assessment of Effect of Supervision, 1979 and 1983 Federal Employee Attitude Surveys, 1992 Survey of Federal Employees

Question	Strongly Disagree	Disagree	Neither Agree nor Disagree	Agree	Strongly Agree
		1979			
Performance appraisals do influence personnel actions taken in this organization.	5.1	17.1	18.9	49.1	9.8
When an employee continues to do his/her job poorly, supervisors here will take the appropriate corrective action.	15.3	32.8	11.7	34.8	5.4
		1983			
Performance appraisals do influence personnel actions taken in this organization.	5.4	15.7	25.5	44.0	9.4
When an employee continues to do his/her job poorly, supervisors here will take the appropriate corrective action.	15.6	29.3	14.6	34.3	6.2
		1992			
I can expect to receive a pay raise or a cash award if I perform exceptionally well.	14.6	19.6	16.3	36.2	13.3
The performance appraisal system in this agency motivates employees to perform well.	15.3	32.0	33.2	17.4	2.2
Pay raises and cash rewards around here depend on how well you perform.	15.2	22.5	23.3	31.6	7.5
My supervisor deals effectively with poor performers.	12.0	21.5	33.1	25.6	7.9
High performers tend to stay with this organization.	9.0	20.6	30.9	32.3	7.2
Low performers tend to leave this organization.	13.2	31.4	29.4	13.8	2.1

Note: Cells are percentages weighted by probability of selection.

badly." It is possible that the 1979 supervisors may have agreed with the statement in 1992, since "disciplining" employees falls under fewer regulations than "removing people from their jobs."

But supervisors couldn't hire. In 1979, nearly two-thirds of the supervisors agreed that they did not have enough authority to hire competent people when they needed them. Even when phrased in a more positive form, more than half of the supervisors in 1992 disagreed that they had enough authority to hire people.

Nor could supervisors promote. Supervisors in 1979 agreed by nearly two-thirds that they did not have enough authority to promote people, while slightly less than half of the supervisors in 1992 disagreed that they did have the authority.

TABLE 4.10. Supervisors' Assessment of Effect of and Constraints on Supervision, 1979 Federal Employee Attitude Survey and 1992 Survey of Federal Employees

Question	Strongly Disagree	Disagree	Neither Agree nor Disagree	Agree	Strongly Agree
		1979			
Supervisors here feel their ability to manage is restricted by unnecessary rules and regulations.	1.8	23.6	23.6	43.1	7.9
I do not have enough authority to remove people from their jobs if they perform poorly.	3.4	23.2	9.4	44.5	19.5
I do not have enough authority to hire competent people when I need them.	2.6	23.3	8.3	43.1	22.8
I do not have enough authority to promote people.	2.8	24.9	9.0	44.3	19.0
I do not have enough authority to determine my employees' pay.	1.2	12.9	10.2	51.9	23.8
		1992			
I have enough authority to discipline employees if they perform badly.	10.9	15.8	13.9	48.1	11.3
I have enough authority to hire competent people when I need them.	24.9	28.2	14.9	26.4	5.6
I have enough authority to promote people.	21.0	28.5	14.6	30.9	5.1
I have enough authority to determine my employees' pay.	37.1	35.5	14.0	11.7	1.7

Note: Cells are percentages weighted by probability of selection.

Nor could supervisors exercise much control over subordinates' pay. Nearly three-fourths of the supervisors in 1979 felt they did not have enough authority to determine their employees' pay. And nearly the same fraction of supervisors in 1992 disagreed that they had enough authority.

What kinds of capacities do the supervisors in 1992 have? The 1992 supervisors believe that they have authority to discipline poor performers at a higher rate than the 1979 supervisors felt they had the authority to remove poor performers. Part of the difference in the level of support has to be due to the more lenient sanctioning in the later study. But at least half of those supervisors felt that they had some sanctioning capacity. Their capacity to influence pay, hiring, and promotions is much more limited. In fact, in terms of their influence over subordinate pay, the proportions are approximately the same across both years, even with the switch in the positivity of the statement.

The supervisors' assessments of capacity clash with the subordinates' assessments. Subordinates felt that supervisors exercised little control over poor performers, although the supervisors (in 1992) agreed that they had the authority to discipline those who perform badly. Subordinates felt that very high performance appraisals (completed by the supervis or) would lead to pay raises (although they also felt that appraisals in general did not have much bearing on pay); supervisors felt most constrained in their influence over subordinates' pay. Subordinates felt that performance appraisals did influence personnel actions; supervisors felt more constrained in hiring and promotions than they did in discipline.

The story that percolates from the first two sections of this chapter is one of disconnection between incentives and consequences. First and foremost among the preferences of subordinates are the kinds of pecuniary rewards that the formal models of the firm assume as the basis of employee motivation. But present in the mix of preferences is a strong component of a functional attachment, and a modest component of solidary attachment to the organization. Subordinate performance was at best weakly related to acquiring those pecuniary rewards: performance appraisals work only for the extreme employee. Furthermore, supervisors felt highly constrained in their abilities to issue those pecuniary rewards.

If one were constructing a model solely on the basis of pecuniary rewards, this kind of disconnection between incentives and consequences of performance would lead one to expect significant degrees of shirking. If employees were solely motivated by pecuniary rewards, yet were not rewarded for good performance, why would anyone work hard? Yet if the mix of motives includes nonpecuniary motives such as functional or solidary attachments, it may be entirely possible for subordinates to acquire nonpecuniary rewards at work. In the next section, we demonstrate that the bureaucrats believe themselves to be hard workers.

How Hard Do Bureaucrats Work?

A half-caution is warranted: In this chapter, we allow bureaucrats to evaluate themselves. Respondents presumably exaggerate how hard they work, and underreport shirking. (In subsequent chapters we have the benefit of others' observations about how hard any individual employee works, providing another angle on the problem.) But this is only a half-caution: it is surely better to examine the biased self-assessments of activity than it is to assume minimal activity without the benefit of any data. We will show that not only do bureaucrats think that they themselves work hard, but that most of their fellow employees work hard; that supervisors of those bureaucrats tend to believe that subordinates work hard; and that every twist on the question of whether an individual works hard consistently shows an active federal workforce. In subsequent chapters on bureaucrats at other levels, we will rely upon not only self-reports, but independent assessments and administrative records.

In 1979 and 1983, the Federal Employees Attitudes surveys asked the respondents to agree or disagree with the simple statement "I work hard on my job" (table 4.11). Overall, more than 92 percent of the respondents agreed, and the percentages are strikingly uniform. In 1979, the lowest percentage of respondents agreeing with the statement was in the Department of Education (85 percent), and the highest was at NASA (96 percent). In 1983, the lowest percentage agreeing occurred in HUD (80 percent), and the highest in the Departments of Energy and Justice (95 percent). But even at the department with the least numbers agreeing with the statement (HUD), there was a majority of respondents who "strongly agreed."

An alternative phrasing of the questions (not in the table), asked the respondent "Please rate the amount of effort you put into work activities during an average workday" on a scale from "No Effort" (1) through "Some Effort" (3) to "Extreme Effort" (5). The midpoints (2) and (4) appeared unlabeled in the questionnaire. More than 80 percent of the respondents, uniformly across the departments, put themselves at either 4 or 5 on the scale. In 1983, the respondents were asked to "Please rate the amount of effort you put into work activities during an average workday":

- I give no real effort at all (0.1 percent);
- I give enough effort to get by and keep my job (1.1 percent);
- I give the amount of effort expected for the job—I give full services for what I am paid (26.5 percent);
- I work very hard on my job—I put much more effort into my job than is expected of me (55.8 percent);
- I am one of the hardest workers in my office—I often work more than 8

hours a day, take few breaks, and rarely waste time on personal matters (16.5 percent).

Again, a supermajority of the respondents work very hard on the job. And one in six of the respondents perceive themselves to be one of the hardest workers in their offices.

Yet another alternative is to ask questions indirectly related to the effort that the employees expend on the job. In 1979, more than two-thirds of the respondents disagreed with the statement "I have too much work to do to do everything well." In 1992, nearly 85 percent of the respondents disagreed with "Generally, I don't have enough work to do to keep me busy." More than 80 percent of the 1992 respondents agreed with "When I don't feel well in the morning, I still try to come to work because I know my contribution will be missed." And more than 80 percent of the respondents said "People in my unit are expected to work hard." More than a third of the 1992 respondents indicated that they worked overtime, and one in six of the 1992 respondents said that when they worked overtime they received no pay at all.

When one asks the supervisors about how hard people work, the numbers increase. While 79 percent of the nonsupervisory employees agreed that "people in my unit are expected to work hard," 87 percent of the frontline su-

TABLE 4.11. Employees' Evaluation of How Hard They Work, 1979 and 1983 Federal Employee Attitude Surveys, 1992 Survey of Federal Employees

Question	Strongly Disagree	Disagree	Neither Agree nor Disagree	Agree	Strongly Agree
		1979			
I work hard on my job.	.5	4.4	4.6	56.3	34.1
I have too much work to do everything well.	7.5	59.9	8.5	17.1	7.0
		1983			
I work hard on my job.	.3	2.8	3.4	54.8	38.6
		1992			
People in my unit are expected to work hard.	1.5	4.4	13.4	53.6	27.0
Generally, I don't have enough work to do to keep me busy.	53.8	31.4	6.9	5.0	2.9
When I don't feel well in the morning I still try to come to work because I know my contribution will be missed.	2.1	7.7	19.0	52.0	19.2

Note: Cells are percentages weighted by probability of selection.

pervisors and 95 percent of the mid- or upper-level managers agreed. While 75 percent of the subordinates disagreed with "The work in this unit could be accomplished by fewer employees," 83 percent of the frontline supervisors and 87 percent of the mid- or upper-level managers disagreed.

Overwhelmingly, federal employees consider themselves to be hard workers, and consider their coworkers to work hard as well. Overwhelmingly, their supervisors agree that their employees work hard.

Conclusion

A model of federal bureaucrats based wholly on pecuniary preferences is inadequate for understanding the preferences and behavior of federal employees. In this chapter we demonstrated that federal bureaucrats express preferences for pecuniary benefits first and foremost, but not solely. More bureaucrats say that a sense of accomplishment is an important aspect of their job than any other aspect, including job security. Bureaucrats find friendships on the job and the respect of their colleagues to be rewarding.

Supervisors feel constrained in their ability to issue pecuniary rewards, and subordinates appear to know as much. Few subordinates believed that pay raises and cash awards depended on performance appraisals. Fewer subordinates believed that their supervisors were able to correct poor performers.

One reason that nonpecuniary motives matter is that the link between performance and acquiring pecuniary rewards is not very strong. Pecuniary rewards depend on the agency that a bureaucrat works for, but nonpecuniary rewards are under the control of the bureaucrat himself or herself.

Yet the employees believe that they work hard, they believe that other employees work hard, and their supervisors tend to concur. Why would bureaucrats work hard, if they saw few financial returns? The next chapter analyzes what accounts for variation in bureaucratic performance.

CHAPTER 5

Working and Shirking in the Federal Bureaucracy

Federal bureaucrats favor pecuniary rewards. Few are satisfied with their current pay, but most feel that there is very little they could do to secure greater pecuniary rewards. Federal bureaucrats consider themselves to be hard workers, an opinion shared by fellow bureaucrats and their supervisors. The puzzle is, what accounts for high levels of working among federal bureaucrats, given that the most preferred return is relatively difficult for employees to obtain and for supervisors to dispense?

It is a puzzle only if one limits the composition of the preferences of bureaucrats to pecuniary returns. In this chapter, we demonstrate that those employees who are motivated by functional preferences are the hardest working federal bureaucrats, linking empirical evidence with the analysis presented in chapters 2 and 3.

The central model that we will explicate in this chapter aims to explain variation in how hard the federal employees report working as a function of subordinate preferences and supervisor characteristics. Following the theoretical approaches of chapters 2 and 3 and the empirical explorations in chapter 4, we consider pecuniary, functional, and solidary preferences, and the subordinates' assessments of the strength of supervision. Our argument in chapters 2 and 3 leads us to expect that functional preferences should dominate over other potential influences over subordinate performance.

We will again rely upon the surveys of federal employees from 1979, 1983, and 1992. The question batteries vary across surveys, and few questions are exact replicates. In order to achieve comparability across the three surveys, and to avail ourselves of the breadth of questions, we generate a series of scales based upon confirmatory factor analyses of the surveys. The first section of this chapter compares across the three surveys the levels of work, preferences (pecuniary, functional, and solidary), strength of supervision, and other potentially important characteristics of federal bureaucracies as organizations. The second section of this chapter explores the relationship between these scales, where we calculate the effect of changes in the strength of subordinates' preferences and the efforts of supervisors upon the extent to which subordinates work.

93

Comparing Preferences across Surveys

With such a diverse base of questions across the three different surveys, we need to achieve some degree of comparability in order to assess what accounts for a greater or lesser degree of working across the different federal employees. We generate base scales for the key concepts (working, preferences, supervision, and organizational attributes) via confirmatory factor analysis. The idea behind confirmatory factor models treats the questions as indicators for latent variables (which are not measured directly). Confirmatory factor analysis is no form of alchemy generating gold variables from leaden questions. But the base idea should have intuitive appeal: using multiple questions to tap into indirectly measurable phenomena lets us pool the information from the multiple questions.

Confirmatory factor analysis entails some assumptions. Perhaps most significant among the assumptions is that the collection of questions really refers to the same latent measure. The actual confirmatory factor models appear in Appendix C (Estimates), including the complete question text. We encourage the reader to evaluate the scales we derive in terms of these questions. In order to help explicate our confidence in the scales we generate, we produce a series of plots to convey the general shape of the distribution of the scales, and their striking degree of comparability across the three surveys. As the reader will see, our method "works" in that it produces highly similar scales across diverse surveys.[1]

After generating the raw scales for each of the key variables, we then rescale these variables to run from 0 to 1. The effect of rescaling the variables is that the scales are now strictly relative to the set of indicators for the one year, referring to the minimum and maximum measured levels of the latent variables. This means, for example, that a "0" on the working scale does not mean total shirking, but instead refers to the lowest measured amount of working for a given year. (As such, we will note the range on the figures from "minimum" to "maximum.")

Figure 5.1 displays a smoothed histogram of the distribution of the "work" scale for the 1979 and 1983 Federal Employees Attitude survey, and the 1992 Survey of Federal Employees. A first point of note is the skew of the working scale toward the high end. As the reader should recall from the previous chapter, the vast majority of respondents assessed themselves as hard workers,

---

1. We also make some technical assumptions. We assume that measurement errors for each indicator are correlated when the indicators load on the same latent variable, but uncorrelated otherwise. Furthermore, we assume that each indicator measures one and only one latent variable. The goodness-of-fit indices for the three confirmatory factor models for this chapter are respectable (.69, .74, and .70), especially considering the number of indicator variables.

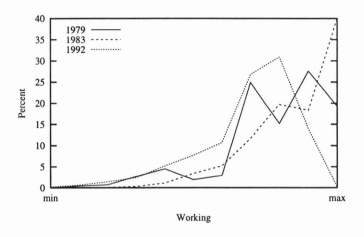

Fig. 5.1. Distribution of "Working" (scale), 1979 and 1983 FEA, 1992 SOFE

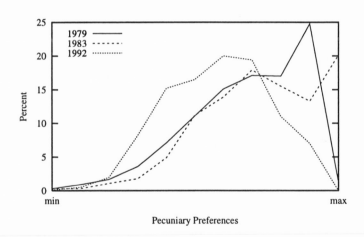

Fig. 5.2. Distribution of "Pecuniary Preferences" (scale), 1979 and 1983 FEA, 1992 SOFE

across all the variations of the questions. Since all the indicators were skewed toward the high end, we should expect the distribution of the latent measure for work to be skewed as well. What this means is that when we refer to variation in the degree to which federal employees are working or shirking, we are really speaking about a relatively narrow range of (self-assessed) levels of working.

Secondly, it is interesting to observe that the skewed pattern of working

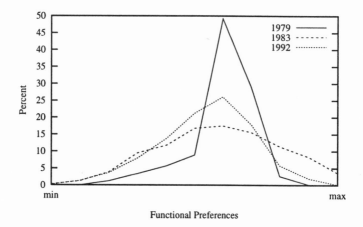

Functional Preferences

Fig. 5.3. Distribution of "Functional Preferences" (scale), 1979 and 1983 FEA, 1992 SOFE

in the scales generated from the three surveys strongly resembles one of the simulated distributions of work generated by the imitation model of chapter 3 (the one that begins with positive predispositions). Work tilts toward the positive extreme.

The scales are remarkably similar across the three years. Even though the indicators themselves are different, the latent variables have very similar distributions across 1979, 1983, and 1992. (The mean level of the work scale for the three years is .75, .80, and .77 for 1979, 1983, and 1992, respectively.) This should provide some confidence that our approach for this chapter is generating a reasonable and consistent picture of the degree to which federal employees believe themselves to work.

The next three figures depict the scales of pecuniary, functional, and solidary preferences for the respondents (figures 5.2–5.4).   With one exception, the distributions of the three scales are very similar in shape, even if the peakedness (degree of concentration) may increase in some years for some measures.

Like the working scale, the distribution of the pecuniary preferences scale is skewed toward the maximum. As chapter 4 detailed, the federal employees preferred pay raises and cash bonuses over other rewards, and expressed dissatisfaction with their current levels of pay. The federal bureaucrats of these surveys are no different from what we must conjecture are ordinary people's reasonable preferences for pecuniary rewards.

One minor variation from the shape of the distribution of pecuniary pref-

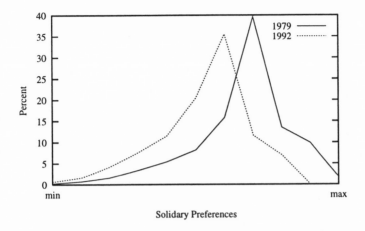

Solidary Preferences

Fig. 5.4. Distribution of "Solidary Preferences" (scale), 1979 and 1983 FEA

erences in 1992 from the previous years is that this scale is more central than tilted toward a maximum. (This is a consequence of producing a scale where there are respondents who place themselves in the middle on some of the questions.) The mean level of pecuniary preferences in 1992, however, is close to the means for 1979 and 1983 (.69, .73, and .61, respectively).

The functional preferences scale (figure 5.3) is more centralized than skewed, with wide variability across the respondents for each year. The distributions for 1983 and 1992 are very similar, while the distribution for 1979 is clearly peaked (with nearly half of the respondents falling around the .6 level on the scale). In other words, most of the respondents expressed only moderate functional preferences. (The means were .65, .67, and .63 for 1979, 1983, and 1992.)

The distribution of solidary preferences (figure 5.4) is similar to those for functional preferences: peaked and centralized, indicating that most respondents expressed moderate solidary preferences. (We are able to produce scales for 1979 and 1992 only, due to the absence of appropriate indicators in the 1983 FEA. The means were .74 for 1979 and .59 for 1992.)

To summarize the state of preferences across the three scales and the three different surveys, federal employees overwhelmingly prefer pecuniary rewards, and moderately favor functional or solidary rewards. There are, however, some employees who express very strong functional and solidary preferences.

The argument that supervisors are able to wield rewards and sanctions in such a way as to discourage shirking and/or encourage working is the chief

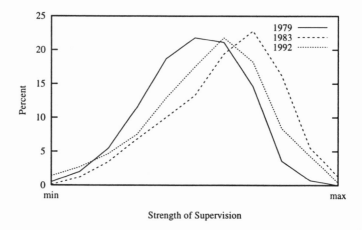

Fig. 5.5. Distribution of "Strength of Supervision" (scale), 1979 and 1983 FEA, 1992 SOFE

rival hypothesis to our argument that it is the subordinates' functional preferences that account for how hard they work. In figure 5.5, we display the scales for the three surveys on the respondents' assessment of the strength of supervision. We find here evidence for only moderate supervisory influence. These distributions are again remarkably similar across the three years, with the scale from the most recent survey falling in the middle of the two previous studies. The distribution is centralized, and somewhat peaked (much the same as the distribution of the functional and solidary preferences). (Means were .44, .64, and .59.)

In addition to our measures of the bureaucrats' incentives and the strength of supervision, we develop scales for hypotheses relevant to other scholarship on bureaucracies. A sociological lens examining bureaucracies points to different aspects of the organization that can emphasize autonomy, lead to a sense of normlessness (or anomie), or lead to the rigidity of the organization. To paraphrase the argument in Hummell (1987), bureaucracies encourage the development of a bureaucratic personality where the employee feels unable to control his or her surroundings. By the bureaucratic personality argument, the more a person feels in control of his or her surroundings, the more we should see the employee work rather than shirk.

Figure 5.6 displays the distribution of our scales for sense of autonomy. Again, the distributions are somewhat centralized, although favoring the higher end of the scale. The implication is that most of the federal employees feel a moderate degree of autonomy on the job, quite in contrast to popular spec-

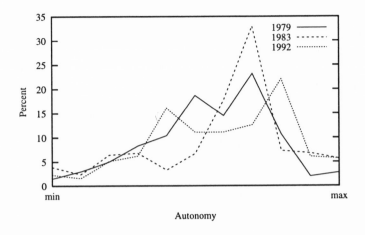

Fig. 5.6. Distribution of "Autonomy" (scale), 1979 and 1983 FEA, 1992 SOFE

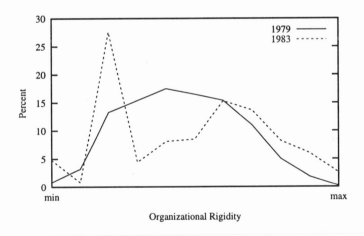

Fig. 5.7. Distribution of "Organizational Rigidity" (scale), 1979 and 1983 FEA

ulations about bureaucrats in faceless jobs with little control over their own circumstances. Our scale is, however, consistent with the "street-level bureaucracies" approach (e.g., Lipsky 1980), noting the wide latitude that bureaucrats may have in enforcing policy. (Means are .64, .65, and .43.)

If bureaucrats have a modest sense of autonomy over their own jobs, they may also have some sense that the bureaucracy itself is rigid in terms of its procedures and rules. Figure 5.7 displays the distributions of our scales of

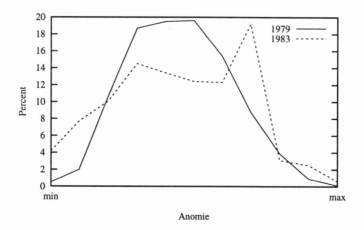

Anomie

Fig. 5.8. Distribution of "Anomie" (scale), 1979 and 1983 FEA

"organizational rigidity" for 1979 and 1983 (the only years for which we had appropriate indicators). Here, the distributions for the two years are quite dissimilar. The two scales do show a sense of organizational rigidity that can be quite variable. (The means are .47 for 1979 and .46 for 1983.)

Finally, we produce a scale of "anomie" or normlessness. The sociological tradition (especially Durkheim) suggests that bureaucracies foster a sense that promotions and rewards are disconnected with performance and are instead attached to particularistic criteria (such as favoritism). Anomie is related to our observation from the previous chapter that most employees did not see a connection between performance on the job and rewards, but it differs in that rewards are connected to other systematic (although inappropriate) criteria. We have scales of normlessness for both 1979 and 1983 (figure 5.8). The distributions are both centralized, with considerable variability in the sense of normlessness across the employees. (The means are .46 for 1979 and .55 for 1983.)

These scales allow us to assess what accounts for variation in the (relatively high) level of work among federal bureaucrats. In turn such analysis provides a perspective for empirically evaluating the findings drawn from chapters 2 and 3. It is to the enterprise of evaluating the effect of variation in preferences, supervision, and organizational characteristics that we now turn.

Estimating the Effect of Preferences and Supervision on Work

We now require an appropriate statistical tool in order to understand what causes some bureaucrats to work harder than others. This tool must be able to replicate the unusually high and uniform level of work among the employees, and to be sensitive to the possibility that the forces that might cause one worker to work hard might not be the same that could also cause that same worker to shirk. We will again rely on the beta distribution (described above in chapter 3) for analyzing the level of work, this time with the federal employee data.

The actual maximum likelihood estimates for the beta distribution can be found in Appendix C, "Estimates." Maximum likelihood estimates may not be as directly and easily interpretable as ordinary least squares, but their results are certainly interpretable nonetheless. In order to facilitate the interpretation of the results from the beta model estimates, we estimate the *effects* (as opposed to simply their *coefficients*) of the preferences, supervision, and organizational characteristics on working in table 5.1. We compute the effects on the basis of a comparison of the change in the level of work from the mean for the variable to its maximum, holding all other variables at their means. (We again use the technique of representing the symmetry or asymmetry of statistical significance with the symbols ◁, ▷, and ⋈.)

For several of the more substantively interesting variables, we also display graphs of the projected distributions of working under the minimum, average, and maximum levels of the particular variable. This is especially useful for understanding the effect of pecuniary preferences, since the average is so close to the maximum.

What is the effect of a change in the preferences of the employee? In every

TABLE 5.1. Estimated Effect of Preferences and Organizational Characteristics on Working, 1979 and 1983 FEA, 1992 SOFE

Variable	1979	1983	1992
Pecuniary preferences	.01 ⋈	.002 ⋈	.05 ⋈
Functional preferences	.20 ⋈	.12 ▷	.08 ⋈
Solidary preferences	.19 ⋈		.03
Strength of supervision	.05 ⋈	.07 ⋈	.03 ◁
Autonomy	−.03 ⋈	−.001 ⋈	−.03 ◁
Anomie	.03 ⋈	−.002 ⋈	
Organizational rigidity	.06 ⋈	.00 ◁	

Note: Cells are estimated change in level of working (scale from 0–1) due to a shift of the variable from the mean to the maximum, holding all other variables at their mean. ◁ means shirking parameter significant at $p < .05$, ▷ means working parameter significant at $p < .05$, and ⋈ means both parameters significant at $p < .05$.

case, the stronger the pecuniary, functional, or solidary preferences, the more that employee works. The sign of the effect of each form of the subordinates' preferences on work is always positive and in many cases quite substantial.

Nevertheless, the relative levels of the effects of functional preferences are consistently the strongest effect in the entire table. In 1979, a shift from the average to the maximum in pecuniary preferences would account for a 1 percent increase in work, while a similar shift for functional preferences would account for a 20 percent increase. In 1983, the effect of a shift in pecuniary preferences accounts for a substantively trivial .002 percent increase in the level of work, while a similar shift in functional preferences would lead to a 12 percent increase. In 1992, the effect of changes in functional and pecuniary preferences are closer to one another in magnitude, but still greater for functional preferences.

In other words, the actual effect of changes in pecuniary preferences is quite constrained. Most of the employees expressed relatively high pecuniary preferences, so that a shift to the maximum can only have a very small effect. But the shift to the minimum—a relatively large shift—dampens the level of work in only the most minor way.

Solidary preferences have a sizable and significant effect on working in 1979, but a nonsignificant effect in 1992. Solidary preferences are weaker than functional preferences in terms of their effect on levels of work, and occasionally stronger than the pecuniary preferences.

The direction of influence is also interesting: stronger preferences always encourage work, and usually discourage shirking. For each of the three preferences, we find that the coefficient for working is statistically significant (except for the effect of solidary preferences in 1992.) (The actual coefficient for working, found in the table in the appendix, is larger in absolute value than that for shirking in almost every case.) In several cases, but not all, the coefficient for shirking is also statistically significant. One interpretation of the results we see here is that the subordinates' predispositions tend to encourage work.

Another way to illustrate the effect of preferences on the distribution of work from the federal employees is to produce graphical representations. Again as we did in chapter 3, we generate estimated distributions of the level of work for the minimum, mean, and maximum levels of the preferences, holding all other variables at the mean. (Thus the graph of the mean is the same for all.)

The graphs of the estimated distribution of work given minimum, mean, and maximum levels of functional preferences demonstrate that functional preferences significantly affect the level of work (figures 5.9–5.11). The graph of the effect of functional preferences at the mean is, as noted earlier, very similar to the actual distribution of work. Note that a shift from the mean to the maximum generates a noticeable, although perhaps minor, shift in the observed

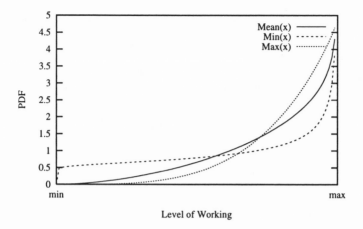

Fig. 5.9. Estimated distribution of work given minimum, average, and maximum functional preferences, 1979 FEA

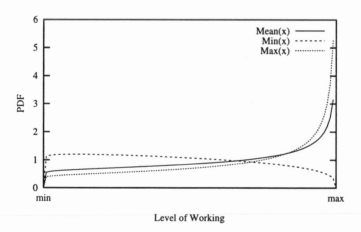

Fig. 5.10. Estimated level of work given minimum, average, and maximum level of functional preferences, 1983 FEA

level of work further toward the extreme. But the shift from the mean to the minimum level of functional preferences yields an entirely different picture: not only is the center of the distribution now shifted well toward the shirking end of the scale, but we can see significant numbers of employees who are distributed all the way along the scale from minimum through maximum.

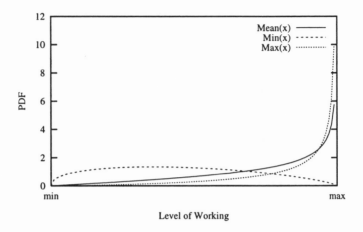

Fig. 5.11. Estimated distribution of work given minimum, average, and maximum functional preferences, 1992 SOFE

Even if the subordinates' pecuniary preferences exercise relatively little effect on the distribution of work, it is still potentially possible for supervisors to influence work through the distribution of rewards and sanctions. The estimated effect (table 5.1) of a shift of the level of supervision from the mean to the maximum has a modest effect on the level of work. In each of the three surveys, the supervisor's effect is greater than the effect of pecuniary preferences. But the effect of the supervisor is always less than both functional preferences and solidary preferences

We generate graphs in order to further demonstrate the (usually) weak effects of supervision (figures 5.12–5.14). The effects of supervision vary somewhat across the three surveys, although the ultimate effect is essentially unchanged. In 1979, the difference between minimum, mean, and maximum supervision is slight: all of the distributions are concentrated toward the maximum. Under minimum supervision, the majority of employees are still working at the maximum, although there is a wider tail, implying a slightly larger number of employees who work at levels below the maximum. In 1983, the basic pattern is that most employees consider themselves to work at the maximum, regardless of level of supervision. The difference between the minimum, mean, and maximum levels of supervision for the estimated distribution of work is absolutely trivial for the 1992 survey. *None* of the three surveys demonstrates any evidence that the highest perceived levels of supervision encourage greater working from subordinates.

Our findings about the strong and consistent effects of functional prefer-

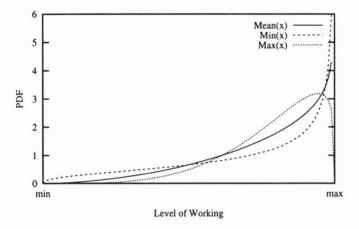

Fig. 5.12. Estimated distribution of work given minimum, average, and maximum level of supervision, 1979 FEA

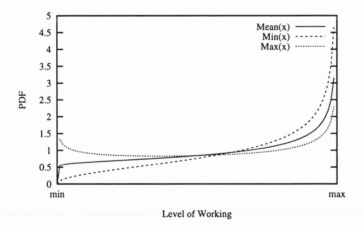

Fig. 5.13. Estimated distribution of work given minimum, average, and maximum level of supervision, 1983 FEA

ences relative to weak effects of pecuniary preferences and supervision confirms the stronger propositions from chapters 2 and 3. Subordinate predispositions matter, and they matter to a greater extent than the efforts of supervisors do.

Expressed in terms of moral hazard and adverse selection, one could con-

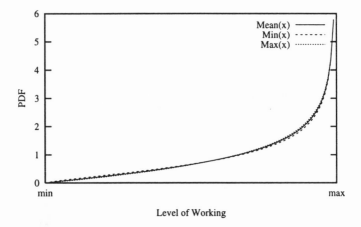

Fig. 5.14. Estimated distribution of work given minimum, average, and maximum supervision, 1992 SOFE

strue poor functional preferences as evidence of the adverse selection problem at work. Employees who enter into the federal bureaucracy without a sense that what they do on the job matters, in a personal way, are concealing information that a prospective employer (the government) would surely wish to know. One could also construe the efforts of the supervisor as an indication of activity by management toward reducing moral hazard. Reflecting our findings presented in chapters 2 and 3, the implication of these results is that adverse selection trumps moral hazard.

The effects of autonomy, anomie, and organizational rigidity turn out to be relatively weak. The more that the subordinate feels autonomous on the job, the less that subordinate works (the effect is negative in every year, and balanced in statistical significance). Our result runs counter to the argument in Hummel (1987) in that the more autonomous employees worked less hard than those with a lesser sense of autonomy. The effect is always weaker than that of functional and even solidary preferences.

The more anomie sensed by the employee, the more that employee shirked in 1983, and the more the employee worked in 1979. Although both results are statistically significant, the substantive effect is slight.

The more that the employee feels that the bureaucracy suffers from organizational rigidity, the more that employee works. The effect is positive for the two available years, although again much smaller than the effect of functional preferences. The effect of organizational rigidity tending to improve work counterbalances the effect of autonomy.

Conclusion

We think it is useful, at this early point of the enterprise of examining the behavior of bureaucrats across all levels of government, to review how the findings of the present chapter relate to our own propositions about what—and who—influences bureaucratic behavior.

The bureaucrats of this chapter prefer the same things that ordinary people prefer. They appreciate monetary rewards for their hard work—above all other kinds of rewards. But these rewards, especially in times of tight governmental budgets, are hard to find. Fortunately for the public, they also value the sense of accomplishment and the feeling of doing a good job (what we call "functional" preferences), and the recognition and association with peers (what we call "solidary" preferences).

We say it is "fortunate" for the public, because having strong functional preferences differentiates the hard worker from other employees. The same is true, to a lesser extent, for bureaucrats with strong solidary preferences. Neither functional nor solidary rewards fall under the domain of the principals, but they are as much the product of the agent himself or herself, the public, and peers.

Put another way, to focus solely on pecuniary rewards really misses the mark in understanding the behavior of bureaucrats. This single-minded focus appears in two seminal economic approaches to organizations. The leisure-maximization approach (Alchian and Demsetz 1972) concurs that rewards may be limited or outside the influence of the subordinate, and so we should expect subordinates to maximize utility by minimizing work. We find no evidence of mass shirking, quite the opposite. The budget-maximization approach (Niskanen 1975) argues that bureaucrats act so as to maximize resources for either the direct pecuniary return, or for the purpose of accomplishing specific policy goals (functional returns). With budgets outside the influence of individual bureaucrats, the pecuniary focus is incapable of understanding what influences the effort bureaucrats put into their jobs.

While Barnard (1938) may have labeled the coercive power of management a "fiction," we find that supervisory authority matters. The degree to which subordinates perceive supervisors to have punishment and reward possibilities does influence how hard they work. These effects are small: those who think supervisors are highly influential work only slightly harder than those who think supervisors are weak.

The results from this chapter are confirmations of four significant aspects of our models in chapter 2 (of individual bureaucrats) and chapter 3 (of networks of bureaucrats).

Supervisors are constrained. In chapter 2, we argue that with respect to individual bureaucrats making decisions in isolation, supervisors are constrained in their ability to monitor subordinates (consistent with the central argument in the principal agency tradition) and also in their ability to sanction. Sanctioning is costly, spending from a limited base of resources for influencing subordinates. In chapter 3, we argue that under certain conditions of multiple subordinates learning in networks, monitoring and sanctioning has a limited effect on work, even when monitoring and sanctioning are allowed to rise to their maxima. In this chapter, we observe that no matter how strong a subordinate believes his or her supervisor's authority to be, subordinates work about the same.

Subordinate preferences consistent with work are the most efficient means to encourage work. In chapters 2 and 3, we explicitly model the amount of effort that a subordinate puts into the job as a function of the subordinates' preferences and the sanctioning power of the supervisor. What mattered the most for obtaining work from subordinates were subordinates who preferred to work. The strong effect of functional preferences on the efforts of subordinates confirms our propositions.

(We do not yet have evidence that subordinate preferences for shirking or for sabotage follow the same patterns. For this, we will turn to our data on other bureaucrats in the shirking and sabotage of social workers [in chapter 6], and of police officers [in chapters 7 and 8].)

Subordinates derive utility from fellow subordinates. In chapter 3, we argued that the behavior of bureaucracies could not be fully understood without examining interactions among subordinates. Although by no stretch the most significant stream of benefits that bureaucrats receive, the recognition and association with their peers yield strong positive returns for many employees. Furthermore, these strong returns can also encourage work, if not to the same extent as the preferences individual bureaucrats may have for work.

(We do not yet have evidence of intersubordinate learning of how to behave in allocations of work. In chapter 7, we will demonstrate that fellow officers exert a strong influence on the shirking of police officers.)

Working may be skewed to the extreme. Chapter 3 assumed that subordinates learn how to behave in the workplace on the basis of imitation and their own experiences, and that the resulting behavior could be skewed toward an extreme. We do not have direct evidence, yet, of learning by imitation in bureaucracies, but we can replicate the resulting behavior.

Perhaps this is the most striking finding that stands out from not only the present chapter but the former: *Federal bureaucrats are hard workers.* An image of bureaucrats as lazy and indifferent, propagated by politicians, the public, and even some scholars, is wholly inaccurate. Not only do bureaucrats consider themselves to be hard workers, they consider one another to work hard, and this opinion is one shared by their supervisors.

CHAPTER 6

Working, Shirking, and Sabotage in Social Work

We shift the lens of our study of bureaucracy away from the federal government toward local government and the activity of social workers. One theme of our book is that scholars can acquire new insights by thinking about bureaucrats as individual actors with varying preferences for pecuniary, functional, or solidary rewards. As the reader will see in this chapter, social workers express very strong functional preferences, to a degree unmatched by the federal bureaucrats of previous chapters. Since the social workers we study in this chapter work for a local (county) government, we also gain purchase on the potential effects of different political principals. It is, after all, quite possible that the size of the federal government precludes influence by political principals over subordinate bureaucrats. Would the principals of smaller, local governments fare any better? As this chapter will show, variation in the working, shirking, and sabotage choices of social workers depends principally upon their solidary and functional preferences.

Some readers might find it curious that we consider social workers to be "bureaucrats." The image of a bureaucrat as a paper-pusher behind a desk might be common, but it is simply wrong. By the principal scholarly definitions of bureaucracy and bureaucrats, social workers are an excellent fit.

Weber's *The Theory of Social and Economic Organization* (1947) stands as the classic description of the ideal-type bureaucracy as "rational legal authority." According to Weber, bureaucracies can be characterized as well-defined hierarchical organizations where the official functions are bound by rules, operating within a specified jurisdiction. The rules specify such aspects of the organization as a clear division of labor and the appropriate exercise of authority by members of the bureaucracy. Virtually every act of a bureaucracy ("administrative acts, decisions, and rules") is put in writing, "even in cases where oral discussion is the rule or is even mandatory."

Social workers are exemplars of what Lipsky called the "street-level bureaucrat." Social workers work directly with citizens. Social workers are at the front lines of significant levels of interaction with their communities, as groups and as individual clients. Unlike the police officers of the next two chapters, social workers are in a position to dispense resources of the state to individual citizens: social workers certify eligibility for welfare payments, provide child welfare services, and (in some states) administer mental health programs. Like police officers, social workers also wield discretion over the punitive aspects of the state, in forms that can be devastatingly harsh (such as removing children from the custody of their parents).

Consider the terms of Weber's classic definition of a bureaucracy, and social work fits to a T. Social workers operate under well-defined rules and procedures. Social workers also complete enormous amounts of paperwork tracking their cases. Social workers often have significant initial training, in the form of a degree in social work.[1] A social worker could establish a career in social work, and many do.

In one significant sense the supervision of social workers does not fit the role of the supervisor as a wielder of rewards and punishments, characteristic of the model of supervision in the economics of the firm. Most social work supervision texts refer to "peer" supervision: the supervisor's role becomes more of a mentor and less of a boss. Kadushin (1992), for example, refers to the role of the supervisor as concerned with education and support as much as with administration. "Education" means that the supervisor identifies the appropriate activities of the subordinate, in a teaching capacity. "Support" refers to the role of the supervisor in helping subordinates manage the considerable stress of the job. "Administration" refers to the role of the supervisor in evaluating subordinates' performance, issuing reprimands, or dispensing rewards. Neither "education" nor "support" fit the role of supervisor that our project has thus far detailed.[2] In fact, Kadushin (1992) considers the reward and coercive aspects of supervisory authority to be relatively weak in supervision of social work. Rewards tend to be shunned by social work supervisors because they run counter to "the ethos of social work [which] favors equality of rewards and decries competition involved in striving for rewards" (86). Coercion tends to be rare, because social work supervisors express "discomfort with punitive actions" (86).

But it would be an enormous mistake to trivialize the importance of "administrative" supervision, because under most state and case law, the supervisor is responsible for malfeasance on the part of the subordinate. The doctrine of *respondeat superiore* ("let the master answer") holds the supervisor liable for the actions of the subordinate. This doctrine means that the supervisors have every incentive to minimize violations on the part of social workers, to an extent which is not felt by any of the other supervisors we have covered in this book. The lines of responsibility are more clearly marked in social work than

---

1. Many of those who perform social work–like tasks, however, may perform their jobs on the basis of no more than a college equivalency.

2. We note, however, that these roles may be particularly important ones for understanding subordinate compliance, although outside the scope of this book.

in many other aspects of public service. As such, the "administrative" aspects of supervision of social workers represent an excellent test of our arguments about the responsiveness and performance of social workers.

Add the widely varying ways in which a subordinate might fail to comply to the problems posed by the supervisor's liability for subordinates' actions, plus unique problems for supervision, and we have all the ingredients for classic principal–agency problems. Kadushin (1992) describes multiple circumstances for social worker noncompliance, several of which fit our description of "sabotage."

> For instance, during the 1960s, social workers in West Coast public welfare departments were fired after they refused to conduct "midnight raids" to check on the continued eligibility of AFDC clients. They strongly felt that such procedures were a violation of clients' rights and their own professional standards. (121)

Other settings for subordinate noncompliance arise when rules are contradictory, when client groups are in conflict, or when policies require interpretation. In all these cases, one could well argue that noncompliance by the subordinate is motivated by policy-oriented reasons, running counter to official department policy. There is also, to be sure, the possibility that social workers engage in more mundane forms of shirking, motivated chiefly for purposes of maximizing leisure.

The social work supervisor faces unusually severe problems of monitoring the subordinates' performance. Due to the need to preserve the confidentiality of the clients, direct observation by the supervisor of the subordinates' activities is somewhat rare. According to Gummer (1979),

> In social agencies supervision is based on the workers' reports of what they are doing rather than a supervisor's direct observation of the work. Organizations with this structure have significant control and accountability problems since the line workers are able to operate with a high degree of autonomy and can screen their behavior from the direct surveillance of administrators. These structural conditions promote discretionary behavior of workers, who in the privacy of the interviewing room are free to interpret and apply agency policy and procedure as they see fit. While confidentiality is designed to protect the client, it protects the worker as well. (200)

Furthermore, the nature of the tasks that social workers perform means that it is nearly impossible to significantly reduce their levels of discretion. As

Lipsky (1980) puts it, the situations encountered by social workers "involve complex tasks for which elaboration of rules, guidelines, or instructions cannot circumscribe the alternatives" (15).

In this chapter, we examine working, shirking, and sabotage by social workers along multiple dimensions. We examine one measure of the working–shirking continuum: whether the social workers take their paperwork home to complete. We explore three distinct measures of sabotage: whether subordinates fudge the paperwork in order to keep a client eligible, bend the rules in order to get things done, and whether they perceive others as breaking the rules. In order to explore these different aspects of the performance of social workers, we conducted a small survey of social workers and workers in related fields in the Durham (NC) County Department of Social Services. The next section of this chapter details the methods by which we collected the data. The subsequent sections analyze our measures of subordinate performance.

Survey of Durham County Social Services

Our survey examined the attitudes of public servants in the Durham County Department of Social Services toward their clients, their jobs, and their supervisors. Specifically, we intended to identify the attitudes of the social workers and caseworkers[3] toward their sense of autonomy on the job, the amount of discretion they have in implementing policy, the frequency of supervision, the nature of supervision, the frequency of collateral contacts, the nature of collateral contacts, the economic and other rewards of the job, their allocation of time while at work, their sense of who exercises influence over their choices of allocation of time, and the reasons they have for becoming a social worker or caseworker. Many of the questions in the survey are replications of questions asked in surveys of other public servants in the other survey vehicles used in this book.

On the basis of a listed sample, each frontline employee in the Durham County Department of Social Services (social workers, income maintenance caseworkers, child support agents, human resource aides, or paraprofessionals) received a survey packet. The packet contained the survey questionnaire, a letter personally addressed to each respondent, and a stamped addressed return envelope. The packets were distributed via the DSS internal mail system. The subject pool consists of the entire workforce of the Durham County Social

---

3. Although we will use the label "social worker" to refer to all the subjects of our survey, the term is literally correct only for a fraction of our sample. In addition to "social workers" (all of whom have a Masters in Social Work), there are "income maintenance caseworkers" and "child welfare caseworkers." We use the label "social worker" to refer to the full sample and make distinctions between the categories only when relevant.

Services that interacts directly with members of the public, along with their immediate supervisors. This consists of social workers, income maintenance caseworkers, child support agents, human resource aides, and paraprofessionals. In sum, there are 239 individuals who belong to one of the job categories.

Each return envelope included a number written on the back side, corresponding to a name on the sample list. The purpose of this number was to track whether a particular employee responded to the questionnaire. Once a questionnaire was returned, we noted the date of return on a sample disposition database recording the disposition of each sample case. If we did not receive a questionnaire within seven days of distribution of the questionnaire, we sent a follow-up letter to the nonresponding sample persons. If after a further seven days we did not receive a questionnaire, we called the nonrespondent at the office and offered to conduct the interview over the telephone. If at this last phone call, the sample person refused to participate, we no longer contacted the respondent.

Our response rate using these procedures was excellent for self- returned questionnaires, at approximately 60 percent. There were some systematic patterns to the response rates by department: the lowest response rate was for employees in the food stamps division (34 percent), where the highest response rate was in adult services (73 percent). Given some adverse publicity in local newspapers for child services immediately prior to the time when the survey was in the field, we anticipated a low response rate among child services employees, but the rate for employees was exactly at the average.

Preferences of Social Workers

We begin with an examination of the distribution of preferences for the social workers in our sample. Table 6.1 displays several indicators for functional preferences. All together, the preferences displayed here are quite similar to those expressed by the federal employees in table 4.6. Over 90 percent of the social workers agreed with the statement "Doing my job well makes me feel good about myself as a person," a number quite comparable to the federal employees. Over 90 percent of the social workers supported the similar statement "The things I do on my job are important to me." When put in the negative, over 90 percent of the social workers disagreed with "I care little about what happens to this organization as long as I can get a paycheck." Indeed, one of the interesting characteristics of the distributions for these three questions is that only two individuals in the entire sample expressed functional dislikes.

We also sought to measure the extent of professionalism as a form of functional preferences. Although the percentages supporting professionalism were not as high as those concurring with the functional preferences, they are still sizable. More than 50 percent of the respondents agreed that "A person enters this profession because he likes the work." Just under 50 percent of the respondents agreed that "It is encouraging to see the high level of idealism which is maintained by people in this field." In other words, not only did the respondents express very strong functional preferences when oriented toward their own behavior, they were also likely to identify the same functional preferences among their coworkers.

We also measured solidary preferences, which were also quite strong for the social workers (table 6.2). Well over 50 percent of the respondents agreed that "A person gets the chance to develop good friends here." Nearly 50 percent of the respondents agreed that "Working hard on my job leads to gaining respect from coworkers." Conversely, well over 50 percent of the respondents disagreed with the statement that "The department is really very impersonal." The social workers in our sample expressed support for solidary rewards from their coworkers.

Moreover, we also measured aspects of learning and observation by coworkers that are directly pertinent to the imitation model of chapter 3. The degree to which subordinates are able to observe the performance of fellow subordinates is high: well over 50 percent of the respondents agreed that "My colleagues pretty well know how well we all do in our job." We also found

TABLE 6.1. Functional Preferences, 1994 Survey of Durham County Social Service Employees

	Strongly Disagree	Disagree	Neither Agree Nor Disagree	Agree	Strongly Agree
The things I do on my job are important to me.	0.0	0.7	2.9	52.2	44.2
Doing my job well makes me feel good about myself as a person.	1.5	0.0	2.9	38.7	56.9
I care little about what happens to this organization as long as I can get a paycheck.	41.3	49.3	7.2	1.4	0.7
A person enters this profession because he likes the work.	2.2	13.0	27.5	39.9	17.4
It is encouraging to see the high level of idealism which is maintained by people in this field.	7.6	22.9	26.7	36.6	6.1

Note: Cell entries are percentages of the row. $N = 138$.

evidence that the effect of others' preferences could cause subordinates to act in ways that were not consistent with their own preferences. Slightly over half the respondents agreed that "Sometimes, I go along with what my co-workers want, even if it's not what I want."

Alternatively, when we asked the respondents to list what they liked and disliked most about their jobs, the preferences they expressed were quite similar to those expressed by the police officers in chapters 7 and 8. The two most frequent aspects of their jobs that social workers mentioned in a positive light were functional and solidary. "Helping others" was the single most common reason to like the job, with varying degrees of specificity (68 percent). Many of the respondents answered that they enjoyed helping poor clients get jobs or get off welfare, or that they liked helping children. The social workers in our sample clearly derive utility from the very performance of their jobs.

By contrast, very few of the social workers mentioned pecuniary aspects of the job. Some 10 percent mentioned "low pay" as a reason to dislike the job. Some 13 percent found that the flexible work hours were a plus. Only one respondent complained about long hours. Beyond these few respondents, virtually all of the social workers pointed to different aspects of their job.

The most frequent reason that social workers found to dislike their job, far and away, was "paperwork" (25 percent). Paperwork serves many purposes

TABLE 6.2. Solidary Preferences, 1994 Survey of Durham County Social Service Employees

	Strongly Disagree	Disagree	Neither Agree Nor Disagree	Agree	Strongly Agree
A person gets the chance to develop good friends here.	4.3	5.1	29.7	50.7	10.1
Working hard on my job leads to gaining respect from coworkers.	2.9	23.9	23.9	40.6	8.7
The department is really very impersonal.	6.8	45.1	29.3	14.3	4.5
My colleagues pretty well know how well we all do in our work.	1.5	16.1	15.3	55.5	11.7
Sometimes, I go along with what my coworkers want, even if it's not what I want.	5.1	23.5	14.7	52.9	3.7

Note: Cell entries are percentages of the row. N=138

in social work. It is one of the few means that the supervisor has to monitor the activities of the subordinates. Completion of paperwork provides a case history for the client, allowing later social workers to track what has or has not been done for the client. Paperwork also establishes whether a client is eligible to receive benefits from social services. Paperwork thus represents an amalgamation of functional aspects of the job as well as a means by which supervisors can track performance.

The picture that emerges from our questions about the strength of supervision is quite textured and perhaps at odds with conventional views of the role of the supervisor (table 6.3). A majority of the social workers disagreed with a (strongly worded) statement about the frequency of supervision: "The employees are constantly being checked upon for rule violations." A majority also disagreed with a strong statement of conformity with rules ("Employees are expected to follow orders without questioning them"). At these extremes, social workers do not sense strong supervision.

At the same time, there is also evidence that subordinates perceive that

TABLE 6.3. Strength of Supervision, 1994 Survey of Durham County Social Service Employees

	Strongly Disagree	Disagree	Neither Agree Nor Disagree	Agree	Strongly Agree
The employees are constantly being checked upon for rule violations.	8.8	43.1	21.9	19.0	7.3
People at my level are required to follow certain procedures to do the work—procedures that they would not choose if it were up to them.	2.9	25.5	18.2	40.1	13.1
My department rewards results and goal achievement both formally and informally.	9.8	27.3	23.5	35.6	3.8
Failure to treat customers fairly results in reprimands from supervisors.	2.9	11.8	22.1	54.4	8.8
Employees are expected to follow orders without questioning them.	4.4	47.8	23.5	18.4	5.9

Note: Cell entries are percentages of the row. $N = 138$.

violating policy leads to sanctions: well over half of the respondents agreed that "failure to treat customers fairly results in reprimands from supervisors." Further, there is evidence that subordinates are obedient. Social workers also agreed that they were "required to follow certain procedures to do the work—procedures that they would not choose if it were up to them" (53 percent).

Where the social workers were decidedly equivocal concerned the degree to which the department rewarded good performance. About 39 percent of the respondents agreed, and about 36 percent disagreed with the statement "My department rewards results and goal achievement both formally and informally."

In short, the picture that we have of the preferences of social workers is one which is largely consistent with the preferences of the bureaucrats studied elsewhere in this book. Social workers express strong functional and solidary preferences. Conversely, the social workers' assessments of the strength of supervision is marginally stronger than what we found in the federal bureaucracy.

In this chapter, we take the social workers' sense of the degree of influence as one of the variables that affects their performance. The social workers were asked to assess how influential five different persons or groups were over how they allocated their time at work. Table 6.4 displays the range of responses.

One group stands out significantly over the others as a factor influencing how social workers allocate their time: their customers. Over two-thirds of the social workers placed their customers in the category "great deal of influence" and a further one-fifth put the customers in the second highest category ("some influence"). Considering the service-oriented role of the department—indeed, the profession of social work—it should hardly be a surprise that the clientele has the strongest effect upon provision of services. Unlike the utility regulators

TABLE 6.4. Assessment of Degree of Influence over Time, 1994 Survey of Durham County Social Services Employees

Actor	Great	Some	Little	None
Supervisor	46.3	43.4	9.6	0.7
Coworkers	10.9	38.4	31.9	18.8
Customers	69.1	22.1	5.9	2.9
Workers in other departments	4.3	28.3	44.2	23.2
Director of DSS	26.3	29.2	22.6	21.9

Note: Cell entries are percentages of the row categories in response to the question "For each of the following groups, please tell me how much influence that person or group has over how you allocate your time at work." $N = 138$.

in the ninth chapter, the social workers' jobs necessitate that they come into frequent contact with the public. Parenthetically, the term "customer" is one which is propagated by the department of social services to refer to the clientele and is itself indicative of a service-oriented bureaucracy.

The second most influential group for influencing how social workers allocate their time is their immediate supervisor. Although perhaps at contrast with our arguments about the relative ineffectiveness of supervisory capacity, the reader should also recall that the social work supervisor is, by the textbooks, more likely to be an educator or base of support than an administrator. The degree to which immediate supervisors have an influence over the social workers is not, in and of itself, an indication of the effectiveness of administrative supervision. (We shall have more to say on the relative effectiveness of rewards and sanctions below.)

The other groups fall off rapidly in terms of influence. Social workers were almost uniform in their placement of the director of social services' influence across the four categories. Cumulatively, the director of social services would rank third, closely followed by the coworkers. At the very bottom of the list would be the effect of workers in other departments.

These tables speak to an intermediate stage in our project. Although it is useful to observe the strong functional and solidary preferences, mixed levels of assessments of strength of supervision, and strong role of the customers, these do not speak to the ultimate questions of performance of the social workers. In the next section, we will turn these measures of subordinate preferences, assessments of the strength of supervision, and of the influence of groups into independent variables.

Models of Working, Shirking, and Sabotage

We asked the social workers about a number of different tasks that might be seen as examples either of extraordinary effort or of sabotage on the part of social workers. Part of the academic folklore surrounding social workers is that they manipulate paperwork for the benefit of their clients. And, as we mentioned above, paperwork is a defining aspect of supervision of social workers; paperwork constitutes not only a principal means by which to track the performance of subordinates, but also the means by which clients become qualified for support, the case record in case of problems (or improvements) down the line, as well as documentation for more impersonal evaluations of the success of the policy. As such, we look toward two aspects of their paperwork: whether social workers ever take paperwork home (which would be uncompensated hours) and whether social workers ever "fudge the paperwork" in order to keep a case qualified. The former we take to be a measure of work, the latter we take to be a measure of sabotage.

Like all public bureaucracies, social work agencies are swimming in rules (some 59 percent of the sample agreed with the characterization that "it seems that there's a rule for everything around here"). We also consider two alternative approaches to the rules: whether social workers admit that "to get things done, sometimes you have to bend the rules" and whether other social workers break the explicit rules of the department. Both of these approaches suffer from weaknesses as measures of compliance. The self-report of rule violations would be expected to be underreported. Even though the questionnaire is anonymous, one should always be suspicious of questions that attempt to elicit reports of socially unacceptable behavior. The report about the behavior of others is likewise suspect, since one's impressions of the success and influence of the supervisor are presumably affected by one's observations of rule violations around oneself.

The four dependent variables we explore in this chapter are five-point Likert-type scales, ranging from "strongly agree" through "strongly disagree." These are limited dependent variables, where the transition from one level (e.g., from "agree" to "strongly agree") need not be equivalent to transitions between other levels (e.g., from "disagree" to "strongly disagree"). In other words, we have ordinal, but not interval level data. The analytical technique we will apply for this chapter is the ordered probit approach (first explicated by Aitchison and Silvey [1957]). As with our earlier analysis, we leave the specific details of the likelihood, as well as our method of interpretation, to the appendix, focusing in this chapter upon estimated effects.[4]

Taking Paperwork Home

The first of our dependent variables for this chapter is whether the respondent agreed, disagreed, or neither, to the question "Sometimes I have to take paperwork home in order to complete it on time." Social workers are not compensated for taking the paperwork home—it represents extra hours, performing a task that many, if not most, of the social workers find unpleasant. Table 6.5 displays the estimated effects of preferences and supervision on taking paperwork home.

The first two questions tap into the supervisor's administrative role. The first of these asks about the connection between sanctions and taking on additional work. Here, we find that the more strongly the subordinate perceives

---

4. We should also mention that the extremes of the distribution, especially with our relatively small sample size, require us to do some folding of the data. Instead of estimating over the full five-point scale, we combine the "strongly (dis)agree" and "(dis)agree" endpoints. This proved to be necessary, since the vast majority of the respondents placed themselves on the less strongly worded alternative, and the "strong" extremes were causing severe overestimates of the likelihood of one extreme or another.

the connection between violations and reprimands, the less likely he or she is to take paperwork home. The flip side of administrative supervision—administering rewards—produced only trivial changes in the probability of taking paperwork home.

The next three questions measure aspects of solidary rewards. Here, the picture is admittedly a bit murky. A sense that working hard on the job leads to recognition from others, and that a person gets the chance to develop good friends here, both contributed in a minor way to the chances of taking on additional work (an increase in the probability of agreeing by about 8–9 percent). On the other hand, when we looked at a variable which simply recorded whether the respondent mentioned coworkers as a reason to like or dislike the job, this variable was mildly negatively related to taking on additional work.

We regard the first two questions to be stronger measures of solidary preferences for the group as a whole, since they rely on stimulated responses, but

TABLE 6.5. Estimated Effect of Preferences and Supervision on "Taking Paperwork Home," from 1994 Survey of Durham County Social Services

	Agree	Neither Agree nor Disagree	Disagree
Failure to treat customers fairly results in reprimands from supervisors.	−.17	.10	.07
My department rewards results and goal achievement both formally and informally.	.02	−.01	−.01
Working hard on my job leads to gaining respect from coworkers.	.08	−.04	−.04
A person gets the chance to develop good friends here.	.09	−.03	−.06
Solidary like	−.03	.01	.02
Doing my job well makes me feel good about myself as a person.	.14	−.08	−.06
A person enters this profession because he likes the work.	.18	−.04	−.14
"Helping" like	.02	−.01	−.01
"Paperwork" dislike	−.23	.15	.08
Pecuniary like/dislike	.12	−.04	−.08
Influence of immediate supervisor	.01	0	0
Influence of coworkers	.06	−.02	−.04
Influence of customers	.09	−.03	−.06
Influence of director	.09	−.03	−.05

Note: Cell entries are estimated effects based on ordered probit coefficients for the response to the Likert scale questions about "taking paperwork home." "Strongly (Dis)Agree" and "(Dis)Agree" answers have been combined. Effects are estimated by computing probability of each response at mean for all variables, and subtracting from probability of response for maximum for selected variable (all other variables at mean). $N = 126$.

the latter approach might be the most appropriate for those who express sufficiently strong solidary preferences that it comes to the top of the head for the survey answer.

A much clearer picture emerges for the relationship of functional preferences to performing extra work, in the form of the next three questions. The first question directly considers the utility a social worker receives from doing a good job. The effect here is to shift the probability of taking home additional work by 14 percent over the average. The second question examines the connection between a characterization of the profession and work, finding an 18 percent increase in the probability of taking home additional work. The third codes whether the respondent mentions "helping others" as an aspect of the job he or she likes, and shifts the probability of taking home paperwork by a relatively small 2 percent.

Perhaps least surprising of all our findings here is that those social workers who expressed an objection to paperwork are the least likely to take paperwork home to complete it. The largest effect that we observe for this table is for the volunteered dislike for taking home paperwork: These respondents were 23 percent less likely to agree to taking paperwork home, relative to the average. (Note that it is conceivable, although perhaps unlikely, that those who object to paperwork might be those who found it most intrusive on their nonwork time, and would be more likely to take it home.) The implications of the strong effect of disliking paperwork for taking it home for the relative strength of functional preferences are decidedly ambiguous. Since completion of paperwork is such a central aspect of the job of a social worker, disliking paperwork is tantamount to a very specific functional dislike. What we take the meaning of the strong effect here to be is that functional preferences are not an undifferentiated broad support for the tasks of the bureaucracy, but do sensibly vary by the nature of those tasks.

Pecuniary preferences positively affect the chances that the respondent agrees that he or she takes paperwork home, to a degree that is roughly comparable to the functional preferences. We estimate that strong pecuniary preferences will lead to a 12 percent increase in the chances that the respondent agrees to taking paperwork home. The finding here is at variance with the effect of pecuniary preferences on the other bureaucrats of the book. Of course, to the extent that pecuniary rewards are no more forthcoming under the Durham County Social Services, the effect of strong pecuniary preferences upon performance is still relatively weak.

Finally, we examine the effect of the perceived influence of the social worker's immediate supervisor, coworkers, customers, and the director on taking paperwork home. Those respondents who felt that their supervisor exercised a "great deal" of influence over how they allocated their time were only

1 percent more likely to take paperwork home than the average. The strongest effects we observe are for both the influence of customers and the director, with the influence of coworkers falling in the middle. We do note that none of the four actors' degree of influence is as important to the social worker in taking paperwork home as the functional or pecuniary preferences.

In summary for the first of our four measures of the social workers, we find that subordinate preferences continue to be the most important predictor of subordinate performance. Functional preferences again have the strongest effect, although pecuniary preferences are not far behind (a finding in contrast to the other bureaucrats in the book).

"Fudging" Paperwork

We turn next to a measure of the respondents' likelihood of engaging in a form of sabotage: Fudging the paperwork in order to keep a client eligible for support. We produce the estimated effect of our variables on the likelihood of agreeing, neither agreeing nor disagreeing, and disagreeing in table 6.6. The first point of note should be that *none* of the variables exercises a substantively meaningful effect upon the likelihood that any of the respondents would agree that he or she had fudged the paperwork. Indeed, the actual percentage of social workers who admitted fudging paperwork is tiny (2 percent). If we observe any substantively meaningful effects, it is with the shift from "disagreeing" to "neither agreeing nor disagreeing." We should caution that not disagreeing with fudging paperwork is not identical to agreeing: Respondents may have not understood what "fudging paperwork" referred to, may have altered paperwork for other purposes (including making subjects disqualified), may have opted for the middle category due to a failure to deliberate over the content of the question (i.e., choose a noncommittal middle alternative), as well as the possibility that a "neither agree nor disagree" conceals an "agree." We will proceed with our discussion of the variables which affect responses to this question in terms of "not disagreeing." Even though this necessitates a double negative, the positive cannot be sustained from our data.

Supervision yielded among the smallest effects on the chances that a respondent would not disagree with fudging paperwork. The administration of reprimands produced an effect in distinguishable from zero, while the administration of rewards actually appeared to (slightly) decrease those not agreeing with this form of sabotage.

The strongest effects observable upon the respondents who disagree to fudging paperwork occur with those variables which measure solidary preferences. Respondents who felt that working hard on the job leads to respect from coworkers were 46 percent more likely to disagree with fudging paperwork, and those who volunteered a solidary like as an aspect they liked about the job were 34 percent more likely to disagree than the average. These effects are among the largest we display for any variable in any of the four models. The implication is that strong solidary preferences strongly discourages admitting to fudging paperwork. (Whether the respondents actually were desisting from or concealing sabotage is unanswerable from our data.)

Functional preferences affected disagreeing with sabotage only slightly, although all the effects are in a consistent direction. The stronger the subordinate's functional preferences, the more likely the respondent would disagree that he or she engaged in sabotage. The sign of the effect of functional preferences here leads us to prefer an interpretation that disagreeing with fudging paperwork signifies actual, rather than concealed, performance. Respondents who were concealing fudging paperwork would have to maintain the double conceit of concealing both the functional preference and the actual act, whereas

TABLE 6.6. Estimated Effect of Preferences and Supervision on "Fudging Paperwork," from 1994 Survey of Durham County Social Services

Variable	Agree	Neither Agree nor Disagree	Disagree
Failure to treat customers fairly results in reprimands from supervisors.	0	0	0
My department rewards results and goal achievement both formally and informally.	.01	.13	−.13
Working hard on my job leads to gaining respect from coworkers.	.01	−.45	.46
A person gets the chance to develop good friends here.	−.02	−.08	.10
Solidary like	−.01	−.33	.34
Doing my job well makes me feel good about myself as a person.	−.02	−.09	.11
A person enters this profession because he likes the work.	−.02	−.08	.10
"Helping" like	0	−.03	.04
"Paperwork" dislike	.01	.06	−.07
Pecuniary like/dislike	−.01	−.15	.16
Influence of immediate supervisor	0	−.01	.01
Influence of coworkers	0	0	0
Influence of customers	0	−.03	.03
Influence of director	−.02	−.09	.11

Note: Cell entries are estimated effects based on ordered probit coefficients for the response to the Likert scale questions about "fudging paperwork." "Strongly (Dis)Agree" and "(Dis)Agree" answers have been combined. Effects are estimated by computing probability of each response at mean for all variables, and subtracting from probability of response for maximum for selected variable (all other variables at mean). $N = 126$.

respondents who were sincere about their activities would be maintaining consistent preferences and actions. Our preference for interpretation is not testable from the data.

Those who volunteered a dislike for paperwork were 7 percent less likely to disagree to fudging paperwork. The effect is substantively small, although consistent with an interpretation of paperwork as an obstacle to the preferences of keeping clients eligible for support.

Respondents who volunteered a pecuniary like or dislike were somewhat more likely to disagree with fudging paperwork. The effect of pecuniary preferences is on par with the functional preferences, as it was in our analysis of the chances of taking paperwork home.

Other actors, with one exception, do not appear to influence disagreeing with fudging paperwork to a substantively interesting degree. Only the perceived influence of the director has an effect greater than a few percentages, and even here the effect is still somewhat small. Those respondents who felt that the director exercised a "great deal of influence" were about 11 percent more likely to disagree with an admission of fudging paperwork.

Although there is no rigorous way for us to test whether respondents are in fact concealing their performance, we think that the convergence of the effects of solidary, functional, and pecuniary preferences suggests that they are not concealing this form of sabotage. Respondents who derive utility from fellow subordinates, from their jobs, and from the material rewards are more likely to disagree. It takes an elaborate concoction of insincere respondents to make all three of these effects work in a way consistent with hiding sabotage.

Bending the Rules

Our second measure of subordinate sabotage is whether respondents agreed or disagreed with the statement, "Sometimes, you have to bend the rules in order to get anything done." Note that the nature of the question mixes performance ("getting anything done") with violation ("bending the rules"). Bending the rules becomes "sabotage" by virtue of an explicit attempt to undermine a specific aspect of the policy, even if the policy itself is inconsistent with the preferences of the supervisor. Like the police officer who engages in brutality, we cannot rule out the possibility that the social worker is proceeding in a way that is entirely coherent with what his or her supervisor "actually wants." As with our analysis of the incidence of police brutality, we will treat the significant part of the act as the "bending of rules" rather than the productively phrased "getting anything done." Table 6.7 presents our estimates of the effects of the variables.

As with our previous table on the chances a respondent would agree that he or she fudged the paperwork, one of the more striking results is that most of the variables have a very small effect upon admissions of sabotage. Unlike the previous table, there is at least one strong effect on agreeing, and a couple of minor effects. Furthermore, the dynamic we observe in this table is not a movement from "disagree" to "neither agree nor disagree" (as it was in the previous analysis), but a movement to or from "agreeing."

Only one of the measures of supervision—the administration of reprimands—accounts for much of a difference in the chances a respondent would admit to bending the rules. The effect is small, a 10 percent change, although of an expected sign: The more the social worker perceives supervision to be likely, the less likely he or she is to bend the rules.

The story for solidary likes is more ambiguous. One of the variables—working hard on the job leads to respect from coworkers—suggests that the stronger the solidary preferences, the more likely he or she is to bend the rules

TABLE 6.7. Estimated Effect of Preferences and Supervision on "Bending Rules," from 1994 Survey of Durham County Social Services

Variable	Agree	Neither Agree nor Disagree	Disagree
Failure to treat customers fairly results in reprimands from supervisors.	−.10	.07	.03
My department rewards results and goal achievement both formally and informally.	−.02	.01	.01
Working hard on my job leads to gaining respect from coworkers.	.08	.02	.05
A person gets the chance to develop good friends here.	−.21	.17	.04
Solidary like	0	0	0
Doing my job well makes me feel good about myself as a person.	.08	−.02	−.05
A person enters this profession because he likes the work.	−.02	.01	.01
"Helping" like	−.01	.01	.01
"Paperwork" dislike	.01	−.01	0
Pecuniary like/dislike	.08	−.06	−.02
Influence of immediate supervisor	0	0	0
Influence of coworkers	−.03	.02	.01
Influence of customers	.07	−.02	−.04
Influence of director	.01	−.01	0

Note: Cell entries are estimated effects based on ordered probit coefficients for the response to the Likert scale questions about "bending rules." "Strongly (Dis)Agree" and "(Dis)Agree" answers have been combined. Effects are estimated by computing probability of each response at mean for all variables, and subtracting from probability of response for maximum for selected variable (all other variables at mean). $N = 126$.

(although the effect is only 8 percent). A respondent who agreed that "a person gets the chance to develop good friends here" would be nearly one-fifth less likely to agree to bending the rules than the average. Volunteered solidary preferences made no difference whatsoever. We offer no particular reasoning behind why we would see such a mixed picture for solidary preferences.

Likewise, the effect of functional preferences on bending the rules is also a mix. Those who felt that "doing my job well makes me feel good about myself as a person" were slightly more likely to bend the rules (by 8 percent), but none of the other variables were substantively meaningful.

None of the remaining variables were of much significance either: There is a minor (8 percent) increase in agreeing for those who volunteered a pecuniary like and an equivalent (7 percent) increase for those who perceive customers as exerting a "great deal of influence," but neither effect amounts to much.

In fact, the only strong effect in the entire table was the one solidary preference that suggested that those with strong solidary preferences were less likely to break the rules. Given the ambiguity of the question, perhaps the reader should not be surprised at the relatively limited effects we find.

Whether Others Break the Rules

Our final approach to modeling the factors influencing sabotage among social workers turned the dependent variable around: instead of asking for a report about oneself, we ask for reports about what others in the department are doing. There are strengths and weaknesses to this approach: since it does not require a confession to a socially undesirable act on the part of the subordinate, one might expect that the answers here are more genuine and less deceptive. On the other hand, perceptions about the strength of the supervisor might well be the result of the activities of others, and not just the other way around. Table 6.8 presents the estimated effect of the variables on reports of others' sabotage.

One of the more striking results from this table is that the supervisor is now much more influential in deterring the sabotage of others than in the models of self-report. Across the board, all of the variables associated with the supervisors are now substantively and statistically significant. Those who see a strong connection between treating customers unfairly and reprimands from the supervisor were over one-third less likely to see others breaking the rules. The effect of rewards is less strong (14 percent less likely to see others breaking the rules), but of a consistent sign.

Solidary preferences did have a significant effect upon perceptions of others breaking the rules, although not consistent across the variables. Those who agreed that "a person gets the chance to develop good friends here" were about one-third less likely to see sabotage by others. Likewise, those who volunteered solidary preferences as something to like about being a social worker were about 11 percent less likely to see others as saboteurs. (The measure of agreement with "working hard . . . leads to respect" was nonsignificant and of the opposite sign.)

Functional preferences made very little difference to perceptions of others' performance. No effect was particularly large, and none of the variables were statistically significant.

Curiously, those who volunteered a pecuniary like or dislike were nearly one-fifth *more* likely to see others as saboteurs. The sign on this estimated effect is puzzling, since we usually think of sensitivity to material rewards as consistent with the strength of supervision.

Finally, the perceptions of the influence of the four groups of actors confirms the strong role of the supervisor. Those who saw their immediate supervisor as exerting a "great deal" of influence were 42 percent less likely to see sabotage by others.

There are two distinct overall interpretations to be drawn from the results

TABLE 6.8. Estimated Effect of Preferences and Supervision on "Others Break Rules," from 1994 Survey of Durham County Social Services

Variable	Agree	Neither Agree Nor Disagree	Disagree
Failure to treat customers fairly results in reprimands from supervisors.	−.35	.32	.03
My department rewards results and goal achievement both formally and informally.	−.14	.12	.02
Working hard on my job leads to gaining respect from co-workers.	.01	−.01	0
A person gets the chance to develop good friends here.	−.34	.31	.03
Solidary like	−.11	.07	.04
Doing my job well makes me feel good about myself as a person.	.02	.01	0
A person enters this profession because he likes the work.	−.04	.03	.01
"Helping" like	.01	−.01	0
"Paperwork" dislike	−.05	.03	.01
Pecuniary like/dislike	.18	−.16	−.02
Influence of immediate supervisor	−.42	.39	.03
Influence of coworkers	.01	−.01	0
Influence of customers	−.03	.02	.01
Influence of director	.18	−.07	−.11

Note: Cell entries are estimated effects based on ordered probit coefficients for the response to the Likert scale questions about "bending rules." "Strongly (Dis)Agree" and "(Dis)Agree" answers have been combined. Effects are estimated by computing probability of each response at mean for all variables, and subtracting from probability of response for maximum for selected variable (all other variables at mean). $N = 126$.

for this last table. One interpretation would be that this last measure of sabotage is the least suspect to biases due to self-reporting, and that we are finally locating the "real" effect of supervision. Clearly, the dominant effect in this table is that of the supervisor. (We do note that the sign on the perceived influence of the director is counter to that of the supervisor.) This interpretation runs counter to all the other examinations in this book, in that functional preferences make no difference at all to the likelihood of sabotage. Solidary preferences do affect the reported level of others' sabotage, which would be consistent with the other findings of the book.

The alternative interpretation is that the strength of supervision is endogenous to the perceptions of others' performance. Subordinates who see other subordinates as saboteurs might be more inclined to view their supervisors as weak, whereas those in groups with little sabotage are likely to see supervisors as strong. The perception of supervisory strength, in this interpretation, comes *after* the perception of others' activities.

Conclusion

The social workers in this chapter are much like the bureaucrats of the other chapters in terms of the factors that motivate performance, both positive (extra work, in the form of taking paperwork home) and negative (sabotage, in the form of fudging paperwork or bending rules). Where there are some significant points of departure for the social workers, those departures are due to the strength of solidary preferences, which are more consequential for the social workers than for any other group of bureaucrats that we explore in this book.

Social workers express strong functional and solidary preferences. When we connect these preferences to the four dependent variables, we find that functional preferences strongly encourage extra work, only modestly affect fudging paperwork, and have no effect at all upon bending rules or perceptions of others' sabotage. Solidary preferences, on the other hand, modestly affect taking on extra work and bending rules, but strongly affect fudging paperwork and reports of others breaking the rules.

The strength of administrative supervision was quite consistent with what we have found for the other bureaucrats of this book, with the exception of the final analysis. The social workers' assessments of the strength of supervision varied (in the univariate analysis): The social workers did not see themselves as under constant scrutiny, nor did they see much connection between performance and reward, but they did regard the usual social worker as generally obedient and saw that failure to serve clients fairly resulted in reprimands. As far as the effects of supervision on the levels of work or sabotage, in three of the four cases, one could only say that supervision had a small effect (for taking paperwork home, fudging paperwork, or bending rules). Only in the last case, where we asked the social workers to report on others, did the supervisors' performance suddenly matter.

The appearance of strong supervisory effects stands in contrast to the findings of every other model of bureaucratic performance in this book. We do find that there is some ambiguity in understanding the relationship between reports of others and assessments of the supervisor, especially since the assessments of the supervisors' strength were so variable within work groups.

Finally, we looked to the social workers' sense of the degree to which four groups of actors influenced how they allocated their time at work: customers, their immediate supervisor, coworkers, and the director. At a univariate level, the customers were far and away the most influential group in determining how the social workers spent their time, followed by the immediate supervisor. When we turn the questions of degree of influence into variables to predict levels of work or sabotage, in only two cases do we actually find substantial effects. Customers were a strong influence on whether the social workers took paperwork home, but not on any of the forms of sabotage. The immediate supervisor was a strong factor influencing reports of sabotage by others, but not on any of the other forms of sabotage or on extra work.

CHAPTER 7

Donut Shops and Speed Traps

Police officers are a second archetype of the "street-level bureaucrat," closely following the terms of Weber's bureaucracy.[1] Police forces are bound not only by federal, state, and local laws and ordinances, but also by scads of departmental rules and informal practices. These rules specify jurisdictions which, although at times overlapping across levels of government, also provide for means to settle the jurisdictional disputes. There is marked division of labor, with local police forces (especially in major cities) tasked to precincts (division by place) and to specific crimes (homicide, vice, traffic: division by function). Police officers ordinarily undergo significant amounts of training before becoming officers, not only in tactics, but also in procedure and rules. Police officers often choose careers as police officers. The management of the office swims in paperwork, in the form of police reports.

This chapter examines one particular dimension of discretion for the police officer, the amount of time the officer spends working and shirking. In the subsequent chapter, we retain our focus on the police officer, but we look toward their exercise of discretion in the form of police brutality, which we will consider to be a form of sabotage.

Two archetypal settings for the police officer are the donut shop and the speed trap. In the former, we might view the officer as avoiding her or his ordinary duties; in the latter, we might view the officer as enforcing her or his orders with unusual diligence. The amount of time a police officer spends working or shirking—laying an archetypal speed trap or eating an archetypal donut—provides us with an unambiguous measure of the degree of compliance of subordinates and an opportunity to evaluate these different models of supervision.

This chapter proceeds as follows. We start with an explication of the variables tied to the formal models presented in chapters 2 and 3. Next, we present our two data sets, a general model of supervision, and our results from the analysis of these two different data sets. Finally, we discuss the implications

---

1. Portions of this chapter appeared as "Donut Shops and Speed Traps: Evaluating Models of Supervision on Police Behavior," *American Journal of Political Science* (1993) 37:555–81.

of our analyses for understanding police behavior in particular and supervision in general.

Key Independent Variables

Defection and compliance are functions of the payoffs of current or future interactions between subordinates and supervisors. We focus our attention here on several key independent variables: *organizational environment, conformity among subordinates and work context, individual skills and attributes, rewards and punishments,* and *frequency of supervision.* These independent variables allow us to examine principal–agent relationships along several common theoretical dimensions.

Organizational Environment

We examine issues of political and organizational environment by differentiating police departments across cities. Reiss selected three cities, Boston, Chicago, and Washington, DC for his study, each representing a different type of police department. Chicago was chosen as representative of a "modern, bureaucratically organized department based on systems analysis and centralized command and control" (1971: xi–xii). Boston represented the traditional department with personalized administration. "Washington was selected because the department was in the process of professionalizing the staff and moving toward modernization of its command and control system" (1971: xii). Each of these cities' police departments possesses different organizational environments, which in turn affect the nature of supervision and control. We also compare the three cities studied by Ostrom, Parks, and Whitaker (1988): Tampa–St. Petersburg, Rochester, and St. Louis. We propose below that these different organizational environments, in turn, affect the propensity for police officers to defect.

Models of organizational culture argue that defection varies by the attitudes of the subordinates toward policy. This proposition can be drawn directly from the model presented in chapter 3. Such attitudes are largely considered to be products of organizational culture. Miller (1992), for example, proposes that the frequency of working and shirking is proportional to subordinates' adherence to different cultural norms; in this manner, subordinates' efforts are proportional to their collective predisposition toward their jobs and what they produce. In the context of a police agency, attitudes toward particular policies may influence how officers carry out their duties (Brown 1981). These political predispositions are further examined in the following sections.

Conformity among Subordinates and Work Context

Working from the conclusions drawn from the model presented in chapter 3 we contend organizational defection is related to conformity in response among the subordinates.[2] In other words, the degree to which subordinates are interconnected affects their propensity to work. Our conceptualization of organizational culture revolves around the adherence to a set of organizational norms by groups of subordinates, and the only impediment to convergence in the response of subordinates to policy is the absence of connections among subsets of the subordinates.

The organizational psychology literature further emphasizes the importance of the work context. Particularly relevant to a work context is the degree of cohesion within an organization. Behavioral conformity among subordinates is central to such notions of cohesion. The issue of conformity in a police agency is closely related to the notion of a police culture. A police culture is the informal organization that operates within a police agency (Brown 1981; Manning 1982; Van Maanen 1983). This notion of interconnectedness is consistent with Brown's observation:

> The police culture demands of a patrolman unstinting loyalty to his fellow officers, and he receives, in return, protection and honor: a place to assuage real and imagined wrongs inflicted by a (presumably) hostile public; safety from aggressive administrators and supervisors; and the emotional support required to perform a difficult task. (1981: 83)

In chapter 5 we found that such a sense of connectedness played a significant role in shaping patterns of working and shirking. Conformity among subordinates toward policy also varies by the network of associations among subordinates. In those police organizations where shirking or sabotage is considered to be acceptable among a network of subordinates, we would expect to see a greater propensity for defection.[3] We examine the role of police conformity by looking at frequency of contact between subordinates as well as expressions of solidary attachments exhibited in police agencies. Organizational disaffec-

---

2. The notion that solidarity can shape subordinate behavior has been around for some time. See for example Blau (1940).

3. Barker's study of police deviance in a southern city is particularly relevant. Fellow officers perceived police brutality to be less deviant than sleeping on duty, sex on duty, police perjury, or drinking on duty. Corresponding to this finding, they responded that they would be more likely to report a fellow officer for sleeping on duty than for the use of excessive force. Drinking on duty was considered to be the most deviant (Barker 1978.) Considering what we find in our next chapter, this is especially interesting. Also see Matza (1964) and Rubinstein (1973).

tion is also hypothesized to be related to the frequency of defection. In the following section we examine the role of police conformity by looking at expressions of solidary norms exhibited by police officers.

Individual Skills and Attributes

In the reforms to the police force in many cities (including Los Angeles), supervisors emphasized the importance of "professionalism" as a way to regulate the behavior of officers.[4] This is very much in sync with those principal–agency approaches which regard adverse selection as a threat to cooperation by subordinates. Reiss (1971) is quite explicit about the professional status of police officers: "The police in America belong to one of the few occupations that includes all of the essential elements to qualify as a profession. They possess the power of coercive authority, and through their power to arrest and book for offenses, they control the fate of 'clients' " (123). One hypothesis is simply that professionalism decreases the probability of defection.

Note that different aspects of the officer's skills and attributes argue for different policies. It is entirely possible that police schools could train officers to become more professional. It may also be possible to train officers to improve their human relations skills. We are skeptical as to whether any program could improve officer's intellectual involvement with the job, short of extensive screening at the hiring stage.

Rewards and Punishment

Most principal–agent models propose that the frequency of an individual's compliance is directly proportional to his rewards and inversely proportional to his punishments. For such models rewards and punishment play an important role in inducing compliance among subordinates. Such a relationship, however, may be indirect. For example, Kreps (1984) and Miller (1992) posit that the effectiveness of rewards and punishment is conditional on the cultural norms operating in an organization. In the specific context of a police agency, Van Maanen (1983) discusses how police supervisors use nonmonetary incentives and disincentives that are not governed by civil service procedures. The general empirical model presented later in this chapter examines the role of rewards and punishment in shaping the propensity for subordinates to work.

---

4. Moe (1984) writing about organizations in general discusses the special problems of adverse selection facing a police force. To overcome these problems, police academies are designed to screen, train, and evaluate police recruits so as to foster professionalism. Also see Bittner (1971), Manning (1977: 193–97), and Sykes (1985).

Frequency of Supervision

Many principal–agent models also focus on the limits to the frequency of supervision and the role this limitation serves in shaping agent compliance. The models presented in chapters 2 and 3 focus on broader limitations to supervision. Holmström (1982) proposes that the frequency of defection is inversely proportional to the supervisor's frequency of supervision. Nevertheless, the role of the police supervisor on subordinate officer behavior is controversial. We empirically examine this relationship later in this chapter.

From this discussion, we now proceed to evaluate the propensity for organizational defection and compliance in the specific instance of police agencies. To develop a set of testable propositions, we focus on the *frequency of shirking* as our dependent variable. To do this our next step is to describe the data at hand for the problem. Our subsequent step is to develop a general empirical method for evaluating models of supervision.

Description of the Data

The Reiss Data (1971)

A combined observational and attitudinal data set collected over twenty years ago permits an initial examination of these propositions. As part of a project to examine the causes and extent of police brutality, Reiss interviewed police officers in Washington, Boston, and Chicago in 1966 (Reiss 1971). A (largely unutilized) part of his project included attaching observers to each officer who recorded the activities of the officers during their runs. Through this data set, we have a unique combination of observations on the officers' patterns of shirking or working, combined with assessments of their attitudes toward their jobs, their superiors, and their public.

We must warn the reader that there are many serious difficulties in using these data. The documentation is miserable, at best, for the file recording the observer's notes. Many apparently useful measures are uncoded; even more are unexplained.[5] Furthermore, the data gathered by the observers are not directly mergeable with the attitudinal data. For purposes of this initial examination, we use a variation on the multiple-imputation techniques developed by Rubin (1987). Where we are able to directly link an officer in the observational data with an officer in the attitudinal data, we do so. For those officers for whom

---

5. We state these caveats primarily because of the data we are using. After all, the first of our data sets in this chapter is nearly 30 years old. We also express tentativeness about drawing too strong a conclusion about any of the models that are analyzed here.

we are unable to conclusively connect the data sets, we use successive levels of imputation based on precinct, assignment (foot patrol or mobile patrol), rank, race, and age. If we are unable to get a conclusive match on the basis of the five characteristics, we impute the mean value to the observational record. That is, if we have attitudinal records for six officers who share the same five characteristics, we use the mean record as the basis of imputation. If we have missing data on any of the five, we multiply impute attitudinal data to the observational data. At worst, we impute attitudes from precincts to observational data.

Despite the problems in the documentation and mergeability of the data, this is an important and well-regarded collection of data. Our technique of merging the data from one file to another will give us unbiased measures of the characteristics and attitudes of the officers on patrol for each observation, even if the multiple imputation approach leads us to necessarily less efficient estimates. Moreover, the *successive* multiple imputations at each level of the five matching characteristics mean that we have a much more efficient match than we would have if we merged at the highest level alone.

The observational data afford us several important measures. We have a very useful measure of our dependent variable, the fraction of time an officer spends working or shirking, in the observer's record of the amount of time an officer spends "goofing off." Literally, we have the estimated percentage of time on duty that an officer spends "actually off the job by their own volition (not waiting for instructions but just loafing)." Of course, we should suspect that the officer would alter his ordinary shirking behavior when under the guise of an observer. As noted in figure 7.1, there is a considerable variation in the percentage of time an officer shirks, ranging from 0 percent to 80 percent. One would expect that the officers would react to observation in such a manner that they would spend less time shirking or at least remain unaffected by the observer. Fortunately, this works against any findings we might produce, rather than exaggerates our findings (i.e., where officers would spend more time shirking while under observation). So any bias resulting from observation works against rather than toward any results that we report.

The observational data also records the race, rank, age, and assignment of the officers. The assignment of the officers affords us one useful measure of the supervisory constraints. As many authors have noted previously, officers on foot patrol are much more difficult to supervise than officers on mobile patrol (e.g., Reiss 1971, Brown 1988, Lipsky 1980). Officers on mobile patrol might be contacted via the car radio. We also have a record of the observational data of the ethnic, racial, and income composition of the officer's beat.

The attitudinal data provides us with several scales as well as some open-ended questions. The attitudinal scales include the respondents' level of satisfaction with their supervisor, level of satisfaction with their rank, number

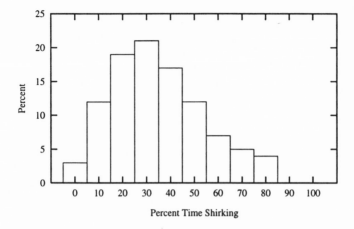

Fig. 7.1. Frequency distribution of the amount of time officers spend shirking, 1967 Reiss data

of times the officers made suggestions to their supervisors in 1965 and 1966, and how often the officers complained to their supervisors about disliked policy or procedures. We code several dummy variables based on responses to open-ended questions asking why the respondents decided to become police officers, what it is they like about their job, and what it is that they dislike about their job. If the reasons offered by a respondent referred to economic conditions (e.g., level of pay or job security), we code the reason as *economic*. If the officer mentioned aspects of the job directly related to performance as a job officer (e.g., interest in law enforcement, making society better, possibility of false arrest), we code the reason as *functional*. If the respondent referred to his/her relations to other officers (such as to friends or family), we code the reason as *solidary*. And in the case of reasons to dislike the job, if the officer mentioned aspects related to supervisors, the courts, or other higher authorities, we refer to the dislike as *political*. (No officer mentioned political reasons as reasons to join the force or to like the job.)

We lack several significant measures. The most conspicuous absence is of any measure of the supervisor's level of tolerance for defection or the level of sanction for defection. Since several models predict that the penalty for defection significantly affects the officer's likelihood of compliance, this is a most unfortunate absence. Nonetheless, we believe that this data set allows us to begin to discriminate among several models of supervision.

The Ostrom, Parks, and Whitaker Data (1988)

Ten years after Reiss conducted his investigation of Police behavior, Elinor Ostrom, Roger B. Parks, and Gordon Whitaker conducted a different (but in many ways similar) study of police services in Rochester, St. Louis, and the Tampa–St. Petersburg metropolitan areas. The data they collected was designed to compare the delivery of police services across comparable neighborhoods. For our purposes we utilize the Patrol Observation General Shift Information. This data file consists of information describing the police shifts (the eight-hour workday) of different officers. As with the Reiss study this data was collected by observers assigned to an officer. The events occurring during the shift, officer attitudes, patrol styles and activities, citizen encounters, and contact with other police officials were recorded. Also like the Reiss study, the observers kept track of how the officers used their time. This gave us access to a comparable measure of police time spent shirking and working.

Shirking can be measured two ways. The first measure is very similar to the one we use to analyze the Reiss data; this is the percentage of total time an officer spent on personal business, not doing police work. The second measure measures the proportion of encounters that were not part of an officer's official business, such as meeting with a friend while "on duty." Figures 7.2 and 7.3 show the frequency distribution of these two measures of shirking with the Ostrom, Parks, and Whitaker data set. As opposed to the Reiss data, with these measures of shirking we see less variation in the percentage of time an officer shirks, ranging from 0 percent to 38 percent, but much greater variance with shirking as a proportion of encounters ranging from 0 percent to 100 percent. Note also that both of these distributions are sharply skewed toward compliance (minimal shirking).

Officers' attitudes and comments were coded from overt statements. We took this information and developed several scales. *Solidary attachments* ranges from −1, dissatisfaction with the squad (the immediate working group) to +1, satisfaction with the squad. *Satisfaction with supervisor* also ranges from −1 to +1 depending on whether the officer expressed dissatisfaction or satisfaction with her or his immediate supervisor. *Supervisory contact* is a count of all the contact an officer has with supervisors during the shift, including all face-to-face contact, radio contact, and stops at the station (other than returning at the end of a shift). On the other hand, *contact with other police officers* is a count of all the face-to-face contact an officer has with other officers and detectives (who are not supervisors). *Functional likes* and *functional dislikes* are scales which measure aspects of the officers likes and dislikes directly related to the job of being a police officer (comments relating to patrol style and satisfaction with the officer's beat).

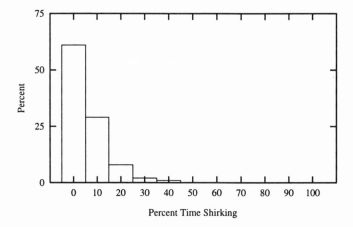

Fig. 7.2. Frequency distribution of the percentage of time officers spend on personal business, 1977 Ostrom, Parks, and Whittaker data

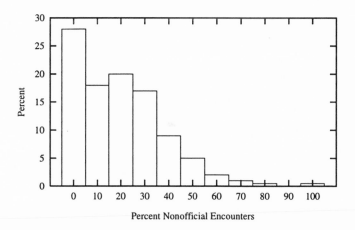

Fig. 7.3. Frequency distribution of the percentage of encounters which are not official business, 1977 Ostrom, Parks, and Whittaker data

With this data set we have better measures of contact with supervisors and fellow workers. Unfortunately we do not have data on the racial composition of the precincts patrolled, nor do we have measures of professionalism. As with the Reiss data we also lack data on supervisors' attitudes, particularly with respect to their tolerance for defection. Nevertheless, these two data sets provide important insights into the forces that shape organizational defection in a police force.

Results

As with chapters 3, 5, and 6, we utilize beta estimates to model police supervision using these two police behavior data sets. The dependent variable is the rate of shirking by the officer for that run, as recorded by the observer. We take two approaches in interpreting the beta-model coefficients. The first point of note is to observe whether an explanatory variable is a statistically significant predictor of either compliance or defection. Here, we attend to whether the coefficients are more strongly associated with ν (defection– shirking) or ω (compliance–working), and whether the estimated coefficients are at least twice their standard errors. This first approach is very much akin to the way one might look for statistically significant predictors in an OLS model. (We will again employ the $\lhd, \rhd$, and $\bowtie$ symbols as per our previous chapters.) Our second approach will be to examine the substantive effect by considering first differences. Since shirking is scaled from 0 to 1, a first difference of .25 means that the explanatory variable encouraged an additional 25 percent goofing off.

In the first model, we include a mix of variables from the Reiss data set that denote characteristics of the officer's precinct, shift, and attitudes toward the job. We evaluate whether the officer's city of residence makes a difference for the rate of shirking. We use two dummy variables, *Boston* and *Chicago,* to denote the city where the police officer works. (Washington is the omitted category.) We include two variables measuring the racial composition of the officer's precinct, *Percent Black* and *Percent White* (coded from 0–1). (Because of nonwhite and nonblack presence in precincts, these two variables are not mutually exclusive.) *Professionalism* was recorded by the observer for each shift, and represents a scale from 0 ("Lackadaisical, sloppy, irresponsible") through .5 ("Takes work as just a job") to 1 ("Serious, businesslike, responsible"). We code two expressions of dislike for the job, and one for likes for the job. *Functional dislike* denotes those officers who expressed a dislike for the duties of being a police officer (such as arresting people, intervening in fights, etc.). *Solidary dislikes* denote those officers who disliked their job for reasons associated with the other officers (e.g., "can't get along with other officers"). *Solidary likes* records the opposite: officers who expressed positive attitudes toward other officers as a reason for liking the job. *Satisfaction with supervisor* is a scale coded from 0 (very dissatisfied with supervisor) through 1 (very satisfied with supervisor). Finally, we use a dummy variable, *Mobile patrol*, to denote whether the officer is assigned to a mobile patrol.

In the second model, we draw our variables from the Ostrom, Parks, and

Whitaker data. As with the model based on the Reiss data, we distinguish between those officers serving in Rochester, Tampa–St. Petersburg, or St. Louis. (We use *Rochester* and *Tampa* as the distinguishing dummy variables.) *Functional likes* and *functional dislikes* also resemble the measures derived from the Reiss data; they measure an officer's likes and dislikes about the duties of policing. *Solidary attachments* reflect in a single variable *solidary likes* and *solidary dislikes*, measured from −1 (dislikes) to +1 (likes). *Satisfaction with supervisor* is measured along a similar scale from −1 to +1. To measure frequency of supervision we use *contact with supervisor* which counts the frequency of contact an officer has with his or her superiors during a single shift. *Contact with other officers* similarly counts the frequency of contact an officer has with his peers. The third model we evaluate uses all of these explanatory variables, but relates them to a different measure of shirking. While the first two models measure shirking as the percentage of time spent "goofing off," the third model measures shirking as the percentage of encounters engaged with purely private business. These three models offer insight into the factors that shape patterns of compliance and defection.

Table 7.1 reports the beta analyses of police shirking. The column headed

TABLE 7.1. Estimated Effect of Preferences and Organizational Characteristics Effects on Shirking by Police Officers, 1966 and 1977 Police Behavior Data

Variable	1967	1977a	1977b
Boston	−.02		
Chicago	.07 ⋈		
Rochester		−.20 ⋈	−.03◁
Tampa		−.21 ⋈	−.20 ⋈
Percent black	.16 ⋈		
Percent white	−.03		
Professionalism	−.46 ⋈		
Functional dislike	.20 ⋈	.11 ▷	.07
Functional like		−.13 ▷	−.09
Solidary dislike	.04 ▷		
Solidary like	−.10 ▷		
Solidary attachments		−.08	−.08
Contact with other officers		.09 ⋈	.02 ⋈
Satisfaction with supervisor	.03 ⋈	.09 ◁	.05◁
Mobile patrol	.27 ▷		
Contact with supervisor		.09 ⋈	.04 ⋈

Note: Shirking measures for 1967 and 1977a are in terms of time allocation. The shirking measure for 1977b is in terms of total encounters. Cells are estimated change in level of working (scale from 0–1) due to a shift of the variable from the mean to the maximum, holding all other variables at their mean. ◁ means shirking parameter (v) significant at $p < .05$, ▷ means working parameter (ω) significant at $p < .05$, and ⋈ means both parameters significant at $p < .05$.

by 1967 designates our analysis of the Reiss data. The second column designated with 1977a draws from the Ostrom, Parks, and Whitaker data and uses the shirking as percentage of total time as the dependent variable. The third column, 1977b, draws also from this same data, but uses the shirking as percentage of encounters as the dependent variable. We now turn to the relationship between these dependent variables and the explanatory variables.

Do the Boston cops goof off more or less than the Washington or Chicago cops? As one can readily see from the beta estimates in Table 7.1, being an officer in Chicago affected the officer's performance. Both the v (shirking) and ω (working) coefficients on the dummy variable for Chicago are statistically significant at $p < .05$.[6] Substantively, we can interpret the first difference such that an officer in Chicago in 1966 is likely to shirk 7 percent more than officers in other cities, controlling for the other variables. Recalling the enthusiastic response of the Chicago officers to a peculiar form of law enforcement just two years later (during the Democratic convention), the level of shirking among Chicago officers (in contrast to Boston or Washington officers) is surprising. Note that the Boston officers shirked marginally less than the Washington or Chicago officers.

Are there similar differences between the police in St. Louis, Tampa, and Rochester? Our results are statistically significant for both city dummy variables with the Ostrom, Parks, and Whitaker data; both the v and ω coefficients on both dummy variables are significant using the first measure of shirking (shirking as a percentage of total time) and both the v and ω coefficients for the Tampa dummy are significant for the second measure of shirking (shirking as a percentage of all encounters) while only the shirking parameter for the Rochester dummy is significant at $p < .05$. We see both police officers in Tampa and Rochester differ considerably from the behavior of their counterparts in St. Louis using either measure of shirking. St. Louis cops are more likely to shirk than the police in the other two cities. In fact the biggest first difference values are evident here with these two variables. For the first measure of shirking we see that Rochester and Tampa–St. Petersburg officers are 20 percent and 21 percent less likely to shirk than St. Louis police. Clearly, where one works affects how hard one works.

We find conformity among workforces with respect to compliance. This first finding is consistent with our model presented in chapter 3.[7] (This is also consistent with Brown's observation, noted above, about police culture.) Of course, in and of itself, the coefficients on the city dummies do not demonstrate

---

6. See Appendix C for tables C.7, C.8, and C.9 which provide a complete listing of the values of the v and ω coefficients.

7. Other models make a similar prediction. For example, Bianco and Bates's (1990) model implies that such conformity is due to the supervisor's specific efforts, whereas the Kreps (1984) and Miller (1992) models imply imply conformity arises out of adherence to cultural norms.

the presence of a police culture, but they are consistent with the predictions of conformity from both models.

The measures of the race of the citizens in the precinct is the next pair of variables to consider. Unfortunately, we only can draw on the Reiss data to explore this issue. While this model is not directly applicable to models of supervision, it is certainly of concern with respect to current debates about the interactions of police and minorities. Note that the v and ω coefficients on the percent of blacks in the officer's precinct are statistically significant at $p < .05$, where the effect of the race of the precinct is clearly more sizable on compliance than on defection.[8] From the first difference for this coefficient, we note that officers in 100 percent black precincts were likely to shirk their duties 16 percent more than officers in precincts of average racial composition.[9] This result is of compelling public policy concern: Citizens who live in majority black precincts receive far less services from police officers than those citizens who live in majority white precincts. At least as of 1967, there is a significant and jarring difference in level of police protection in these three cities.

By far the most substantively significant variable in the model used to analyze the Reiss data is the role of professionalism. Both the v and ω beta coefficients on professionalism are substantially larger than their standard errors. The most professional officers shirked 46 percent less than the average officer, according to the first differences computed from the beta model. The effect of professionalism on working and shirking is of direct public policy concern. The goal of many police reform programs in the decades since Reiss's original study has been to bolster the professionalism of officers. In fact, Reiss himself called for greater attention to the professionalism of officers (Reiss 1971: 121–24).[10] Professional norms constitute a significant aspect of police culture and a mechanism for regulating the behavior of officers. Note that professionalism, while a component of policy, is contingent upon the extent of cooperative cultural norms in the police force. Seen from the perspective of principal-agent approaches, academies and professionalism serve to counter problems of adverse selection (Moe 1984: 760).

Also of substantive importance are the measures of the extent of shirk-

---

8. We have reestimated this model controlling for the race of the officer, and it does not appear to be the case that it was white officers shirking their duties in black precincts, but that the race of the officer did not matter.

9. It has been pointed out to us that this finding is not directly applicable to charges that police officers are more likely to brutalize black citizens than white citizens. A black citizen undergoing a beating by police officers might well prefer that those officers were shirking their duties instead. Moreover, as we discussed in chapter 2 and examine in detail in chapter 8, there are distinct modes of subordinate behavior that are neither working nor shirking.

10. Also see Bittner (1971), Manning (1977: 193–97), and Sykes (1985) for more on the need for police professionalism. Police academies are designed to foster professionalism by screening, training, and evaluating police recruits.

ing by officers' likes and dislikes for the job. In our first model (1967) officers who express a functional dislike for the job (e.g., dislike arresting people) shirk 20 percent more than the average officer. Compare these results to those for the Ostrom, Parks, and Whitaker data (1977a), where we find that functional dislikes and functional likes are significantly associated with working parameters, but not the shirking parameters. The signs of the first differences are in the expected directions; functional likes are positive and functional dislikes are negative. Clearly in these two models, the attitude with which an officer approaches his job affects how hard he or she works.

For the Reiss data (1967), officers who express solidary dislikes shirked at about the average rate, while officers who express solidary likes shirked 10 percent less than average officers. Note that the effect of solidary likes and dislikes is asymmetric with respect to compliance and defection. The v coefficients for both are small relative to their standard errors, whereas the ω coefficients are statistically significant. The implication is that solidary likes and dislikes affect propensity to shirk, but not propensity to work.

The models used to analyze the Ostrom, Parks, and Whitaker data (1977a and 1977b) utilize one measure of solidary attachment ranging from -1 to $+1$. Here we found no relationships significant at $p < .05$; however for the 1977b model (where shirking is measured as a percentage of time), the working parameter for solidary attachments is significant at $p < .06$. We found better evidence to support the important role played by networks of subordinates with the contact with other officers variable. Here we found significant relations for both the v and ω parameters for both measures of shirking, suggesting that contact between subordinates does make a difference.

We take these results to be a contribution to the thinking in political science about compliance by agents. In recent years, political science has adopted a set of models that from the outset regard the fundamental connection in organizations to be between agents and principals, not between the agents. The importance of solidary likes and dislikes in the first empirical model suggests that the relations *between* agents may be as important as any between agents and principal. Further, the role of solidary likes and dislikes adds to evidence about the presence of a police culture, and the role of that culture in setting standards for working and shirking. The importance of solidary likes and dislikes is tangentially related to the importance of the network of subordinates for conformity seen in the model presented in chapter 3. More directly related to the concept of networks is the frequency of contact between agents. We find that such contact is significantly related to both the propensity for working as well as shirking.

These findings are further enhanced by the relative surprise embedded in attitudes toward the supervisor. According to the beta estimates, the more satisfied the officer is with his supervisor, the more likely that officer is to work. The officers who expressed the most satisfaction with their supervisor are the most likely to work. The effect of satisfaction with one's supervisor in the first model (1967) leads us to interpret that the most satisfied officers shirked 3 percent more than average officers. For the next two models we only found significant relationships with the shirking parameter, but the pattern across all three empirical models was very similar. One could interpret the magnitude and sign of these first difference measures in one of two ways. Either officers are satisfied with their supervisor because the officer can shirk more, or officers shirk more because they are satisfied with their supervisors. The latter is consistent with the organizational culture models if one takes shirking to be independent of the officer's attitudes toward supervision. Another way of looking at this coefficient, and at the sharp divergence in the two interpretations, is that this measure is endogenous. Merely because we have adopted more appropriate statistical models for the movement of the dependent variable does not eliminate any simultaneity problems. Corrections for simultaneity in this context are beyond both the data and the scope of this essay.

We can also ascertain how the officers' patrol assignment affects their propensity to shirk. In the 1967 model we include one dummy variable denoting whether the officers are assigned to mobile patrol or otherwise (foot patrol, lockup, desk duty, etc.). As we mention above, a supervisor is somewhat better able to attend to the actions of officers on mobile patrol than those on other assignments. Officers on mobile patrol may be dispatched to new locations or have their current locations monitored over the radio. The unambiguous interpretation of the first differences reported in table 7.1 is that officers on mobile patrol shirk substantially more than officers assigned to other duties: 27 percent more than the average.

However, we acknowledge several reasons to remain skeptical about this finding. First of all, it is entirely likely that our measures of shirking for officers on mobile patrol are not strictly equivalent with the measures for the other officers. Officers on foot patrol might feel more conspicuous when taking time off than officers on mobile patrol. Secondly, the duties of mobile patrol officers differ from those of the other officers. Mobile patrol officers spend a great deal of their time on "routine, preventive patrol" (Gates and Worden 1989). The mere presence of a police vehicle in a neighborhood acts as a deterrent. Consequently, what might appear to some observers as additional time spent loafing may actually be time spent in this passive style of deterrence. Third, we do not have measures of the sanctions or tolerance of the officers. As a result, we do not know whether it is the supervisor's observability or the sanctions available to the supervisor that accounts for the greater time spent shirking by mobile patrol officers.

With the models used to evaluate the Ostrom, Parks, and Whittaker data 1977a and 1977b we can more directly evaluate the effects of supervision frequency. We find that the number of contacts with a supervisor are significant at $p < .05$ for both working and shirking. We find here that those officers watched the most are those that receive the greatest attention. Recall this conclusion from the model presented in chapter 2.

Conclusions

We emphasize our finding of the overwhelming importance of attributes of the organizational culture in determining the subordinates' levels of compliance. There is an acute need in current scholarly concerns about bureaucratic responsiveness as well as current policy concerns about police behavior to assess the differences between the theoretical perspectives of these models. As we suggest with the model presented in chapter 3, one must change the organizational culture that, in turn, shapes the predispositions and attitudes of the officers if we are to hope that bureaucratic regulations will moderate officers' behavior. . Our results indicate that norms of police professionalism could play a significant role in altering these attitudes and predispositions.

If one were to return to the disjuncture between the aggregate observations of bureaucratic responsiveness (e.g., Moe 1982, Wood 1990) and the individual level analysis noting widespread discretion for subordinates (e.g., Kaufman 1960, Heclo 1977, Lipsky 1980) that we present in our introductory chapter, we believe our work points to a possible resolution. Many agencies, perhaps most, are staffed by policy bureaucrats with strong policy interests. Many subordinates put in long hours, yet may receive few direct rewards for extensive service (Feldman 1989). As we observe with the levels of shirking by police officers, a productive avenue for research would be to explore the culture of the agency. Do the bureaucrats express strong solidary likes about their jobs? Or do they express dislikes toward the very functions they are asked to perform? To what extent does subordinate professionalism carry throughout the agency, and to what extent does that professionalism reflect working over shirking? Perhaps the resolution to the discrepancy between wide latitude for subordinate bureaucrats and productive agencies washes out when both agent and principal share the same preferences.

Likewise, we believe our analysis has a theoretical contribution to make to the principal–agency approaches. As we demonstrate here, attitudes and the frequency of contact among subordinates to one another affect the level of shirking to a much greater extent than does the observability of the subordinate by the supervisor.

We have seen some surprises that inform the general discussion about supervision and control. We see that the officers' city matters, which is consistent with those models that predict conformity among workforces. We see that the officers' attitudes toward their jobs affect their rates of compliance. With special interest we note the imortance of solidary and functional attitudes. The frequency of interaction between officers is also shown to be significant. The clear implication for a police agency is that if we want to discourage shirking by police officers, we want to encourage the officers to develop friendships with other officers and to develop a sense that they are doing the right thing. We also see that the officers' attitudes toward their supervisor affect their compliance, although in a way some observers might find surprising. Officers who are more satisfied with their supervisors shirk more frequently. When is it time to lay down a speed trap or to go to the donut shop? Our research suggests that the answer lies in the norms of the network of officers.

CHAPTER 8

Policing Police Brutality

Trials of police officers in the early 1990s for beating black motorists in Los Angeles and Detroit demonstrate that police brutality persists as a compelling public policy issue. Police brutality is an exceptional case of defection— defection against the public, against the law, against simple decency. The public policy problem of regulating brutality makes this a worthy subject of analysis per se. Further, analysis of brutality provides an opportunity to expand our theoretical understanding of general problems of supervision and control.

While the great preponderance of principal–agency models treat compliance and defection as if they simply fell along a continuum, we argue that forms of cooperative and noncooperative behavior differ fundamentally. We have already demonstrated in chapters 5, 6, and 7 that working and shirking are motivated by different sets of factors (i.e., that variables that reduce shirking do not necessarily have a simultaneous effect of increasing work). Moreover, in chapter 2 we distinguished between two principal forms of defection, shirking and sabotage. A subordinate shirks when he does not work at full capacity. A subordinate engages in sabotage when he actively undermines the supervisor's policy. Clearly, police brutality is not a variety of shirking. Police brutality is much closer to the idea of sabotage, an explicit violation of the law.

Some skeptical readers will question whether police brutality constitutes "sabotage" if it accomplishes the public's, and the principal's, goal of reducing crime. Such skepticism is, in fact, opposite of public preferences over the appropriateness of brutality. Public preferences are quite clear, and exceptionally stable. Figure 8.1 plots the percentage of respondents to the 1972–93 General Social Survey agreeing with each of the following questions:

- Are there situations that you can imagine in which you would approve of a policeman striking an adult male citizen?
- Would you approve of a policeman striking a citizen who had said vulgar and obscene things to the policeman?
- ... was being questioned in a murder case?
- ... was attempting to escape from custody?
- ... was attacking the policeman with his fists?

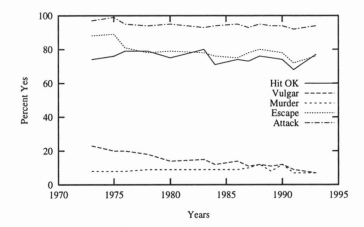

Fig. 8.1. Public approval of policeman striking adult male citizen, 1973–93 General Social Survey

By overwhelming margins, the public supports police violence, of a very limited form, only under narrow circumstances: to protect the officer and to prevent flight. Respondents opposed the use of force in murder interrogations in excess of a ten-to-one margin.

Still, some scholars of police behavior (see Reiss 1971), as well as many of the officers themselves, regard police brutality as the exercise of unusual means to accomplish the social goal of punishing criminals. In this manner, police brutality could actually be condoned by superiors and may constitute compliance rather than defection. Unfortunately, we have no data to evaluate supervisors' attitudes toward police brutality. For the purposes of evaluation of the problems of supervision in this chapter, we assume that brutality is illegal and not condoned by police departments.

At minimum, we will demonstrate that brutality is distinct from working, and that different forms of police brutality are explained by very different factors. We hope that the reader shares our conception of police brutality as a kind of criminal behavior on the part of police officers and thus a form of sabotage.

This chapter consists of two distinct parts. The first and larger part utilizes the Reiss data (Reiss 1971) described in chapter 7. This data provides a combined observational and attitudinal perspective of individual police officers. The second part of this chapter analyzes organizational data regarding police use of force, more specifically involving official reports, citizen complaints, and legal consequences (Pate and Fridell 1994).

In the first part of this chapter we address a common problem in the analysis of social phenomena, the examination of rare events. Brutality is a rare event relative to all other police activities. Similarly rare, but no less important, events happen elsewhere in politics—wars, coups, assassinations, and riots are just a few examples. We employ two principal methods in order to analyze these rare but substantively important events. The first approach involves analyzing police brutality with simple dichotomous choice models, using a special link function in order to compensate for the few cases in one tail of the distribution. The second approach utilizes a censoring model where we differentiate police officers who contemplate abuse from those who do not contemplate abuse. This second approach is perhaps closer to the actual public policy problem, although we are able to proceed with the approach with only one form of police brutality.

A problem that we have with the analysis of the police encounters data is that the presence of observers might induce police officers to behave differently. In order to address this possible "Hawthorne Effect," we rely on administrative data of the records of public complaints about police use of force. This second part of the chapter employs event count analysis using Poisson regression models to examine citizen complaints filed against police officers. (Unlike the other data collections we examine in this book, the unit of analysis in this second part is the department, not the individual officer.)

This chapter proceeds as follows. In part one, where we examine the behavior of individual police officers, we start with an explication of a set of propositions regarding the relationship between factors that are theoretically linked to different forms of police brutality. Next, we describe the Reiss data set (1971), our methods to analyze incidence of brutality, and the results of this analysis. In part two, where we examine police use of force across different organizations, we start with an overview of propositions regarding organizational oversight and supervision. We then describe the Pate and Fridell (1994) data set, the analysis we employ to analyze these events, and our results. Finally in the conclusion, we discuss the implications of our analysis for understanding police behavior in particular and supervision and organizational oversight in general.

The Behavior of Individual Police Officers

Questions of supervision and control inherently revolve around issues of compliance and defection (or cooperation and noncooperation). Most works looking at this issue focus on one type of defection, shirking. Indeed, our own chapters 5–7 examine the factors that motivate working and shirking. In chapter 2, on the other hand, we argue that sabotage is a clear case of organizational defection qualitatively distinct from any variety of shirking (motivated either through policy motivations or for leisure). In this chapter and chapter 6 we examine the factors that motivate sabotage.

Police brutality can be perpetrated in a variety of ways. The most obvious form of brutality is most literally defined as unnecessary force, but verbal brutality (threats and ridicule) exists, too: "the use of undue or unreasonable physical force in some aspect of police action. . . Another level of definition for police brutality is verbal or psychological brutality" (Radelet 1986: 191–92). We expect that some readers will trivialize verbal brutality. We would hope that most readers recognize that a police threat of violence constitutes "assault," even if it is not "battery." In this chapter, we identify brutality as any excessive use of police authority in the officer's interaction with a civilian.[1] Unnecessary frisks, ridicule, threats, as well as excessive use of force constitute different forms of police brutality that we examine in this chapter.[2] In the pages that follow we explicitly examine whether different forms of brutality are statistically distinct from one another in their interaction with a common set of independent variables.

Factors that Influence Defection

Several common themes emerge from models of supervision and compliance. Defection and compliance are functions of the payoffs of current or future interactions between subordinates and supervisors. We focus our attention here on five sets of independent variables: *organizational environment, work context, individual skills and attributes, predispositions* and *circumstances of the encounter* We explicitly employ sets of variables from several levels of organizational analysis for a multilevel approach, where relationships are posited among variables that apply at two or more levels.[3] We have also attempted to utilize the same independent variables that we used in the previous chapter when we examined shirking in police agencies. This allows us to not only compare different forms of brutality but to compare these varieties of defection with shirking.

To a large extent our choice of variables in this section of this chapter very closely resembles our analysis in chapter 7. For *organizational environment* we look for differences across cities (police agencies). For *work context* we

---

1. See Carter who similary defines brutality as the abuse of authority (Barker and Carter 1991: 197–217).

2. Pate and Fridell's 1994 data categorizes citizen complaints about the excessive use of force by the police. These categories include: unnecessary force, false arrest, illegal search, verbal abuse, misuse of authority, and demeaning lanuage. In neither set of analysis however, do we explicitly examine police use of deadly force.

3. See Rousseau (1985) for her discussion of compositional, multilevel and cross-level organizational research.

use a measure of solidary likes as an indicator of individual affinity for the organization. *Individual skills and attributes* are analyzed using measures of human relations skills, intellectual involvement, and professionalism. Each of these variables has been discussed in previous chapters, so we spare the reader a redundant discussion of how these factors may influence behavior. *Circumstances of the encounter* and *predisposition*, on the other hand, possess characteristics that are more particular to questions of brutality. We discuss these two variables in greater detail below.

Circumstances of Encounter

The specific circumstances of a police encounter may also influence the propensity for a subordinate officer to engage in brutal activity.[4] Three features of the Rodney King case are quite relevant: the number of other officers, the differences of races, and the character of the alleged offense.

The number of officers might influence the probability that an officer would defect, but the direction of influence is quite unclear. If police officers resort to brutality because they need to assert control, we would expect that officers would be less likely to brutalize civilians with a large number of other officers at the encounter. Conversely, officers might be tempted to brutalize as a demonstration of power to their peers. We remain agnostic about the direction of the relationship between the number of officers and frequency of defection.[5]

A salient charge against the police officers, indeed the LAPD and its chief, is that the officers acted out of racial animosity against King. Charges of racism underlie the long-standing concerns about police brutality (Wilson 1968, Reiss 1971). This is a testable hypothesis in principle; unfortunately, in the data at hand, the race of civilians is suppressed in the collection.

The type of alleged crime may also affect brutality. Officers investigating felonies (not all of which are violent) may be more likely to brutalize than officers investigating misdemeanors. We would not ordinarily expect brutality to occur when officers investigate relatively minor offenses. Officers investigating violent crimes (not all of which are felonies) may be more likely to brutalize civilians than officers who are investigating nonviolent crimes.

Chapters 2, 5, 6, and 7 demonstrate that defection varies by the attitudes of the subordinates toward a policy. In the context of a police agency, attitudes

---

4. A large number of studies have examined the influence of situational factors on police behavior. See for example Black (1980), Smith and Visher (1981), and Worden (1989)

5. A related issue is whether an incident of brutality stems from malfeasance (a wanton desire to defect) or misfeasance (unintentional violence resulting from incompetence) (Frye 1986: 467). Either problem theoretically could be addressed through appropriate training.

toward particular policies may influence how officers carry out their duties (Friedrich 1980, Brown 1981). The frequency with which subordinates comply is positively related to subordinates' affect for and initial responses to a policy. It follows that the frequency of defection is positively related to the subordinate's predisposition toward defection. In this specific case a police officer's attitude toward brutality is seen to influence a subordinate officer's propensity to engage in brutality.

Officers express a wide variation of likes and dislikes about their jobs (as would any set of employees). As in chapters 4 through 7, we distinguish between likes and dislikes in terms of broad references. *Functional* likes and dislikes refer to how the officer feels about the duties of being a cop: An officer who dislikes arresting people expresses a functional dislike, while the officer who likes the idea of enforcing the law expresses a functional like. *Solidary* likes and dislikes address the officer's feelings about fellow officers.

As seen in chapter 7, our analysis of shirking by police officers found that likes and dislikes strongly influenced the extent to which officers shirked. If Reiss's argument about the reasons for brutality holds true, then we would expect that officers who express a political dislike for the job would be more likely to brutalize than other officers.

From these theoretical observations, we now proceed to evaluate models of organizational control in the specific instance of police brutality. The general task is to determine whether police brutality can be controlled by supervisors or by fellow subordinates, or if it is simply a very rare event.

Description of the Reiss Data

As with chapter 7 we utilize the Reiss data (1971) in this chapter. This data set affords a unique opportunity to examine the behavior of "street-level bureaucrats" in their encounters with citizens. In addition to the observational data, we also draw upon the interviews with the officers about their feelings toward their jobs, their superior officers, and the public.

There are three separate data collections that we merge together in order to examine our propositions. Two of these are on the basis of observer's records: the "runs" and "encounters" files. The "encounters" file treats each service- initiated[6] police–citizen encounter as a single observation. We have recorded in the "encounters" data the officer's attributes (e.g., rank, age, race, assignment, precinct), characteristics of the encounter (e.g., number of officers, whether the crime is a felony or violent), and the types of interactions (e.g., whether unnecessary force, unnecessary frisks, ridicule, or threats were used).

---

6. At this time, we have not included records of citizen-initiated encounters.

The "runs" file represents an entire shift for the officer.[7] Each run contains multiple encounters. It is relatively straightforward to merge the encounters and runs data.

Several different types of brutality and harassment are recorded in this data set. These acts include the use of unnecessary force, unnecessary frisks, threats of violence, and ridicule. The frequency of these incidences of brutality in terms of the total number of citizen–police encounters is tiny: .2 percent for unnecessary force, .7 percent for unnecessary frisks, 1 percent for ridicule, and 6 percent for threats. These are our dependent variables for examining police brutality. We also utilize information regarding officers' attitudes toward physical abuse of suspects. This information is used to differentiate officers according to their propensity to be physically brutal.[8]

It should be immediately apparent to the reader that there is a significant risk of a "Hawthorne effect" causing the officers to alter their behavior under the scrutiny of an observer. One would expect that the officers would react to being observed by restraining any inclinations they might have to engage in brutality. In fact, it is noteworthy that any brutality took place in front of these observers. For two reasons, we argue that it is well worthwhile to proceed with the analysis of these observations, despite the obtrusive nature of the measurement of our dependent variables. First, while our suspicions are that the officers suppressed noncooperative behavior under observation, these suspicions are probably an exaggeration. In our study of police working and shirking in chapter 7, we found a surprisingly high incidence of shirking despite the presence of an observer. Other analysts of police behavior (Worden 1989, Black 1980, Brown 1981) report that officers are relatively unconstrained by observers. Second, if this is a "censored data" problem, the effect of the censoring on the dependent variable produces attenuation of the coefficients. In other words, the effect of the observers is likely to undermine the findings we report here by reducing the magnitude of the coefficients toward zero, not to exaggerate them. While the incidents of brutality are rare, if one considers all the police–public encounters, there are an amazing number of cases involving brutality.

We lack several measures with the current data, although we amend the omissions in the subsequent data set. The most conspicuous absence is of any

---

7. The "runs" file constituted the data set for our previous analysis of shirking. As we note in Chapter 7, there are many serious difficulties in working with the "runs" data. Chief among the difficulties was that the attitudinal data did not cleanly merge with the data recording what happened on each shift. We construct the combined runs–attitudinal data set through straightforward merges of officer's records where possible, and imputation where a merge is not conclusive. Further details on the procedure for merging appear in chapter 7.

8. We lack any comparable measure for other types of harassment or brutality.

measure of the supervisor's level of tolerance for defection or the level of sanction for defection. We address both of these absences with the administrative data below. This data set allows us to make several observations about police brutality, which, in turn, aids our understanding of organizational defection, supervision, and control.

Models for Analysis of Rare Noncooperative Behavior

We employ two very different approaches in our analysis of the incidence of police brutality in its several guises (unnecessary force, unnecessary frisks, ridicule, and threats). One approach is simply an analysis of each police–citizen encounter as a dichotomous dependent variable, and applies a method similar to the more conventional probit or logit. Our approach recognizes that the underlying choice process is highly asymmetric, and uses a link function (the Gompertz curve) which recognizes, relative to all police–citizen interactions, that brutality is rare. (We supply more complete details about our "gompit" approach in Appendix B [Distributions], and comparisons of the probit and gompit estimates in Appendix C [Estimates].)

The second, very different, approach proceeds from the question, Why is brutality so rare? Here, we will use a "censored probit" approach (Dubin and Rivers 1990) in analysis of the incidence of unnecessary force. The motivation for using a completely different method is that the question of the reasons for the relative infrequency of brutality strikes to some very basic public policy questions. (Again, full details about the censored probit method appear in Appendix B [Distributions], and the actual estimates in Appendix C [Estimates].)

Armed with these estimation techniques, our enterprise is to produce estimates of the effect of various characteristics of the precinct, the officer, supervision, and the alleged crimes on the incidence of brutality. We turn to an examination of the effects of the officers' attributes and predispositions, and the circumstances of the encounter, on all four forms of brutality.

Results for 1966 Police Encounters Data

Our selection of variables replicates our analysis of shirking by police officers (making use of a different part of the same data set) in chapter 7.[9] Table 8.1 displays the estimated effect of each of our explanatory variables for the four forms of police brutality. (The probit and gompit estimates may be found in Appendix C [Estimates], in table C.10.)

---

9. The coding procedures used for these variables are described earlier in this chapter or in chapter 7.

Our imitation model (chapter 3) implied that we will see convergent behavior across subordinates in the same workforce. Models of informational cascades, in much the same spirit as the imitation model, likewise lead to predictions of convergent behavior under these conditions of very high uncertainty. There is also strong evidence from social psychology that individuals in conditions of uncertainty look toward "like others" in order to identify appropriate behavior.[10] And with our analysis of police shirking, we found striking convergence among officers in the same city in the levels of shirking. Does the same pattern persist for the four varieties of brutality?

At least one city coefficient using the gompit model of each form of brutality is statistically significant, and usually both. Boston and Chicago officers are more likely to engage in unnecessary force or employ threats, while less likely to use unnecessary frisks or ridicule, than the Washington, DC officers.[11] Each of the models in table 8.1 confirms the hypothesis that there are differences by city (across organizational environments).

The imitation and enhanced principal–agent models of subordinate compliance (presented in chapters 2 and 3) make the strong claim that the predispositions of the subordinates are what determine compliance. Likewise, the

---

10. See chapter 3 for more detailed discussion of "social proof" models of persuasion.

11. Note that the first differences for all variables are small. (Because the constant term is substantially negative, the base probability on which we evaluate the probit and gompit estimates is very small, and hence only small changes are possible with the first differences.) Nonetheless, these first differences are substantively important: when one considers the hundreds of thousands of encounters between police and citizens across the country each year, first differences of .8 percent (as in use of ridicule by Boston officers) refer to hundreds of cases of brutality.

TABLE 8.1. Effects of Officer's Attributes, Preferences, and Circumstances on Measures of Brutality, 1966 Police Behavior Data (Gompit Estimates)

	Unnecessary Force	Unnecessary Frisks	Ridicule	Threat
Boston	.0046*	−.0030*	−.0077*	.0122*
Chicago	.0035*	−.0009	−.0050*	.0163*
Human relations skills	−.0003	.0000	.0014	.0029
Intellectual style	.0001	−.0005	−.0009	−.0103*
Professional dimension	.0000	.0015*	.0027*	−.0021
Felony	.0015	.0078*	.0018	−.0130
Violent	.0018*	−.0015	.0025	.0366*
Number of officers	.0250	.0298	.0095*	.2201*
Solidary likes	−.0006*	−.0019*	.0016	−.0089*
Functional likes	−.0008*	−.0028	.0135*	−.0168*
χ^2 (15 df)	4774	4564	4411	3260

Note: * = statistically significant at $p < .05$. $N = 3507$.

problem of "adverse selection" in the principal–agent context emphasizes the predispositions of subordinates prior to entering into the game. In our analysis of shirking by police officers, we were surprised to discover that human relations skills, professionalism, and intellectual style did *not* affect the incidence of shirking.

The results of the present analyses of incidence of the different forms of brutality largely bear out observations about shirking seen in chapters 5, 6, and 7. It is particularly important to point out the similarities with chapter 7, where the same data and independent variables are used in the analysis. With few exceptions, none of the estimates of the effects of human relations skills, intellectual style, and professionalism are distinguishable from zero. There are some important exceptions to this general rule, worthy of comment. Professionalism is positively related to both the incidence of unnecessary frisks and of use of ridicule. In other words, the more professional officers were more likely to engage in these forms of unprofessional behavior. One explanation might be that the more professional officers learn to resort to these lesser forms of brutality instead of the more violent forms. However, one would then expect that professionalism would be negatively associated with unnecessary force or threats, which is not the case, at this level of analysis. (As the reader will see in the next section, this pattern reverses in the censored probit approach.)

We also examine the relationship between the circumstances of the encounter and the incidence of brutality. We know the number of officers on the scene, and the type of alleged crime to be investigated. Here, there are some strong patterns across all four forms of brutality. In general, felonies did not encourage more brutality. Although the effects of type of crime are usually positive for all but incidence of threats, they do not meet conventional statistical significance levels. Violent crimes are positively associated with use of unnecessary force, ridicule, and threats, but negatively associated with incidence of unnecessary frisks. The number of officers at the scene is positively associated with all four forms of brutality. (Recall that we were agnostic in our hypotheses about the direction of the relationship between number of officers and the incidence of brutality.)

At the maximum number of officers in the data collection (99), the probability of threats increases by about 10 percent, unnecessary force by 1.3 percent, unnecessary frisks by 3 percent, and ridicule by 6 percent. What are we measuring with the number of officers? We are probably accounting for two phenomena simultaneously: The presence of others observing the action of the officer, as well as the likelihood that a very unusual situation is at work. The present analysis can not discriminate between these sharply divergent reasons for the magnitude of the first difference.

In our analysis of shirking by police officers in chapter 7, we found that the officers' likes and dislikes for being an officer strongly affected the extent to which they shirked. Officers who expressed a functional dislike for the job (e.g., disliked the duties of being an officer) shirked 72 percent more than the average officer. Conversely, officers who expressed a solidary like for the job (e.g., enjoyed the company of the other officers) shirked 63 percent less frequently. In the context of incidence of brutality, one common explanation (see Reiss, above) is that officers resort to brutality when they feel stymied by the courts.[12] If so, we should expect that those officers who express dislikes about the politics of being an officer would be more likely to resort to brutality.

Although singularities in the overlap among the likes and dislikes with the incidence of brutality prevent us from including all the likes and dislikes officers expressed for their jobs, the present study does include the effect of solidary and functional likes on the four forms of brutality. Solidary and functional likes are *negatively* associated with unnecessary force, unnecessary frisks, and threats. The interpretation is that officers who like their jobs for reasons associated with connections to fellow officers or for the duties of being a police officer are less likely to engage in these more violent forms of brutality. The pattern reverses for the incidence of ridicule: Officers who express functional likes for the job are more likely to ridicule citizens than those who do not.[13]

These four models provide a glimpse at the factors influencing the incidence of police brutality in these three cities in the 1960s. Several points should be clear. First, defection is not an amorphous black box of subordinate behavior; there are distinctly different forms of defection, which are governed by very different factors. Even though the preponderance of formal models treats noncooperative behavior as one, uniform, response, there are clearly ma-

---

12. See Klockars (1980) for a similar discussion.

13. A few words about the "fit" of the models. The constant term for every one of the models of brutality is huge and negative. Hence, the naive hypothesis that brutality does not occur clearly overwhelms the data. One traditional measure of the "fit" of the model is a comparison of how well the model predicts cases relative to the modal value. The size of the constant term relative to the substantive coefficients means that all of these models lead to predictions that are identical to the naive hypothesis.

An alternative measure of goodness of fit is to compare the log-likelihood for the substantive model against the null model: minus two times the ratio of the log-likelihoods is distributed as a χ^2 with 11 degrees of freedom. In each of the four models, the χ^2 is quite significant. Unfortunately, the striking skewness of the dependent variable in the four models means that this log-likelihood ratio test is approximately equal to the number of cases in the sample (cf. McCullagh and Nelder 1983). Surely one would not regard sample size as a measure of goodness of fit! Furthermore, this log-likelihood ratio test cannot discriminate between the probit and gompit estimates: The link functions do not affect the likelihood. Indeed, one of the virtues of maximum likelihood estimation is invariance to reparameterization, and so the log-likelihoods for probit and gompit models will be identical (with the occasional slippage due to rounding error).

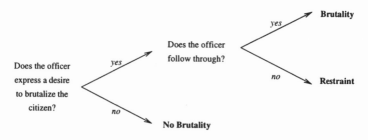

Fig. 8.2. Police brutality as a censored data problem

jor differences in the empirical explanations among different forms of defection. Shirking, sabotage, and brutality as different forms of defection differ, as do the varied manifestations of brutality, in terms of explanatory factors.

In fact, we can obtain a direct statement of the noninterchangeability of the different modes of brutality via the definition of conditional probability. The percentage of encounters between police and citizen that include either unnecessary frisks, ridicule, or threats is 7.32 percent. The percentage of encounters where unnecessary force is used and any of the other forms also occurs is .05 percent. Therefore, the probability of unnecessary force given an occurrence of one of the other modes of brutality is .0005/.0732, or .7 percent. While all forms of police brutality are relatively rare, far rarer still are occasions when the forms of brutality overlap. The variation in propensity for the different forms of brutality by city confirms our proposition that different modes of brutality are influenced by a variety of different factors. We take this finding as indirect evidence of varying incentives among the officers for different forms of defection.

Is brutality rare because there are very few circumstances in which brutality is remotely possible, or is it because principals have been able to control the behavior of the agents? One probably would not expect brutality in most citizen–police encounters, perhaps the overwhelming majority of such encounters. The difference between these two questions is substantively critical: If the incidence of brutality is solely a function of the predispositions of the officers to act in a brutal fashion in certain encounters, then the principal–agent problem becomes irrelevant. We might expect brutality to become more frequent during crime waves, or as the recruitment patterns for officers change, or as peripheral circumstances change, but the characteristics of reward and punishment and of supervision might make very little difference. Conversely, the principal–agent problem of regulating police brutality is not a problem if the officers do not express an inclination to brutalize citizens.

If we treat the principal–agent problem of regulating brutality as arising *only* in those circumstances where an officer has a predisposition to brutalize, then we transform the statistical problem from the simple dichotomous dependent variable problem to a problem of selection bias in dichotomous models. Figure 8.2 displays the selection bias underlying the decision tree. The first branch of the tree discriminates between circumstances where a police officer is or is not predisposed to brutalize the citizen. The second branch of the tree denotes whether the officer, in fact, brutalizes the citizen or restrains him/herself. The gompit method folds together all those encounters where the officer does not wish to brutalize the citizen as well as the situations where the officer does want to brutalize the citizen, but holds back. Our analysis of brutality will be censored by the first stage, the question of the predisposition of the officers. The substantive importance of the censoring is that we will underestimate the effect of every variable on the incidence of brutality.

We have a crude measure of the predisposition of the officers in the record of whether officers avoided action because they felt such action was prohibited. The language of the codebook is instructive: "wanted to beat a little more on street but couldn't as others around"; "would like to bang the punks heads together"; "knock him out and make it easier for everyone"; "I'd like to show them." If we treat this first variable as a dichotomy, coded 1 for officers who used excessive force or expressed supervisory prohibition to using excessive force, 0 otherwise, we have a crude measure of the first selection stage. The second, outcome stage of this process is coded 1 for officers who used excessive force, 0 for officers who felt such actions were prohibited, and missing data for all others.

If, as we argue, the selection bias approach is most apt for the particular problem, why do we bother with the first two? Unfortunately, we only have purchase on the selection stage with the most extreme form of police brutality, use of unnecessary force. This same kind of selection process is likely to be at work with all the manifestations of police brutality. Due to the nature of the data at hand, we are only able to estimate this selection bias model with the use of unnecessary force. The record of "prohibited actions" does not include mentions of the other forms of brutality, and it is the basis for our coding of the first stage of the decision tree. Were one to consider a replication of Reiss's original data collection, we would strongly encourage the development of measures of restraint for the alternate forms of brutality. In order to gain limited understanding of the less extreme modes of brutality, we need to use the uncensored gompit method, recognizing that the coefficients are likely to be attenuated in the uncensored models.

Table 8.2 displays our estimates of the effects of officer's predispositions, attributes, and the circumstances of the encounter on the probability of use of unnecessary force, given a predisposition to brutalize. (Table C.11 presents the probit and censored probit estimates for our model, in Appendix C [Estimates].)

(Although not shown in the present text, we use three independent variables to predict the first stage in this selection process.[14] Three measures appear to do reasonably well in predicting whether an officer expresses a desire to brutalize a citizen: *authoritarian* demeanor, *number of officers* at the encounter, and whether the alleged crime was *violent*. The top half of table C.11, in Appendix C [Estimates], reports the probit estimates for the selection process. A couple of points are worth noting in the selection model. The authoritarian demeanor of the officer is far and away the most important predictor of a predisposition to brutalize. This variable comes from the encounter data set itself, and is probably endogenous to some degree with respect to brutality [i.e., observers might classify officers who brutalize citizens as authoritarian, by definition]. The coefficient on violent crime is also interesting: As one might expect, officers investigating a violent crime have a predisposition that [marginally] favors brutality over officers who are not investigating violent crime. And the coefficient on the number of officers suggests that officer's predisposition to brutalize civilians is enhanced by the presence of other officers, not diminished.)

Unlike the prior results, both coefficients for the officer's city are now statistically significant. Again, the first differences remain somewhat small: officers in Boston were 1 percent and those in Chicago 2 percent more likely to use unnecessary force given a predisposition to brutalize.

---

14. Unlike the Heckman (1976) or Achen (1986) two-stage approaches to selection bias, the Dubin–Rivers estimator uses full information maximum likelihood, estimating both stages simultaneously. We refer to the "first stage" only to make it clear that predispositions censor our observations of brutality in the second stage.

TABLE 8.2. Estimated Effect of Officer's Attributes, Preferences, and Circumstances of Encounter on Use of Unnecessary Force by Police Officers, Censored Probit Estimates, 1966 Encounters Data

Boston	.0114*
Chicago	.0195*
Human relations skills	−.0214
Intellectual style	.1420*
Professional dimension	−.0225*
Felony	.0051
Violent	.0792*
Number of officers	.9103*
Solidary likes	.0059*
Functional likes	.0200*

Note: * = statistically significant at $p < .05$. $N = 3507$. $\chi^2 =$ 4774 with 15 d.f.

The officers' attributes yield some of the more important substantive findings from the censored probit approach. Professionalism has an important effect on the officer's decision to follow through on a predisposition to brutalize, and in the direction one might anticipate. More professional officers were less likely to use unnecessary force. Note that this is opposite to the findings displayed in table 8.1, where more professional officers were more likely to resort to unnecessary force, unnecessary frisks, or ridicule than less professional officers. The implication we draw from the censored probit is that we were confounding a desire to brutalize suspects with an actual incidence of brutality. Similarly, officers with better human relations skills were also less likely to use unnecessary force. Here, the first differences are still small, but theoretically significant in their implications. In contrast, officers who were more intellectually engaged were more likely to brutalize civilians than those who were less engaged. Whereas the simple probits tended to disconfirm our proposition that professionalism reduces brutality, the censored probits confirm this posited relationship.

The circumstances of the encounter between police and citizen significantly affected the likelihood of use of unnecessary force. Officers investigating a violent crime were about 8 percent more likely to follow through on their predispositions to brutalize, by the first differences. Officers who were investigating a felony were also slightly more likely to follow through on predispositions to brutalize. But the most striking effect is of the number of officers. If there were the maximum number of officers (99) on the scene, and the officer under observation expressed a predisposition to brutalize, then it is almost a certainty that the officer followed through with that predisposition: The first difference is 91 percent, meaning a 91 percent increase in the probability of unnecessary force over the average. With twelve other officers on the scene, the probability of unnecessary force given a predisposition to brutalize was about 33 percent. We take these results as confirmation of our propositions that organizational defection is associated with the circumstances of the encounter; more specifically, associated with the number of officers present, whether the crime is a felony or whether or not it is violent. Again, we are unable to separate the effects of social proof (due to the presence of like others) from the admittedly unusual circumstances where there would be so many officers.

Finally, we turn to the effect of the officer's solidary and functional likes for the job. Unlike the simple probit coefficients, both solidary and functional likes are positively related to the officer's chances of following through on a predisposition to brutalize. One interpretation of the difference between the effect of the same variables in the two approaches is that officers who expressed solidary or functional likes were less likely to be in situations where they had a predisposition to use unnecessary force. In contrast to the more optimistic findings associated with trainable aspects of the officer's job (i.e., professionalism and human relations skills), the effect of the solidary and functional likes on the officers' willingness to follow through on a predisposition to brutalize is disconcerting. One might well expect that as the officer's tenure as a policeman lengthens that he/she would develop more solidary likes, and perhaps more functional likes. The implication of this last table is that these officers will be more likely to use unnecessary force, given situations where unnecessary force is on the officer's mind.

Citizen Complaints About Police Use of Force

What role does the citizenry play in regulating excessive police violence? Previous analysis in this chapter and preceding chapters reveals that direct supervision plays a limited role in inducing compliance. Given these results about direct supervision, are there other avenues for oversight? For example, are there institutional mechanisms by which citizens at large can redress or attempt to alter police behavior? In this section we focus on citizen-initiated complaints regarding police use of force.

We examine the factors that affect the incidence of police misconduct at the level of the agency as opposed to the level of the individual. In terms of specific institutional mechanisms available to a police department, we propose a number of factors that could mitigate the incidence of police misconduct. Again, we test the proposition that sanctions deter inappropriate behavior. We also take into account to what extent police agencies have counseling services available. Counseling could reduce the officer's predisposition to commit violence, or such services may merely provide an outlet for officer's frustration.

Along the lines of sanctions and counseling, we also examine the role of a police department's policy on violence. The department's explicit policy provides the best handle on the conjecture that police brutality is consistent with the principal's preferences. Such policies provide a monitoring mechanism that in turn can be used to regulate violence in a police force. Many of the policies regarding violence establish procedures for recording violent activity that involves an officer. Each of these variables is conceptually related to moral hazard at the level of the organization. Such institutional mechanisms are designed to control the behavior of police officers, to induce them to not engage in inappropriate activities.

Moe (1984) writing about organizations in general discusses the special problems of adverse selection facing a police force. To overcome these problems, police academies are designed to screen, train, and evaluate police recruits so as to foster professionalism.[15] This is very much consistent with those principal–agency approaches which regard adverse selection as a threat

---

15. Also see Bittner (1971), Manning (1977: 193–97), and Sykes (1985).

to cooperation. To examine this aspect of adverse selection we analyze the relationship between departmental training programs and the incidence of different forms of police misconduct that they experience. Relatedly, we look at average education levels across police agencies. The posited relationship here is that officers with greater degrees of formal education will be less likely to engage in brutal or demeaning activities while on duty.

In this part of this chapter, we also examine the role of external mechanisms designed to curb moral hazard problems. In particular, we examine the role individual citizens play in mitigating the incidence of different forms of police misconduct. Police agencies can encourage such external oversight by providing as many opportunities as possible for citizens to register complaints. This means having many access points, few restrictions on reporting, and disseminating information about access and reporting to the citizenry at large. We posit here that ease of reporting mitigates police violence and other forms of misbehavior. In this way, we examine the role institutional mechanisms can play in controlling problems of moral hazard and adverse selection in a police force.

The Police Use of Force Data Set

For this part of this chapter, we draw on the data set developed by Antony M. Pate and Lorie E. Fridell (1994) under the auspices of the Police Foundation.[16] This data was collected from a stratified random sample survey of all law enforcement agencies in the United States. The survey examines police department policies and experiences regarding police use of force. Our analysis in this section examines citizen complaints regarding police behavior. More specifically we focus on sustained charges initiated by citizens against police officers. Such citizen-initiated charges include: excessive/undue/unnecessary use of force (brutality—including use of weapons, cuffs, etc.); false/unlawful arrest/imprisonment, improper detention/interrogation (false charges filed); illegal/unlawful search or seizure; harassment, intimidation, threats, verbal abuse; abuse/misuse of authority (conduct unbecoming of an officer); and improper language (demeaning ethnic/racial slur). This data provides a different perspective on police brutality than the Reiss data in that it uses a different level of analysis and it comes from the same era as the prominent cases of excessive police violence in Los Angeles and Detroit. While we use similar dependent variables in our analyses of these two data sets, the Pate and Fridell data set offers a glimpse of how police department policies and citizen complaints are related to the incidence of police use of force.

The biggest distinction between these two data sets is that the Reiss data

---

16. *Police Use of Force [United States]: Official Reports, Citizen Complaints, and Legal Consequences, 1991–1992*

examines the behavior of individual police officers, gathering data regarding attitudes and behaviors. The Pate and Fridell data, on the other hand, is collected at the departmental level, regarding the experiences of departments as wholes. Incidents of brutality are recorded as events that had transpired during 1991 and 1992. In general, the sample size for these dependent variables is approximately 815.

We constructed several scalar variables from this data set to test our propositions. To examine citizen initiated complaints we utilize an *ease of reporting* variable, which is an additive scale of all the different institutional mechanisms by which citizens can register complaints regarding police misconduct. *Counseling* is another additive scale measuring the number of counseling services available to officers. To develop a variable for *crime* we added all types of arrests and citations recorded by each police department; in turn, we take the natural log of this number which we use in our analysis. For *sanctions* we used the number of officers whose jobs were terminated as a result of a sustained decision regarding a complaint against the officer for using excessive force. *Training* is another additive scale of all the hours of different training programs provided by each sampled department. A department's *policy on violence* is another additive scale of all the written policies a police agency has regarding the use of lethal force, less than lethal, pursuit, body armor, and whether or not there is a regular review and investigation of the use of force. *Education* is the percentage of officers in a department with an associates degree or higher.[17]

Results of Analysis of Citizen Generated Complaints Regarding Police Use of Force, 1991–92

To examine the data on specific counts of incidents of sustained cases of citizen generated complaints about police misconduct, we utilize a Poisson regression analysis. Appendix B (Distributions) provides further elaboration on the Poisson models. Six dependent variables measuring different forms of police brutality are analyzed with respect to a common set of independent variables. So we can compare the factors that are associated with sustained citizen complaints regarding *unnecessary use of force, false arrest, illegal search, verbal*

---

17. In particular each of these independent variables is created from the following Pate and Frieden survey questions: *ease of reporting* is associated with Q16–Q23; *counseling* with Q57–Q58; *crime* with Q67AA–Q67NJ; *sanctions* with Q56D; *training* with Q76A–Q76V; *policy on violence* with Q61–Q62; and *education* with Q3A–Q3E. Unfortunately we are missing information which would be valuable for our analysis. Particularly useful would be more data on race, the race of the charged officer as well as the involved citizen. In general, more specific information regarding each incident of police misconduct would be useful. The problem is that even when Pate and Frieden attempted to collect such data, most reporting police agencies lacked or did not report this information. Such large amounts of missing data inhibited our analysis.

abuse, misuse of authority, and the use of *demeaning language.* The common independent variables include: *counseling, crime rate, reporting ease, sanctions, training, policy on violence,* and *education level* of the force.[18] The results of these analyses are presented in table 8.3.

Poisson regressions (with a linear link, as we use here) are somewhat unique for maximum likelihood estimates in that the coefficient estimates can be interpreted in a way similar to OLS coefficients. For example, the coefficient on the additive scale for ease of reporting and incidence of unnecessary force is .25. This means that if a department initiated four new modes facilitating citizen reports of police brutality, that one should expect one additional sustained case of unnecessary force.

Can police departments alter the propensity for violence? What tools do they have at their disposal that can serve to limit police use of force? One

---

18. The coding of these variables is discussed in the preceding section.

TABLE 8.3. Poisson Estimates of Different Forms of Police Brutality Based on Sustained Cases Initiated by Citizens, 1991–92 Police Use of Force Data

Variable	Unnecessary Force	False Arrest	Illegal Search
Constant	−7.33*	−3.97*	−6.57*
Counseling	−.18*	.12	−.24
Training	.00*	−.00	.00
Policy on violence	.11	−.17	.15
Sanctions	.28*	.37*	−.00
Log of crime	.18*	.10*	.01
Reporting ease	.25*	.06*	.14*
Education	−.13	.97*	.40
N	500	493	492
χ^2	364.5	18.3	16.2
	Verbal Abuse	Misuse Authority	Demeaning Language
Constant	−3.37*	−3.72*	−6.79*
Counseling	−.06	.09*	.02
Training	.00	.00*	.00*
Policy on violence	.24*	−.08*	.02*
Sanctions	.34*	−.02	.07
Log of crime	.12*	.16*	.16*
Reporting ease	.06*	.11*	.17*
Education	−.69*	.81*	.56*
N	491	492	491
χ^2	108.9	388.9	441.7

Note: The dependent variables are events; counts of the number of sustained citizen-initiated cases against officers in each sampled police department. * = statistically significant at $p < .05$.

potential tool is counseling. We find that counseling depresses the rate of sustained citizen charges of police use of excessive force, to a statistically significant degree. However, greater access to counseling in a department is associated with greater incidence of abuses of authority, again to a statistically significant degree. There were no other significant effects of counseling on the other dependent variables. The picture of the effect of counseling is decidedly mixed.

A second tool for departments to reduce unnecessary force is additional training. By our estimates, additional training was accompanied with slightly greater incidence of excessive use of force, abuse of authority, and the use of demeaning language. The effects, although statistically significant, were substantively trivial.

The department's policy on violence is a third potential tool to reduce police brutality. We find that the department's policy did not affect violence in general, and it was actually positively associated with verbal brutality. Where the relationship is statistically significant, we find that the presence of a violence policy was accompanied by greater incidence of verbal abuse and the use of demeaning language. It may be that violence policies, in the minds of police officers, do not address verbal altercation with the citizenry.

Do sanctions curb police misconduct? We examine only an extreme measure of sanction, the termination of an officer's job. We find that the incidence of such a sanction is statistically significant and positively associated with the use of unnecessary force, false arrests, and verbal abuse cases. Of course, the relationship between sanctioning and incidence of brutality might be backwards: some departments sanction many officers because there are many cases of brutality. It is entirely possible that these sanctions tend to occur in those departments with the biggest problems with police conduct. Termination, in this way, does not seem to deter the use of force; then again, it is unlikely that sanctions of this type actually induce officers to use more force. To further explore this endogeneity problem, we ran these analyses with a wider scale of sanctions. Unfortunately, the sample size is markedly reduced in this case (from approximately 500 to 135); nevertheless, the results do not change significantly. The same relationships appear to be significant and the coefficients show the same signs. We also ran our analysis without a sanction variable. Again, there were no big changes in our results from those reported above. Despite the obvious causal ordering problems, it should be apparent that there is no evidence that sanctioning deters any of the forms of brutality.

Does the composition of the police force make a difference? We examine the relationship between the education level of an agency and the incidence of police misconduct. We find that as a department becomes better educated, occurrence of verbal abuse cases declines. On the other hand, the higher the level of education in the department, the more likely that citizens were able to sustain cases of abuse of authority and use of demeaning language. Unfortunately, the sample size for the education level of the specific officer under question was too small for reliable analysis ($N = 117$), compelling us to instead utilize aggregated figures from each survey police agency.[19]

Can citizens regulate police misconduct? Evidently not. We found that the easier it was for citizens to report brutality, the more likely it was that there would be sustained cases of brutality, for every one of the six forms. We can conjecture that police departments with problems of police violence respond by allowing for more opportunities for citizens to register complaints, but the actual ease of reporting is not associated with a decline in the incidence of police misconduct.

We also examined one environmental control variable, the crime rate. We assume that communities with higher crime rates will experience more incidents of police misconduct. This is evident in our results. Crime rate (scaled as a natural log) is significantly and positively associated with all forms of sustained citizen-generated police misconduct except for the incidence of illegal search.

As a way of summarizing these results, is there any pattern that emerges across these different types of police misconduct? As with our analysis of the Reiss data, we find considerable differences across our dependent variables. Yet while there are differences across these different forms of police misconduct, we found few differences between the results of our analysis of citizen generated and internally generated complaints.[20] Only in our analyses of verbal abuse are there any appreciable differences between the significant independent variables found to be associated with citizen-generated as opposed to internally generated sustained complaints. In none of our tests do we find a sign change for a significant variable. For the most part, we see far greater differences between different forms of police misconduct than we do between citizen-generated and internally generated complaints.

---

19. We also had a problem with too many missing cases when we attempted to examine the role of race. In particular, we lack adequate information on the race of the officer and the civilian who leveled the charge. Again as with our analysis of the Reiss data, this is unfortunate.

20. We also examined the aggregated numbers for all citizen-generated complaints (those sustained as well as those unfounded, exonerated, not sustained, and pending). We experienced some problems getting convergence on many of these tests. Where we did get convergence we saw very little difference between sustained citizen-generated complaints and the sum of all citizen-generated complaints across the different forms of police misconduct.

Conclusions

The first of several general points to be drawn from our analyses is that there is resounding confirmation of our opening hypothesis: Agents have many ways to defect, and the factors influencing different varieties of defection are themselves quite variable. Across the different forms of brutality (and other forms of police misconduct), there are few instances where potent explanatory variables worked in the same way. And in contrast to our findings about shirking by the same police officers, it is quite clear that all these forms of defection are also quite different from shirking. This finding leaves us with a new set of unanswered questions. Do we take this to mean, in principal–agency terms, that the games are different? Are there different incentive and enforcement structures for unnecessary force, unnecessary frisks, ridicule, and threats? Do these incentives or enforcement structures affect the officer's behavior? Or do the differences in the patterns for the four varieties of brutality arise from circumstances related to the encounter? Or do they arise from different predispositions by the police officers? At the very least, we take the findings in this chapter to argue that we have to be very careful about the application of deductive models to the empirical analysis of subordinate behavior.

The most significant of our substantive findings is that professionalism safeguards against brutality. If the question is not why officers become angry enough to brutalize civilians, but why they follow through, professionalism aids the officer's self-restraint. Unfortunately, the magnitude of the effect of professionalism, as seen in this data, appears to be somewhat marginal. There appear to be significant variations in the incidence of brutality by city, suggesting that the officers arrive at some level of conformity in response to police-citizen encounters. Unfortunately, we have no real way of assessing whether this conformity stems from solidarity with peers or supervisory tolerance for brutality.

We find that counseling inhibits the unnecessary use of force (whether the complaint is generated from a citizen or from within the police department). Counseling is generally not significantly related to the other forms of police misconduct and is positively associated with the abuse of authority. The role counseling plays in mitigating violence should be further pursued. This is quite a different role for the supervisor, one more akin to education than administration.

Finally, we look toward the events in Los Angeles and Detroit and ask which of our findings illuminates the situation. Of course, some of our data are from a much earlier time period and in different cities. The number of officers at the scene of the Rodney King beating suggests that the beating was inevitable *given that the officers had a predisposition to brutalize*. We do not know whether the officers arrived at the scene with such a predisposition. Nor do we know whether the effect of the number of officers comes because of the unusual nature of the situation with so many officers present or because so many fellow officers pressured the police into brutality.

The archetypal street-level bureaucrats, police officers and social workers, look very much the same. This is perhaps surprising to some, since we don't usually think of the sorts of people who become police officers as at all similar to the sorts of people who become social workers. What we have demonstrated is that the functional and solidary preferences of both groups are the most significant influences on their performance, and that the first link in the chain of command, the immediate supervisor, is weak. We would not go as far as Barnard (1938) to call the coercive power of supervision a "fiction," but the results from these chapters do suggest that it is an awfully short story.

CHAPTER 9

Smoke Detectors or Fire Alarms

In one of the most influential arguments on political oversight of bureaucracy, McCubbins and Schwartz (1984) observe that congressional committees need not be actively involved in the policing of administrative agencies in order to exercise significant control over the performance of those agencies. Instead of regular and intensive scrutiny of the performance of federal agencies (the "police patrol"), McCubbins and Schwartz argue that committees construct mechanisms that encourage interest groups to attend to the activities of agencies and devices ("fire alarms") to encourage interest groups to signal their objections to agency performance. Considering the extensive demands on the members of Congress, it is eminently rational for Congress to prefer fire alarms over police patrols as a means of oversight. The significant implication is that the potential sanctions of Congress (or any other politically superordinate body) affect the performance of agencies more than the infrequent occasions when these sanctions are actually applied.

The fire alarm device is an answer to the persistent question of how democratic publics are able to control the behavior of nonelected public officials. If we regard the members of Congress and other varieties of political superordinates[1] as the elected principals to whom bureaucratic agents must respond, it is quite appropriate that the discipline devote extensive efforts both to formalize the nature of the oversight process as a principal–agency problem[2], and to evaluate empirically the success of congressional committees in influencing bureaucratic behavior.[3]

In this chapter, we look beyond congressional oversight to examine, more generally, the role political superordinates play in bureaucratic oversight. In chapters 4 through 8, we examine bureaucracy across a wide variety of environments, from federal bureaucrats (those most directly under the watchful

---

1. We use the unfortunately cumbersome term "superordinates" to distinguish between a subordinate's immediate supervisor and any supervisor up the chain of command, or even a political principal.

2. See McCubbins et al. 1987; Weingast and Moran 1983; Hill 1985; Banks and Weingast 1992; Lupia and McCubbins 1993.

3. See Wood 1988, 1990; Wood and Waterman 1991.

eyes of Congress) to police officers and social workers. This chapter shifts the focus of our analysis away from an internal examination of bureaucratic agencies (specifically examining the relationship between supervisors and subordinates) to an examination of the relationship between bureaucrats and actors from outside their agency. In this chapter we throw a wider light on the question: *Who, or what, controls the policy choices of bureaucrats?*

The path from citizen through elected official to unelected bureaucrat is not the only means by which a democratic public might influence the behavior of bureaucracies. We contend that, in fact, it may make considerably greater sense for individual citizens (or groups of individuals organized as interest groups) to directly exert influence over bureaucrats than it is for a citizen to expect intervention from some political superordinate on the question. In fact, it may be easier for the individual citizen or interest group to try to modify the behavior of bureaucrats directly than to appeal to an elected official to intervene on her behalf (e.g., "case work" appeals, à la Fiorina [1977, 1982, 1986]).

Our intent here is to examine the sources of pressure and influence that are brought to bear on bureaucracy. We are not saying that politically superordinate bodies are inconsequential to oversight—far from it: Congress (in particular) plays a large and significant role by shaping the broad policy environment. However, to examine how bureaucracies respond to pressures from competing sources, we need to focus on bureaucracies themselves. Political superordinates may shape the policy agenda and the political environment in which bureaucracies must operate, but questions involving oversight are not necessarily the same as issues of bureaucratic responsiveness.

Emphatically, this chapter does not contend that political superordinates (congressional committees in particular) are irrelevant in their construction of fire alarms. Fire alarms matter, in part, because they affect broad policy decisions and allow for public debate and reprimand for agency malfeasance. Nor would we wish to imply that the casework of individual politicians is not a potent means for satisfying constituent demands or for constituencies to exert influence over recalcitrant bureaucracies. Instead, we wish to draw attention to a complementary mode of citizen control: think of the bureaucrat as a smoke detector for the individually minor but cumulatively significant daily complaints that we have with bureaucracies. A citizen who has a grievance with the local department of social services might be more inclined to raise that grievance directly with the social worker than to notify a higher authority. The social worker remedies the problem before it becomes more severe, akin to the way a smoke detector notifies the home owner of an emergency before the need to notify the fire department.

When we view the behavior of individual bureaucrats, we expect that bureaucracies will appear to be more responsive to individual citizens, client groups, and interest groups than they will to superordinates.

Direct bureaucratic response to citizen demands may not be an entirely good thing. When bureaucrats are responsive directly to individual citizens or interest groups we expect three separate dilemmas to emerge: capture by disproportionately influential interests or responsiveness to a pluralist system; responsiveness to democratic republics or responsibility to serve good government; and broad political control over bureaucratic behavior or micromanagement of individual choices.

Our chapter proceeds in four steps. We first explicate some propositions about why bureaucrats as smoke detectors are likely to be the most visibly responsive aspect of this multistep chain of democratic command. We then turn to methods by which we can empirically evaluate these propositions, and explain our analysis of a data set observing the behavior of public utility commissioners (Gormley 1985). Next, we evaluate these propositions using the beta distribution to develop maximum likelihood models of varying responsiveness. Finally, we turn to some implications of the smoke detector argument for democratic control and connect the results of this chapter to our other analyses.

Bureaucrats as Smoke Detectors

The general logic of our argument is that, for the average citizen's encounter with a specific bureaucrat, it makes considerably greater sense for that citizen to attempt to influence the bureaucrat directly than it does for her to attempt to elicit the aid of an oversight committee or a specific elected official. Furthermore, because the daily weight of sanctions (even if individually minor) is greater from citizens, we expect that bureaucrats will be more responsive to citizens than to their political superordinates.

The essential difference between a "smoke detector" and a "fire alarm" is that with a fire alarm an external party is called in to take care of the problem. With a smoke detector, the citizen takes care of the problem herself. In the case of a fire alarm, a political superordinate is expected to address the issue for the citizen or interest group. In the case of a smoke detector, a citizen or interest group directly addresses the problem through the bureaucracy itself; political superordinates do not play a role.

We delineate three assumptions regarding smoke detectors and fire alarms.

TECHNOLOGICAL ASSUMPTION: *Citizens and interest groups have two modes of recourse to a complaint of a bureaucrat's performance: contact a political representative (sound a fire alarm) or to attempt to persuade the bureaucrat to change his behavior (touch off a smoke detector). Interest groups and citizens choose the mode of recourse that brings the highest expected change in bureaucratic behavior, less the cost of applying that change.*

From the interest group or individual citizen's point of view, both the fire alarm and the smoke detector are costly. For a citizen to touch off the smoke detector, it requires that the citizen invest the time and energy to contact an elected representative (or to contact an interest group who contacts the representative). For the citizen to raise a complaint directly to the bureaucrat, it requires not only the time and energy to try to persuade the bureaucrat, but also, potentially, personally embarrassing or stressful costs resulting from complaining about another's behavior. In this respect, an interest group may regard such an encounter as less stressful than an individual citizen.

RESPONSIVENESS ASSUMPTION: *Bureaucrats will respond (change behavior) to a requester in a way that maximizes their own policy goals or minimizes their effort (absent policy goals), subject to any sanctions applied by the requester for failure to comply.*

Our "responsiveness assumption" is hardly revolutionary. For instance, Downs (1967) proceeds from a similar assumption that bureaucrats, like all social actors, "seek to attain their goals rationally" where the goals may include "power, income, prestige, security, convenience, loyalty (to an idea, an institution, or the nation), pride in excellent work, and desire to serve the public interest" (2). The responsiveness assumption does explicitly include the predispositions of subordinates, which we have demonstrated throughout this book to be the dominant influence on their behavior.

We wish to draw further attention to two particular features of the responsiveness assumption: the role of policy goals and the role of supervisory sanctions. Prior literature on the principal–agency problem notes the difficulty a superordinate may have in encouraging compliance from subordinates. Although some argue that the principals may be effective in inducing compliance under some circumstances, few would dispute that exacting compliance from agents is a theoretical and political challenge when those agents have a significant advantage in their information about their own capabilities and performance. We have argued in Chapters 5 through 8 that inducing compliance from subordinate bureaucrats is far more likely with bureaucrats who share the principal's policy goals (or are at least nonhostile to those goals) than with bureaucrats who hold policy goals contrary to the goals of the principal.

SANCTIONING ASSUMPTIONS: *(1) Political superordinates are able to exact sanctions that increase in magnitude with the relative distance between superordinate and the subordinate bureaucrat. (2) The likelihood that a sanction will be applied to an individual bureaucrat decreases proportional to the distance between the bureaucrat and the political superordinate. (3) Clients are able to exact minimal (but nonzero) sanctions, with certainty.*

By these assumptions, we agree that political superordinates (such as a member of Congress) may be very powerful. A political superordinate might be able to bring significant and real sanctions upon low-level bureaucrats by threatening the agency with budgetary cutbacks, greater scrutiny over the performance of the agency, or indirect sanctions upon the lowest of bureaucrats. (Note that this is a very charitable grant of authority to the political superordinate. It is ordinarily very difficult to bring severe sanctions down upon the behavior of individual bureaucrats, especially at the career civil service level.)[4] At the same time, as the hierarchical distance lengthens between the political superordinate and the subordinate bureaucrat, the range or number of bureaucrats increases. The risk that any one bureaucrat faces sanctions declines with each increase in political distance. At the same time, we argue that although individual citizens or interest groups may exert only minimal sanctions over bureaucrats, they always have the opportunity to exact those minimal sanctions.

The citizen's choice about whether to pull a fire alarm or to trigger a smoke detector depends on the nature of the functional form of the relationship between severity of superordinate sanction, likelihood of application of the sanction, and the political distance. For the sake of illustration, let us suppose that the probability that a political superordinate will apply the sanction is inversely proportional to the distance:

$$\text{Probability of Sanction} = \frac{f}{\text{Distance}} \qquad (9.1)$$

where f is the frequency of sanction per unit distance. In other words, the further up a political hierarchy a superordinate is from the subordinate, the less likely the superordinate is to sanction the subordinate. Hierarchical distance should be inversely proportional to the chances that the superordinate actually applies a sanction. Likewise, let us suppose that the magnitude of the sanction is directly proportional to distance:

$$\text{Severity of Sanction} = S \times \text{Distance} \qquad (9.2)$$

---

4. See Johnson and Libecap 1994.

where S is the magnitude of the political superordinate's sanction. In other words, the further up the hierarchy a political superordinate is from a subordinate, the more severe the sanction she can bring to bear. Hierarchical distance should be directly proportional to the weight of the sanction.

Consider the setting where the bureaucrat has some policy goals pertinent to the behavior in question. Let D denote the extent to which the bureaucrat would be willing to endure a penalty in order to accomplish a policy goal. Under the fire alarm scheme, a bureaucrat would change his behavior if the expected gains from keeping the policy (D) are less than the expected sanction (note that "Distance" cancels out):

$$D < fS. \tag{9.3}$$

Under the smoke detector scheme, a bureaucrat would change his behavior if the expected gains from policy are less than the sanction (with certainty) delivered by the citizen:

$$D < s \tag{9.4}$$

where s denotes the interest group or citizen's level of sanction applied directly to the subordinate. Under these conditions, a citizen should pull a fire alarm if the weight of the (certain) sanction is less than the (expected) weight of the superordinate's sanction, *and* the expected weight of the superordinate's sanction matters:

$$s < fS \text{ and } fS > D. \tag{9.5}$$

The citizen should trigger a smoke detector if the weight of the personal sanction is greater than the expected weight of the superordinate's sanction, *and* the personal sanction matters:

$$s > fS \text{ and } s > D. \tag{9.6}$$

The citizen should signal neither a fire alarm *nor* a smoke detector ("swallow his or her lumps") if neither the personal sanction nor the expected value of the superordinate's sanction are greater than the bureaucrat's value of retaining the policy:

$$\max(fS, s) < D. \tag{9.7}$$

What do we know about the relative values for f, S, s and D? For one, D

may be quite large. Indeed, the overwhelming evidence in our book is that bureaucrats are unresponsive to sanction. The implication is that neither fire alarms nor smoke detectors are likely to be cumulatively effective in changing policy. From the individual bureaucrat's point of view, while S might be significant, f is likely to be quite tiny. This is especially likely the further down the bureaucracy the contact takes place, and to the degree to which civil service protections limit S. (In fact, given these civil service constraints, the coarseness of the budget as a sanctioning tool, and the arguments of this book about the inadequacies of coercive supervision, s and S may be quite similar in magnitude.) Under quite plausible values for these variables, it makes more sense for the citizen to apply her own minor sanctions than it does for that citizen to take recourse to political superordinates.

This leads us to our first two propositions:

CITIZEN INITIATIVE PROPOSITION: *Citizens (or client groups) will take their complaints to the bureaucracy first, and more frequently, than they will to political superordinates.*

STREET-LEVEL RESPONSIVENESS: *Street-level bureaucrats are more influenced by their clients than by their political superordinates. Street-level bureaucrats are less likely to shirk and less likely to engage in policy sabotage when stimulated by a request from citizens than by a request from political superordinates.*

We had direct evidence for this latter proposition from the social workers, who assessed their clients as the most influential group of actors over how they allocated their time at work. (The state utility commissioners are not at "street level" and hence provide no further insight on this proposition.)

At the same time, interest groups or citizens bear a disproportionate cost in trying to influence the behavior of bureaucrats when they have a complaint. This leads to two further propositions:

DISSATISFACTION AND ACCOMPLISHMENT: *On the whole, the experience that citizens (and client groups) have with bureaucracies will be both more frustrating (incur greater costs to the citizen or client group) and more successful (be more likely to lead to the interest group or citizen's wishes) than the experience that citizens (or client groups) have with such political superordinates.*

DISPROPORTIONATE INFLUENCE: *Because some citizens and groups will be better able to subsidize the costs of sanctioning individual bureaucrats underprivileged*

> *better than others, those with more political resources are more likely to employ "smoke detectors" than those with fewer resources. The bureaucracy in the aggregate will then be more responsive to wealthier groups (in the sense of political resources) than poorer groups.*

The enterprise of the next two sections of this chapter is to develop empirical tests for these propositions. In particular, we turn to what we believe is the most controversial of our propositions, that street-level bureaucrats are more responsive to citizens than to political superordinates. The unit of analysis in the street-level responsiveness proposition is the bureaucrat. Some of the other propositions require study of client groups' and citizens' experience with bureaucracy and represent a very different unit of analysis. While we don't directly test the other three propositions, we believe that our results with respect to the street-level responsiveness proposition are informative to the remaining propositions. We turn first to a discussion of our reanalysis of a data set collected by William Gormley Jr. on public utility commission officials, and then to a discussion of our tests.

Influence over Utility Regulators

In this chapter we compare the responsiveness of Public Utility Commission (PUC) officials across political superordinates, individual citizens, and interest groups. In this chapter, we utilize the interviews conducted by William Gormley Jr. in the late 1970s and early 1980s with public utility commissioners, citizen groups, proxy citizen representatives, and utility company representatives.[5] Our switch to public utility commissioners expands the scope of our analysis of bureaucracy in two distinct directions by looking at the state (instead of the federal or local) levels of bureaucracy, and by looking at mid-level bureaucrats, rather than those at street level (as in chapters 6–8), or without regard to level (as in chapters 4 and 5)..

As the reader may recall, the late 1970s and early 1980s were especially controversial times for the management of public energy resources. Between supply pressures in the form of the energy shortages induced by the fall of the shah of Iran, and the rise of modestly sized antinuclear power groups and groups representing the financial hardships of the poor and the elderly, the public utility commissioners of the time were beset with massive technical and political problems. By the fire alarm logic, these highly salient issues with wide dispersion of information present exactly the sorts of circumstances where one might expect significant leadership from political superordinates, in

---

5. See Gormley 1985, ICPSR 8080.

this case, the governors, the attorneys general, or the legislatures of the various states, and perhaps even the Department of Energy. To the contrary, some of the political actors chose not to become involved in the daily management of the policies of the utility commissions (shunning police patrols). As Gormley observed in his analysis, state legislatures shunned energy politics nearly completely. The fact that the state legislatures stayed out of energy politics hardly disconfirms the fire alarm logic—in fact, the fire alarm logic would predict that state legislatures should stay out of the day-to-day policing of energy policy, opting for interest group attention as a way of signaling when the legislature should intervene. Our point is that the performance of the public utility commissioners should vary closer to the preferences of the client and citizen groups and be more influenced by their activities than by the activities of the political superordinates (attorneys general, governors, or state legislatures).

Gormley interviewed public utility commissioners and staff, citizen group advocates, and utility company representatives in twelve states in late 1979 and early 1980. There were a total of 284 interviews across the twelve states, where the states varied in the levels of citizen group activity (from "grassroots" to "acquiescent"). With only a few exceptions, the interviews were conducted face-to-face, with a tape recorder to record open-ended comments. Gormley himself conducted about two-thirds of the interviews, with the remaining third conducted by Charles Williams. The total response rates were quite high (with response rate calculated as percent interviewed out of those who were requested to be interviewed by Gormley or Williams): They ranged from a low of 73 percent for the utility company officials to a high of 95 percent for the proxy advocates. Gormley masked demographic variables prior to release by the ICPSR in order to preserve the confidentiality of respondents.

Our strategy in the reanalysis of Gormley's data is to use confirmatory factor analysis to extract latent variables that correspond more closely to the parameters of our model and to use extremely flexible maximum likelihood methods to analyze what accounts for movement in the main dependent variables in our model.

We will explore a series of measures denoting the extent to which the respondent perceives any of eight different groups as having a very low to very high degree of impact. The eight groups included the attorney general, business groups, citizens' groups, individual citizens, labor groups, municipalities, the Public Utility Commission staff, and utility companies. These are, of course, only the respondents' perceptions about who is influential. As such, these perceptions are likely to inflate the importance of the most visible actors, while depressing the importance of less visible actors, who may be more influential but more dispersed. This style of question would be biased against both our argument that individual citizens matter and against the McCubbins

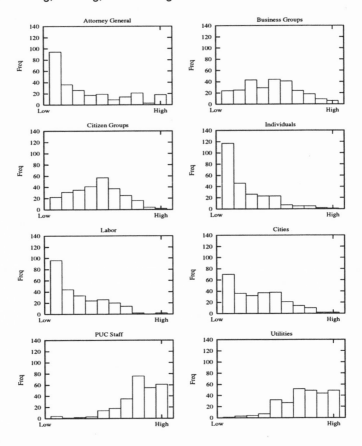

Fig. 9.1. Respondent's assessment of actors' degree of influence

and Schwartz argument that oversight committees matter more than the mere measurement of their use of sanctions.

This dependent variable provides a reasonable test of our proposition that citizens initiate conflict with the bureaucracy and of the responsiveness of bureaucrats to citizens and clients over political superordinates. Our aim is to demonstrate that the activities of citizens can enhance the influence of some of these groups (individuals, citizens' groups, business groups, and the attorneys general), while the activities of the governor and legislature should increase the influence of political superordinates, but not necessarily of citizens.

Figure 9.1 provides histograms of the eight different measures of the extent of influence, recoded to fit to a scale from 0 to 1.0. There is quite a range of influence among the eight actors. Actors that exerted a good deal of influence would be concentrated towards the "high" mark on the right side of the graph. Among the diverse groups of respondents, there was relative consensus that the utilities and the PUC staff were highly influential on the PUC decisions: both of these groups are packed towards the right. To a lesser extent, citizens' groups and business groups were also of modest influence on the PUC decisions. The least influential actors included individuals and the attorney general. The former may appear to run counter to our argument about the importance of individual citizens in bureaucratic decisions; as we will demonstrate below, citizens' groups may increase the importance of individuals to the process. (The next set of graphs demonstrate that citizens may not have needed to intervene.) The latter might also be something of a surprise, since the attorneys general are the chief legal officers of the states, and often the states' formal advocate for citizens in the regulation of utilities.

The second category of dependent variables include a series of rankings of issues by the various types of actors in the PUC study. Gormley asked the respondents to rank a series of eight different goals: clean air, economic development, energy conservation, energy supply sufficient for demand, fair return for utility company investors, low rates for residential consumers, low rates for business consumers, and special protection for the very poor.

Figure 9.2 presents eight different histograms that measure the ranking of different energy regulation issues. In this case, consensus about a high priority would be represented as a cluster towards the left of the graph. The rankings of these issues vary considerably from issue to issue. However, there was relative consensus that energy conservation and energy supply sufficiency were extremely desirable, receiving widespread high rankings. This makes sense for the time: Energy policy analysts were quite concerned about the "energy crisis" perceived as a shortage of energy supply.

Respondents also largely agreed that low business rates and a fair return to investors were less significant issues, receiving the lowest rankings. Among concerns that might appeal to citizens, air quality, low residential rates, and economic development received more mixed support. Protecting the poor received either strong support or low rankings with little moderate support.

We see provisional evidence in these rankings illuminating the potential magnitude of the value of policy to the bureaucrats (D, in the notation of the discussion above), and perhaps some reasons for relatively infrequent involvement by citizen groups and even less frequent involvement by citizens. By far the most favored policies were those consistent with what experts of the time argued should be most important: energy conservation and energy supply. The next categories of priorities were those that would have been shared by citizen groups: the importance of clean air, low residential rates, economic develop-

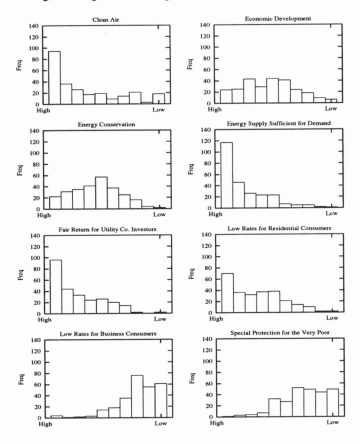

Fig. 9.2. Respondent's rankings of energy issues

ment, and protection for the poor. At the bottom of the list of priorities were those that would be favored by utility investors: fair return for utility investors and low rates for business consumers.

Still, the basic question is whether citizen activity is capable of stimulating policy change. We will approach this question by examining how perceptions of influence change as various actors become more active. As independent variables for our analyses, we drew upon measures of the degree to which the governor, legislature, citizens' groups, and utilities were active in the regulation of utilities. The scales for the governor and legislature were responses to a question, "How active is your [governor/state legislature] in the public utility policy area?" and coded from 0 (very inactive) to 1 (very active). The participation of citizen groups and utilities were coded from a differently worded question, "How frequently would you say you are visited by [citizens' group members/utility company employees] in your office?" with the response options "once a day/week/month/year." The scales for citizen group and utility participation were recoded to represent the fractions of a year that each group was active in the process.[6]

Besides these measures of activity, we also produce three attitudinal measures derived from a confirmatory factor analysis of questions asking about the costs and benefits of citizens' involvement. (Appendix C, Estimates, contains further details regarding the confirmatory factor analysis and other techniques that were used to construct these independent variables.) One of these scales denotes the extent to which the respondent values citizen participation in utility regulation as accomplishing expressive benefits (e.g., "a voice" or "balances the utilities"). A second scale reflects the extent to which the respondent considers citizen participation to lead to an improvement in services (e.g., "keeps price low"). The third scale measures the extent to which the respondent sees citizen participation as leading to an improvement or worsening of regulation (e.g., "helps the PUC," "increases PUC cost").

We examine how the respondents perceive the influence of different actors in the politics of energy regulation as a function of their involvement. The idea is that if the smoke detector argument holds, we should see that increased involvement by citizens leads to increased perception of their importance.

We again rely on the beta distribution in order to assess the degree to which activity from different actors leads to response from the public utility regulators. We employ this technique again to provide comparability across our analyses, but also because it offers a flexible analytical tool. A quick inspection of the histograms presented in figure 9.1 demonstrates that the distributions of the dependent variables vary considerably and often are quite clearly nonnormal. The beta distribution is a sufficiently flexible analytical tool to be capable of making comparisons across these measures of influence.

From the histograms in figure 9.1, we know that certain actors are relatively uninfluential in the regulation of utilities. The respondents assessed both the attorneys general and individual citizens at the bottom of the scale of influence. Our aim in this section of this chapter is to explore the reasons for the relatively low levels of influence of some groups and the relatively high levels of influence of others. Specifically, as citizens become more involved in the process, do they amplify the influence of actors that are closer to their cause?

---

6. We note that these questions were asked only of the public utility commissioners. In order to achieve a more complete sample size, we impute the mean level of activity of each of the four groups by state for all missing data in the state.

Table 9.1 presents the first differences of the maximum likelihood estimates of the beta distribution for six categories of actors. We again use our ◁, ▷, and ⋈ notation to indicate the asymmetry of statistical significance with reference to the factors toward low influence (◁, the ν coefficient), high influence (▷, the ω coefficient), or both (⋈).

Greater activity by the two political principals—the governor and the legislature—has but scant effects upon perceptions of the influence of others. Our estimates of the effect of greater participation by the governor suggests that only cities and the PUC staff would be affected in influence to a statistically significant degree, with cities becoming slightly more influential and the staff less influential. Neither of the estimated effects is particularly large in a substantive sense (and, in fact, less in magnitude than some statistically insignificant results for the governor). Likewise, a more active legislature appears only to boost the influence of citizen groups to a statistically significant degree, and this only to the smallest of degrees: A change from the mean level of activity to the maximum for the legislatures accounted for a 2 percentage point increase in the sense of the influence of citizen groups.

In short, not only do the histograms of actual influence demonstrate relatively uninvolved political principals, our models strongly imply that were these principals to become more involved in the process, that the relative importance of each of the eight groups would be largely unchanged.

The activity of citizen groups strikes closest to our ideas about the potential direct role for citizens in a policy process. Public utility commissioners are, in many ways, quite unlike some of the bureaucrats we study in this book. They are not at the "street level," and their days are not dominated by contact with citizens. Further, the commissioners tend to minimize the role of citizen groups in actual influence and especially to minimize the role of individuals.

As citizen groups become more active in the policy process, we note that many groups change in their perceived influence upon regulation. As citizen groups become more active, business groups decline in influence: in a move from mean to maximum level of influence, business groups would be fully a third less involved in regulation. By contrast, greater activity by citizen groups significantly boosts the perceived influence not only of the citizen groups themselves, but also of individuals. (Cities, too, become more influential as citizen groups become more active.)

Utilities are in some ways in opposition to citizen groups, and as utilities become more active, citizen groups decline in influence (although not to a statistically significant degree). Greater participation by utilities does lead to a greater sense of influence on the part of the utilities.

The contrast is intriguing: As the client groups (citizens and utilities) become more active, they clearly exert changes upon who regulators take to be influential, while a corresponding change by political principals (the governors and the legislatures) does not. Even this middling level of bureaucracy appears to be more responsive (in the sense of perceptions of who is influential) to citizens than to political principals.

The attitudinal measures yield further interesting results. One might take citizen participation simply to be a means for venting spleen or acquiring expressive benefits. And there is modest confirmation of this suspicion: respondents who valued participation for the expressive benefits did tend to see citizen groups and individuals as more influential, but not to a statistically significant degree. Instead, those that saw participation as accomplishing expressive aims tended to see business groups and utilities as less influential (but only the first of these to a significant degree).

We do not see particularly strong evidence to demonstrate a more instrumental connection between participation and utility performance. One of our measures is the respondent's assessment of the value of participation in improving utility services, and it does not affect how influential the respondents believe the different actors to be. Only one of the four effects is statistically significant, and this one is counterintuitive: The more that participation is seen as improving utility services, the less influential labor is seen in policy.

On the other hand, those respondents who believed that participation improves regulation were much more likely to see citizen groups, individuals, cities, and the PUC staff itself as influential, and less likely to see business groups as influential, all of these to a statistically significant degree. To the extent that this last term captures something of the willingness of bureaucrats to change policy in response to external demands, the most intriguing implication of all is that it leads toward citizen influence, not the influence of political principals. Respondents who thought participation improves regulation did see citizens and citizen groups as more influential, but not the attorneys general.

Implications

The deductive arguments in the first section of this chapter lead to a richer set of propositions than are testable within the scope of this book. The empirical test we offer in the second section only touches upon one aspect of the propositions, that citizens can be more influential in a policy process, even if the current evidence suggests that they are not. Still, we are struck by the effects that citizen groups can have upon the influence of a range of political actors.

So, if citizen groups could be more influential than they appear to be, why don't citizens participate more in the process? Our reasoning in the first section of this chapter leads toward two potential explanations: Either bureaucrats themselves are unresponsive to the coercive pressures of either their supervisors or citizens, or citizens do not see the potential gains from participation as being worth the costs. Of course, the dominant argument of this book is that coercive pressure from supervisors is unlikely to influence subordinates, so why should one expect coercive pressure from citizens to be any more influential?

Direct bureaucratic response to citizen demands may not be an entirely good thing. When bureaucrats are directly responsive to individual citizens or to citizen groups we expect three separate dilemmas to emerge: capture by disproportionately influential interests or responsiveness to a pluralist system; responsiveness to democratic publics or responsibility to serve good government; and broad political control over bureaucratic behavior or micromanagement of individual choices.

If, as we demonstrate, citizen groups may affect the regulatory process by directly intervening with bureaucratic regulators, then there arises a significant dilemma. On the one hand, we fear that disproportionately influential interests may have a greater effect on the policy decisions of bureaucrats than other interests. One might expect that those interests would be more likely to be wealthier and probusiness than advocates of the interests of the poor. And there is provisional evidence about the effectiveness of some groups over others: In the respondents' assessments of who was influential, business groups and utilities fared considerably better than did individual citizens. On the other hand, the proponents of the pluralist model of government expected that fairer and wiser policy would be obtained because only those interests that were intensely held would affect the policy process. The unfortunate amplification to this dilemma happens when the decisions by bureaucrats take place out of public scrutiny.

One factor mitigates the seeming lack of influence of individuals. As we note from our results, individuals do seem to present considerable indirect influence over who is influential. Citizen groups channel individual influence, playing a particularly large role in shaping which actors are influential to public utility commissions, including not only citizen groups and individual citizens, but also business groups and cities.

So, who influences bureaucrats? From previous analysis in other chapters, we found only limited effectiveness of direct supervisors. Given limited compliance stemming from direct supervision, can we expect to see effective control to be generated from outside the agency by political superordinates or by the general citizenry? Our analysis in this chapter points to limited influence, but influence nevertheless exists. In general, citizen groups and individuals do *not* influence the regulatory process, but when citizen groups become more active, both citizen groups and individuals become more influential.

TABLE 9.1. Estimated Effects on the Respondents' Assessment of the Degree to Which a Group is Influential

Variable	Attorney General	Business Groups	Citizen Groups	Individuals
Activity of				
Governor	−0.137	−0.000	0.091	0.074
Legislature	−0.099	0.048	0.023 ⋈	−0.043
Citizen Groups	−0.021	−0.337◁	0.270▷	0.174▷
Utilities	−0.047	0.046	−0.270	0.011
Expressive benefits	0.025	−0.137◁	0.116	0.027
Improve services	0.031	0.094	−0.055	0.060
Improve regulation	−0.021	−0.337◁	0.270 ⋈	0.174 ⋈

Variable	Labor	Cities	PUC Staff	Utilities
Activity of				
Governor	0.079	0.019 ⋈	−0.051 ⋈	−0.085
Legislature	−0.004	0.049	0.024	0.067
Citizen Groups	0.140	0.231◁	0.043	−0.109
Utilities	0.012	0.152 ⋈	0.048	0.187 ⋈
Expressive benefits	−0.081	−0.075	0.131	−0.210
Improve services	−0.272 ⋈	0.025	−0.123	−0.001
Improve regulation	0.140	0.231◁	0.041 ⋈	−0.109

Note: Cells are estimated change in degree of influence in policy process (scale from 0–1, uninfluential to influential) due to a shift of the variable from the mean to the maximum, holding all other variables at their mean. ◁ means low-influence parameter significant at $p < .05$, ▷ means high-influence parameter significant at $p < .05$, and ⋈ means both parameters significant at $p < .05$. $N = 284$.

CHAPTER 10

Routes to Democratic Control of Bureaucracy

We have now examined bureaucrats at local, state, and federal levels of government. These bureaucrats perform a wide variety of tasks, but the principal forces that affect how hard they work are strikingly similar. We have two aims in this chapter: to recapitulate our findings in terms of the possibility for democratic control of the unelected bureaucracy and to explicate implications for supervision, leadership, and bureaucratic reform.

It is hardly a new thought to suggest that supervisors in public bureaucracies are constrained as far as their abilities to influence subordinate behavior. Indeed, principal–agency approaches to bureaucracies proceed from insights about constraints. The very raison d'être of delegation is a constraint: Supervisors cannot carry out all of the tasks assigned to the bureaucracy without delegating tasks to others; supervisors are constrained by the volume of work they can accomplish. The process of delegation creates new constraints, in that the supervisor cannot monitor all of the activities of the subordinate (creating moral hazard problems), nor can she identify the true "type" of the subordinate (leading to adverse selection problems). Supervisors in any hierarchical control situation face these kinds of constraints, whether in a firm or a public bureaucracy.

But public bureaucracies, in particular, additionally constrain supervisors. In chapter 2 we focused on the production of policy output. The nature of this policy output distinguishes the work of public bureaucracy from that of many private sector bureaucracies. Many public bureaucracies might be seen as creating no goods at all, merely regulating common property resources.[1] The Environmental Protection Agency monitors encroachments on shared air, water, and land resources, and the Bureau of Lands and Mines administers ranchers' and miners' claims over public lands. Neither is in a position to distribute public resources exclusively to the members of its organization. Put in terms of the economics of the firm, public bureaucracies rarely are able to redistribute the residuals of production.

---

1. To the extent that one regards property rights as a good, then public bureaucracies create a good when they regulate.

191

The goods produced by other public bureaucracies exacerbate constraints on supervisors. In contrast to the goods that private firms create, those public bureaucracies involved in production almost always produce public goods, whether material (roads, bridges, national defense, clean air) or information (inflation and unemployment rates, counts of the population, analyses of disease). When bureaucracies are engaged in the production of information, the supervisor has a much more difficult time assessing "how much" or "how efficiently" a given subordinate produces. That is, even if the subordinate's production were fully visible with zero monitoring costs, production is itself ambiguous. Not only are many public bureaucracies unable to distribute residuals, the very idea of measuring the productivity of employees fundamentally differs from the private sector.

In the case of the production of material goods, the supervisor might be in an easier position to identify production and efficiency (although not always, as "national defense" bears out). Wilson put it succinctly

> To a much greater extent than is true of private bureaucracies, government agencies (1) cannot lawfully retain and devote to the private benefit of their members the earnings of the organization, (2) cannot allocate the factors of production in accordance with the preferences of the organization's administrators, and (3) must serve goals not of the organization's own choosing. (1989, 115)

Furthermore, even the organization's goals might prove contradictory. At the same time we want an agency to be efficient (devote minimum manpower and other resources to a problem), we also want it to be equitable (make sure that all clients receive the same treatment) and fair (make sure that clients receive treatment specific to the circumstances of their case). No wonder that as a public we can maintain such contradictory impressions of bureaucracies as omnipotent, yet inefficient; routine, yet incompetent; arbitrary, yet unresponsive to individuals.

Compound these problems of supervision in bureaucracies with civil service laws that make it difficult not only to sanction, but also to reward employees on the basis of performance. Johnson and Libecap (1994) observe that the creation of a career civil service with the Pendleton Act of 1883 explicitly isolated the day-to-day bureaucracy from the direct influence of politicians.[2] Instead of patronage, merit governed promotions. The effect has been to create an institutional interest group in the form of federal employees that circumscribes the possibilities of bureaucratic reform.

---

2. Subsequent reforms in 1908 and 1923 further insulated the civil service from the patronage politics.

To this mountain of constraints upon the influence of supervisors, we add three new ones. Subordinate preferences, the repertoire of responses available to subordinates, and the means by which subordinates learn to implement rules, procedures, or policy all significantly constrain the supervisor.

In chapter 2, we modeled a supervisor's problems distributing tasks to subordinates, each choosing for themselves how to allocate their level of time and effort across tasks in the form of working, shirking, or sabotage. This constrained optimization problem highlighted several implications. Under some circumstances, the supervisor is best off not devoting any time at all to (administrative) supervision: when the subordinate is already working at a level close to that desired by the supervisor, when the subordinate is relatively unresponsive to supervision, or when the value of the policy in question is low to the supervisor. Supervisors should devote most of the energy toward supervising bureaucrats who are amenable to supervision, or to sanctioning saboteurs when the marginal utility of eliminating sabotage is greater than the marginal costs of additional supervision. The innovation in our model is explicitly to include subordinate preferences as part of the supervisor's problem. The result focuses attention on what may seem to be the counterintuitive group of subordinates: Supervisors are often better rewarded when they focus on amenable subordinates (those who derive utility from work) rather than the saboteur or slacker.

In chapter 3, we extend the model across multiple subordinates, each of whom learns how to respond to policy on the basis of two explicit heuristics: learning from like others and maintaining behavioral consistency. These heuristics are solidly grounded in the psychology of persuasion, in organization theory, and as economically efficient shortcuts for decision. We further examine the capacities of the supervisor in such circumstances, by varying the level of sanction, ease of monitoring (observability of subordinates), and the tolerance of the supervisor for defection. The innovation in this second model is to require that subordinates learn how to respond to new policy on the bases of contact with other subordinates as well as the sanctioning capacity of the supervisor. The results of the model indicate that although supervision (monitoring, sanctioning, tolerance) affects subordinate compliance, subordinate predispositions and repertoire of initial responses dominate the behavior of subordinates. Further, the model is fully capable of generating extreme behavior, toward either working or shirking, where subordinate repertoire tilted toward compliance is a necessary condition for subordinate work over sabotage.

We interpret our theoretical results about the importance of intersubordinate learning, the connections among fellow subordinates, and the repertoire of possible responses to be an alternative conceptualization of the idea of "organizational culture." Organizational cultures, in our concept, arise because they represent common stocks of information. While one might see conformity among subordinates as the result of coercion (e.g., cracking down on rate busters), we see conformity as the result of uncertain individuals looking to fellow subordinates for appropriate responses.

From our models, we conclude that the new constraints of subordinate predispositions, repertoire, and contact are essential elements of any examination of the reasons why bureaucrats work, shirk, or sabotage. In the empirical research of this book, our focus turned toward preferences, the predispositions that shape performance. Beginning with chapter 4, we looked toward pecuniary, functional, and solidary preferences. What was quite apparent was that bureaucrats working for the federal government preferred material or pecuniary rewards over other rewards. As a reward for good performance, increases in base pay or cash bonuses topped the list. But also on the list of desirable rewards were recognition from others (solidary benefits) and a sense of accomplishment (functional benefits).

The problem for the supervisors in the federal bureaucracy was that they felt relatively unable to punish or (especially) reward subordinates. Subordinates tended to see pay raises and cash rewards as disconnected from performance and tended to doubt that poor workers would be moved out of the workforce. One irony is that between 1979 (prior to the full effect of the Civil Service Reform Act) and 1992, the supervisors retain largely similar capacities. The act's establishment of regularized performance reviews was noticeable among the federal employees: The bureaucrats changed their opinions about the uniformity of the reviews. But supervisors were no more capable of sanctioning or removing inadequate workers, or of rewarding exemplary workers.

The second irony is that even though supervisors in the federal bureaucracy were constrained in the use of administrative supervision, the employees' performance tilted toward hard work. Through multiple variations of the questions, respondents to the federal employee surveys regarded themselves as hard workers. More importantly, this opinion was shared by their supervisors.

Over the subsequent chapters, we shift the analysis from one that focuses on subordinates' preferences to asking how changes in these preferences across employees accounts for variation in how hard they work. We consider a diverse array of measures of performance: self-reports, reports of outside observers, and administrative records. We have measures of the working and shirking continuum, as well as measures for forms of sabotage (brutality by police officers, casework manipulation by social workers). Our unit of analysis remains the same—the performance of individual bureaucrats —even as we shift data collections across four different decades, multiple agencies, and different levels of government.

Across all the variation in measures of performance, levels of government, and types of bureaucrats, we find striking convergence of our results. Subordinate performance depends first on functional preferences, second on solidary preferences, and lastly on the efforts of the supervisor. These results suggest that there has been an overemphasis on issues of moral hazard and not enough attention has been given to adverse selection problems. With the three surveys of federal employees, we demonstrate that functional preferences are far and away the strongest determinant of (self-reports of) performance. We also showed that functional preferences tended to affect both working and shirking, whereas the strength of supervision tended only to discourage shirking, while not having a corresponding effect on encouraging work.

In chapter 6, we consider an archetypal "street-level" bureaucrat, social workers. Our survey again gathered information on working, shirking, and sabotage in the form of self- reports. Strong functional and solidary preferences significantly encouraged work (in the form of taking paperwork home to complete), and discouraged sabotage (fudging paperwork or bending rules). Only when we shift the consideration to reports of the performance of others do we find that the strength of supervision affects the level of sabotage.

With the police officers (another archetypal "street-level" bureaucrat), we looked toward an outside observer's estimation of the amount of time officers would spend shirking on the shift. The strongest effects across the models for officers in 1967 and 1977 were functional preferences and the officer's degree of professionalism. Contrary to expectations derived from the role of the supervisor, we found that the officers who were more observable and who had greater contact with supervisors were more likely to shirk than those who were less observable or had less contact with supervisors. Furthermore, we found evidence of the role of solidary attachments and connections among fellow officers, consistent with ideas of "corporate culture" (Kreps 1984, Miller 1992) as well as "police culture." A higher degree of contact among officers yielded conformity in the patterns of working and shirking.

In chapter 8, we considered an alternative aspect of subordinate performance in examining police brutality as a form of organizational sabotage by officers. Whether we examined the outside observers'.tabulation of the incidence of use of force or verbal abuse, or whether we consider the administrative records, the results suggest that use of force and verbal abuse tend to vary in different ways. Professionalism is a significant impediment toward the use of force, but more professionalized officers are more inclined to verbally ridicule, threaten, or abuse. With the exception of ridicule (arguably the least unacceptable manifestation of verbal abuse), functional and solidary preferences tended to discourage brutality. We also saw the negative side of conformity among fellow subordinates, when the presence of other officers at the scene tended to increase the likelihood of the use of excessive force.

Across chapters 4 through 8, the prominent result is that the performance of subordinate bureaucrats is chiefly influenced by the bureaucrats' predispositions and only modestly influenced by the efforts of supervisors. The chain of command looks to be a weak mode for principals—ultimately, democratic publics—to influence the performance of bureaucratic agents. In chapter 9, we offer an alternative mode of democratic influence, where the individual citizen or his/her interest group attempts to directly sway the subordinate's performance. It may be vastly more efficient for the citizen or interest group to attempt to influence the bureaucrat (trip a smoke detector) rather than contact political supervisors (sound a fire alarm).

As a test of our arguments about the potential for citizen influence over bureaucrats, we consider a group of bureaucrats who are ordinarily insulated from members of the public, public utility commissioners. In general, public utility commissioners tended to regard individuals as relatively uninfluential. But as citizen activity increased, public utility commissioners saw citizens having greater influence. At the same time, the more active political supervisors (attorneys general, legislatures, governors) were perceived to influence public utility commissioners only marginally.

We return to the central question of our book: *Who, or what, controls the policy choices of bureaucrats?* As we observed at the outset, there are at least four potential groups of actors that might directly affect a bureaucrat's performance: the bureaucrat himself or herself, fellow bureaucrats, supervisors, and the public with whom the bureaucrat comes in contact. The overwhelming evidence of our book indicates that the bureaucrat's own preferences have the greatest effect upon performance. First and foremost, bureaucrats control their own behavior. Fortunately for the public, the bureaucrats we have seen in our analysis prefer work and serving the public.

Second, bureaucrats control the behavior of one another. We have strong evidence of the effects of fellow subordinates upon a bureaucrat's performance. Solidary preferences were consistently strong determinants of the reasons why a subordinate would work, or would refrain from sabotage. We found evidence of organizational culture in the prominent effects of intersubordinate contacts among police officers, and of significant differences between departments. Given the strong footing of social proof (learning from like others) in the psychology of persuasion, in organizational theory, and even in economics, we should perhaps not be surprised at the significant roles played by fellow subordinates. When the preferences of fellow subordinates are consistent with preferences of the public, then subordinates can be a positive influence. When the preferences of subordinates run counter to the public, and when those subordinates are in a state of great uncertainty, then the role of fellow subordinates can lead to such disastrous breaches of civic authority as police brutality.

Citizens may exercise some control over bureaucrats, under special conditions. We found evidence for the potential influence of citizen clients on the performance of bureaucrats. In the circumstances where bureaucrats came into contact with citizens on a regular basis, we found that citizens significantly affected how those bureaucrats spent their time. Social workers ranked their customers as the most important influence over how they spent their time. Police officers on the beat were less likely to shirk than officers in patrol cars—even though the officers in patrol cars were more easily tracked by supervisors. We even found evidence of the role of citizens among bureaucrats who might ordinarily be seen as insulated from citizen contact. Although the state utility regulators perceived citizens as the least influential, once we accounted for their level of activity, we found that changes in the citizens' level of activity had a greater effect upon the regulators' perceptions of influence than among comparable groups.

Supervisors matter, too, but not to the extent implied by prior principal–agency approaches. Bureaucrats do respond to their supervisors. At no point in this book have we argued that the sanctions of supervisors are irrelevant to bureaucratic performance. But when one considers the dense net of constraints limiting what supervisors in public bureaucracies might do, it should hardly be startling to find that those supervisors are not as influential as it might seem from a crude transposition of models of the firm onto the public bureaucracies.

As should have been obvious from the lengthy survey of the literatures in the first chapter, this book treads upon well-worn ground. The problems of supervision in organizations, democratic control of bureaucracy, the proper role for professionalism, the extent to which individual bureaucrats wield discretion are all recurring themes of a diverse scholarship crafted by many of the best minds in the social sciences. At this point in our book, we want to identify what we consider to be the key points in our research and to relate our observations to the contributions of previous scholars.

Chester Barnard, writing in the 1930s, figures prominently in the scholarship on organizations when he writes that the coercive power of the supervisor is a fiction. Even in his time, Barnard was not alone in his observations about the limits of a supervisor's ability to command (see, especially, Mary Parker Follett's famous address on "The Giving of Orders"). For that matter, the scientific management works implicitly acknowledge limits to a supervisor's abilities whenever they question the appropriate number of employees under her scrutiny (the "span of control"). The idea that managers cannot lead simply by application of sanction or design of appropriate schemes of supervision resounds throughout later work, too. Our book clearly sides with Barnard. Supervisors have limited abilities to influence subordinate behavior even under the best of circumstances. For the application of coercive controls, public bureaucracies are a far cry from those optimal circumstances.

Nonetheless, bureaucracies can be quite functional places. James Q. Wilson's significant volume (1989) notices that despite all of the factors that might limit bureaucratic performance, bureaucracies continue to deliver the mail and police the streets; that, in general, bureaucracies function. These are opinions shared by many (although hardly all) scholars of bureaucracy. Charles Goodsell (1985), in his self-labeled "polemic" for public administration, notes that the federal bureaucracy functions quite well most of the time: "For a fundamental feature of bureaucracy is that it continually performs millions of tiny acts of individual service, such as approving applications, delivering the mail, and answering complaints" (37). (Indeed, the authors share a concern that a reason for rampant public dislike of bureaucracies stems from the isolated cases of bureaucratic misconduct that attract significant press.) Martha Feldman (1989) and Wood and Waterman (1991, 1994) add other, recent, observations about responsive and functioning agencies and bureaus.

We share this general evaluation of bureaucratic performance. To be sure, bureaucracies do, occasionally, break down. We found significant instances of shirking by police officers, and occasional (yet unfortunately all too frequent) instances of the use of police brutality. No doubt, there are some federal workers who just go through the motions and look for opportunities to avoid effort. But the dominant picture of our book should be that bureaucrats devote the majority of their time to working, rather than to shirking or to sabotage. This is a picture that emerges when we examine self-evaluations, when employees are asked to rate each other, when supervisors rate their workforces, when outside observers evaluate performance, and by virtue of external administrative measures.

The reasons for the relative high levels of working (as opposed to shirking or sabotage) stem from attitudes noted by both Anthony Downs and James Q. Wilson. Among the many archetypes of bureaucrats in Downs's (1967) book are the policy-oriented bureaucrats of the single-minded zealot, the advocates loyal to the organization broadly, and the statesmen loyal to society as a whole. We denoted these kinds of preferences as "functional" ones, referring to the extent to which the bureaucrat derives some pleasure from completion of the demands of his or her job. Wilson (1989) points more toward the second alternative class of preferences. Considering both soldiers going into battle and police officers investigating domestic violence, Wilson suggests the importance of the respect of one's peers in guiding their effort. In neither case is it all appropriate to dwell upon "leisure-maximization." Indeed, we found no evidence at all to support leisure-maximization as an explanation for variance in effort.

If we share many of the main points with the established literature in organization theory, we diverge (as the organization theory scholars do) from some of the conclusions derived with more analytically rigorous tools in the economics of the firm. Many of these models lead toward overstatement of the abilities of the supervisor, misattribute preferences by subordinates to favor leisure- or budget-maximization, and ignore policy-oriented preferences and the performance of fellow subordinates. More generally, the principal–agent models which have made their way into the political science literature have overemphasized the importance of moral hazard and ignored issues of adverse selection. We demonstrate that the tools of agency theory themselves identify limits on the capacity of the supervisor and the singular importance of subordinates' preferences. We illustrate the limits of supervisors and the role of subordinate preferences in diverse bureaucracies with statistically appropriate tools. To put it bluntly, we find that the arguments of organization theorists hold under the scrutiny of the more rigorous tools of economics and fare better than many of the models advocated by economists themselves.

We think there are some important implications from our research on the preferences and performance of local, state, and federal bureaucrats. We turn next to consideration of these implications for democratic control of an unelected bureaucracy, for the relevance of the economics of the firm, and for the possibilities of bureaucratic reform.

Implications for Democratic Control

What are the prospects for democratic control of bureaucracy in the United States? If by "democratic" one means control by "legislatures" or "presidential administrations," and if by "control" one means "to cause the members of the bureaucracy to behave in a way other than their preferences," then the prospects are slender.

We do not address questions of the responsiveness of the agency as a whole in a direct way. We can speak to responsiveness of agencies, if the response of an agency is an aggregation of the behavior of individual bureaucrats. Our evidence demonstrates that the immediate chain of command only weakly affects the performance of subordinates. By far the greater effects are to be found among the bureaucrats' functional and solidary preferences than among either the bureaucrats' material preferences or the effects of supervisors. Our theoretical argument identified the web of constraints enveloping a bureaucratic supervisor. To put it bluntly, if the first link in the chain of command is weak, we expect the entire chain to be weaker still.

But these definitions of "democratic" and "control" are needlessly restrictive and eliminate many possibilities for a responsive bureaucracy.

One route to democratic control proceeds directly from the ultimate principals in a democratic process, the citizens, to the bureaucrat. In chapter 9, we argued that the individual citizen evaluating whether to appeal to a political supervisor or try to sway a bureaucrat directly might find the direct route more satisfactory. Our argument in chapter 9 hinged upon the decreasing likelihood that an individual bureaucrat would be punished by an increasingly distant political supervisor. If it is the case that, for example, a social worker has little to fear that he or she would fall under the scrutiny of a state legislature, or that an Occupational Safety and Health inspector would be contacted by a congressman, then the weight of a political supervisor is, in practice, considerably less than the weight of individual citizens.

To be sure, citizens rarely engage bureaucracies in what they consider to be policy making activities. But there is considerable evidence that citizens are likely to contact bureaucrats, perhaps even more frequently than they contact political representatives. Verba and Nie (1972) argued that "citizen-initiated" contacts may be a more rational way to address particularized grievances than other modes of political participation. Their seminal study demonstrated that citizen-initiated contacts with state or local officials originates from different issues and purposes than does participation in broader activity. Jones et al. (1977) explored the response of the Detroit Environmental Enforcement Division to citizen-initiated contacts, concluding (among other findings) that "The records indicate that virtually every citizen contact generated a governmental response in the form of an on-site inspection" (164).

Furthermore, if one limits the role of political supervisors to that of administrative supervision, one severely circumscribes their possible roles. The educational and coordination functions of supervisors may significantly alter the performance of subordinates. As our models in Chapter 2 demonstrated, principals are better off spending resources in supervision of amenable subordinates. This role is considerably closer to education—identifying more efficient ways for subordinates to act in ways that are consistent with preferences shared by super- and subordinates—than it is to administration—sanctioning the inadequate employee.

We choose to emphasize the consonance of subordinate and supervisor preferences as a reason for bureaucratic performance. No doubt, when preferences differ, principal–agency problems appear. But the result throughout our book has been that the strong functional preferences are a better predictor of subordinate performance than any tool available to the supervisor. In other words, when principal–agency problems are most severe, the capacities of the principal are relatively weak, weaker than the positive contributions of subordinates when principal–agency problems are largely irrelevant. It is a bit absurd to construe Congress as in control of, or dominant over, a bureaucracy if the bureaucracy is already doing what the Congress prefers.

All the work in this book does not counter the possibility that Congress and the President can have significant effects upon the performance of bureaucracy, and that bureaucracies might appear to be responsive to the preferences of political principals. Indeed, Wood (1988, 1990, 1991) and Wood and Waterman (1991, 1994) convincingly demonstrate that agencies as a whole can be quite responsive to both presidential administrations and congressional committees. Drawing on time-series data across a plethora of agencies, Wood and Waterman paint a picture of a bureaucracy that is "competitive, adaptive, and dynamic" (154).

The evidence for congressional dominance has to appear in those circumstances where the preferences of bureaucrats differ from Congress. As Shakespeare put it:

> *Glendowner:* I can call spirits from the vasty deep.
> *Hotspur:* Why, so can I, or so can any man;
>   But will they come when you do call for them?
>
> —*King Henry IV, Part One,* Act III, Scene 1

When the preferences of Congress and the bureaucracy diverge, there are some tools available to Congress whereby the effectiveness of those tools is consistent with our results. Members of Congress might try informal, low-level contacts with bureaucrats, rather than engage more formal routes of congressional oversight or budgetary sanctioning. Balla (1994), in an examination of congressional intervention in Health Care Financing Administration fee schedules, found that informal letters from members of Congress had a greater effect upon the outcome of the schedules than either formal or informal participation by interest groups or citizens.[3] The reason for the influence might hinge on implicit threats, or may as well be taken as a source of information about citizens' preferences. There are draconian methods by which Congress and the presidency can become enormously effective in reining in a recalcitrant bureaucracy. When Congress slashes resources, forcing agencies to cut staff, staff output necessarily falls. If Congress intends to reduce the output of an agency, reducing the agency accomplishes the feat, independent of the preferences of individual agents. If the president wants to reduce the writing of regulations, then a presidential policy can force continuous rewriting of regulations, restricting output for the agency as a whole.

There might also be significant positive opportunities for both Congress and the president. The creation of bureaucracy, such as the Department of

---

3. Note that this finding is entirely consistent with our model that argues that members of Congress, when active, exert greater influence over a bureaucrat's decisions than would a citizen. Balla's finding does not speak directly toward our argument about whether a citizen would find it more economically rational to engage the bureaucrat directly or to seek the aid of supervisors.

Energy under Carter or the Environmental Protection Agency under Nixon, defines new goals and new functions under which to recruit staff. At the creation of agencies, presidents and Congress have unique opportunities to set the broad agenda of policy.

Indeed, the strongest and most positive role that our research identifies for the potential of supervisory control over bureaucracy is in the process of recruitment. If our strongest finding is that the stronger a bureaucrat's functional preferences the more likely that bureaucrat is to engage in work, we are essentially arguing that the process of selecting and indoctrinating bureaucrats is the process that matters. Bureaucrats select themselves into bureaucracies, but management also has considerable control over the kinds of bureaucrats they hire. Put in the language of agency theory, our results suggest that the problem of adverse selection trumps the problem of moral hazard. To the extent that professionalism provides a signal to supervisors about a bureaucrat's true type, then professionalism and functional preferences help to solve a significant part of an agency problem.

Ultimately, our data and our models turn the phraseology, if not the meaning, of principal–agency models around: Bureaucracy works in the United States because of "principled agents." We found that federal employees consider themselves to be hard workers, an opinion shared by their supervisors. We found that social workers and police officers rarely engaged in policy sabotage and were highly professional and strongly influenced by principles that cohere with the mission of their organizations. We found that citizens and interest groups could be influential in the policy process, with greater marginal effect than some political elites. Scholars, as well as the public and politicians, need to credit bureaucrats for being public servants, for working as hard as they do, and for being as responsive as democratic government demands.

Appendixes

APPENDIX A

Models

Solutions to the Enhanced Principal–Agent Model

The Subordinate's Problem: A Constrained Optimization Problem

A subordinate's problem is to maximize his utility, subject to both production and work constraints. This is a constrained optimization problem. The first step is to identify the objective function to be maximized, as well as the constraints:

$$\max U_b = u_b(x_{ib}, w_{iLb}, w_{iDb}, (p_{ib})) \tag{A.1}$$

where U_b = a subordinate's utility function; x_{ib} = the quantity of output i produced by subordinate b; w_{iLb} and w_{iDb} are leisure- and dissent-shirking; and $(-p_{ib})$ is the subordinate's disutility associated with the punishment levied for defection. The objective function (A.1) is maximized subject to:

$$x_{ib} = f_{ib}(w_{iWb}, w_{iSb}, s_b, k_b, \theta_{ib}) \tag{A.2}$$

and

$$W_{ib} = w_{iLb} + w_{iDb} + w_{iSb} + w_{iWb}. \tag{A.3}$$

where w_{iSb} is time spent in sabotage; w_{iWb} is time spent working; s_b = the supervisory time subordinate b receives from a supervisor s; k_b = the capital input available to b; and θ_{ib}, a random state of nature.

Using Lagrange multipliers, the equation can be set up to determine the first order conditions. The subordinate's utility function can be expressed as follows:

$$\mathcal{L}(x_{ib}, w_{iLb}, w_{iDb}, (-p_{ib}), \lambda_1, \lambda_2) = u_b(x_{ib}, w_{iLb}, w_{iDb}, s_b)$$
$$-\lambda_1[x_{ib} - f_{ib}(w_{iWb}, w_{iSb}, s_b, k_b, \theta_{ib})]$$
$$-\lambda_2(W_{ib} - \sum_{z=1}^{4} w_{izb}). \tag{A.4}$$

The marginal utility of the time spent producing output is obtained by finding the first order conditions, which are:

$$\frac{\partial \mathcal{L}}{\partial w_{iWb}} = \frac{\partial u_{ib}(X)}{\partial x_{ib}} \cdot \frac{\partial x_{ib}}{\partial w_{iWb}} - \lambda_1(-f_{ib}) - \lambda_2(-1) = 0. \tag{A.5}$$

It follows that:

$$\partial w_{4b}\left[\frac{\partial \mathcal{L}}{\partial w_{iWb}}\right] = \partial w_{iWb}\left[\frac{\partial u_{ib}(X)}{\partial w_{iWb}}\right]$$
$$+\lambda_1(f_{ib})(\partial w_{iWb}) + \lambda_2(\partial w_{iWb})$$
$$= 0. \tag{A.6}$$

Simplifying this:

$$\partial \mathcal{L} = \partial u_{ib}(X) + \lambda_1(f_{ib})(\partial w_{iWb}) + \lambda_2(\partial w_{iWb}) = 0. \tag{A.7}$$

By the same calculus, the marginal value of time spent on sabotage activity is:

$$\partial \mathcal{L} = \partial u_{ib}(X) - \lambda_1(\partial w_{iSb}) - \lambda_2(\partial w_{iSb}) = 0. \tag{A.8}$$

Since, by definition, the value of $x_{ib} = 0$ when subordinates spend their time leisure-shirking or political-shirking (w_{iLb} and w_{iDb}), the marginal value of time spent shirking is:

$$\left[\frac{\partial \mathcal{L}}{\partial w_{iLb}}\right] = -\lambda_2. \tag{A.9}$$

This, in turn, multiplying both sides by (∂w_{iLb}) appears as:

$$(\partial w_{iLb}) \left[\frac{\partial L}{\partial w_{iLb}} \right] = -\lambda_2(\partial w_{iLb}) = 0. \tag{A.10}$$

Simplified, the following expression is derived for the marginal value of time spent leisure-shirking:

$$\partial L = -\lambda_2(\partial w_{iLb}) = 0. \tag{A.11}$$

In the same manner, the marginal value of dissent-shirking is:

$$\partial L = -\lambda_2(\partial w_{iDb}) = 0. \tag{A.12}$$

The second order conditions, in turn, are assumed to be satisfied. Thus, the ratio of marginal utilities for each use of time is seen to be equal. The subordinate thus solves for $w_{i1b}^*, w_{i2b}^*, x_{ib}^*$, dependent on s_b and θ_{ib} at a point in time. When the optimal output is known, the bureaucrat adjusts the time spent producing on each x_{ib} and solves for each $w_i^* (i = 1, \ldots, m)$.

The Supervisor's Problem

Our analysis of the supervisor's problem follows that of the subordinate presented in the preceding section. Begin with the supervisor's utility function:

$$\max U_s = u_s(x_{ib}, x_{is}, w_{iLs}, w_{iDs}) \tag{A.13}$$

subject to a production function:

$$x_{is} = g_{is}(w_{iWs}, w_{iSs}, s_b, w_{iWb}, w_{iSb}, a_s, k_b, k_s, \theta_{is}) \tag{A.14}$$

and a work/time constraint:

$$W_{is} = \sum_{z=1}^{4} w_{izs} + s_b = w_{iLs} + w_{iDs} + w_{iSs} + w_{iWs} + s_b \tag{A.15}$$

where U_s = a supervisor's utility function, and x_{is} = the quantity of policy output i produced by supervisor s; a_s = administrative supervision imposed on supervisor s; k_s = the capital input available to the supervisor; W_{is} = total work time available to s for policy i; $\sum_{z=1}^{4} w_{izs}$ = all manners of allocating work on a policy by a supervisor s, including $w_{iLs}, w_{iDs}, w_{iSs}$, and w_{iWs}; where w_{iLs} = the amount of work spent leisure-shirking; w_{iDs} = the amount of work spent political-shirking; w_{iSs} = the amount of work spent producing negative output $[-(x_{is})]$; and w_{iWs} = the amount of work spent producing and supervising the production of output (x_{is}).

Given this constrained optimization problem, the supervisor solves for λ_s^*, x_{is}^*, w_{i1s}^*, w_{i2s}^*, w_{ib}^* (for $b = 1, \ldots, n$) which, in turn, determines w_{is}^* and s_b (for $i = 1, \ldots, m$ and $b = 1, \ldots, n$) while taking a_s (administrative supervision) into account. This optimization problem reflects that seen with subordinates, demonstrated in the section above.

Identification of Equilibria

Before moving into specific equilibria we can identify a simplified representation of the supervisor's strategies to include only *ignore* and *supervise*. The supervisor does not allocate any supervisory resources (*ignore*) as long as the following condition holds:

$$\frac{\partial U_s}{\partial x_{is}} - \frac{\partial W_{is}}{\partial x_{is}} < 0. \tag{A.16}$$

On the other hand, when the marginal utility of producing the policy output, x_{is}, exceeds the marginal costs, W_{is} the supervisor invests supervisory resources (*supervise*), such that:

$$\frac{\partial U_s}{\partial x_{is}} - \frac{\partial W_{is}}{\partial x_{is}} < 0. \tag{A.17}$$

Incorporating supervision into a subordinate's decision making we can establish the subordinate's strategies to include, *work*, *shirk*, and *sabotage*. We will see *work* when:

$$\frac{\partial U_b}{\partial x_{ib}} - \frac{\partial W_{ib}(s_b)}{\partial x_{ib}} > 0. \tag{A.18}$$

Shirk when:

$$\frac{\partial U_b}{\partial x_{ib}} - \frac{\partial W_{ib}(s_b)}{\partial x_{ib}} = 0. \tag{A.19}$$

And *sabotage* when the marginal costs of producing output taking supervision into account exceeds the marginal utility of producing the policy output, such that:

$$\frac{\partial U_b}{\partial x_{ib}} - \frac{\partial W_{ib}(s_b)}{\partial x_{ib}} < 0. \tag{A.20}$$

These conditions specify the various equilibria that emerge in this game played between a supervisor and subordinate. To derive more specific results we now turn to our assumptions regarding the nature of subordinate responsiveness to supervision. In our description of the game above, we assumed a functional relationship between supervision and subordinate responsiveness. We specified the following relationship:

$$w_{ib}(s_b) = w_{ib}^* - (w_{ib}^* - w_{ib}(0))e^{-\gamma s_b}. \tag{A.21}$$

Given this relationship, two parameters affect the equilibria in this game, γ, which is a measure of subordinate responsiveness to supervision, and $(w_{ib}^* - w_{ib}(0))$, which is a measure of the difference between the amount of work desired by the supervisor and subordinate, respectively.

In terms of the relationship specified in equation 2.6, the conditions that define the six equilibria can be further defined. Essentially this is a game where nature determines how responsive a subordinate is, γ (or in game theoretic terms, the subordinates type), and the interaction of subordinate and supervisor actions define the difference between w_{ib}^* and $w_{ib}(0)$.

First, examine the situation where $w_{ib}^* - w_{ib}(0) < \varepsilon$. In terms of equation A.21,

$$\varepsilon = -\frac{w_{ib}s_b - w_{ib}^*}{e^{-\gamma s_b}}. \tag{A.22}$$

In other words, $w_{ib}^* - w_{ib}(0)$ approaches 0, whenever the subordinate and the supervisor share the same view as to how much time to invest toward the production of some output, whether much or little. This equilibria is pooling on type (meaning that there is no way to differentiate responsive from unresponsive subordinates). In such a situation, the supervisor does not know anything about the subordinate's responsiveness since she does not supervise. Without supervising there is no way to ascertain subordinate responsiveness.

Second, look at the opposite situation where $w_{ib}^* - w_{ib}(0) > \varepsilon$. If this condition holds, we can identify separating equilibria on type. Here we can identify responsive and unresponsive subordinates. If the subordinate is sufficiently unresponsive, no supervisory time is allocated. This occurs when

$$\gamma < -\frac{1}{s_b}\log(\frac{-(w_{ib})(s_b) - w_{ib}^*}{w_{ib}(0) - w_{ib}^*}),$$ (A.23)

or expressed in another way when

$$\gamma < \frac{1}{s_b}[\log(w_{ib}^* - w_{ib}(0)) - \log((-w_{ib})(s_b) + w_{ib}^*)].$$ (A.24)

A responsive subordinate, on the other hand, is defined by

$$\gamma > -\frac{1}{s_b}\log(\frac{-(w_{ib})(s_b) - w_{ib}^*}{w_{ib}(0) - w_{ib}^*}).$$ (A.25)

In such a situation, supervisory time is allocated.

Details of the Imitation Simulation

The simulation begins each replication by establishing initial states for the general parameters for the distribution of responses (w_{b0}), desirability (d_b), observability among subordinates (O_{ij}) and supervisors (S_b), and the supervisor's tolerance (T) and sanction (P). We repeat the cycle of act–punish–learn, Recording variables that change in each iteration: vector of response (response, w_{br}),[1] vector of feelings about the policy (desire, d_b), vector of probabilities of the supervisor seeing each bureaucrat (supobs, S_b^*), a matrix of communication paths among the bureaucrats (obsty, O_{ij}^*), vector of the mean and standard deviation of the response (supoutc, the supervisor's outcome u_s), and the matrix of outcomes for the bureaucrats (buroutc, u_b).

policy begins when a supervisor informs her bureaucrats of the new policy. response (w_{br}), the vector of responses (length numburs), corresponds to the moves for each bureaucrat. response ranges from -1 (total defection) to 1 (total compliance) and is drawn from a normal population with mean and standard deviation equal to the (2 element) vector respparms (μ_w, σ_w^2). desire, the vector of feelings about the policy, ranges from -1 (total revulsion at the policy) through 0 (no feelings) to 1 (totally thrilled by the new policy). In the simulation (during the adapt stage) response changes while desire remains fixed. In other words, the bureaucrats learn what to do with the policy, but how they feel about the policy remains fixed.

---

1. We use a typewriter face to indicate that the variable is part of the simulation.

As a further demonstration of the forces affecting conformity, we include "positively predisposed" bureaucrats as a variation on our simulations. In this variation, the bureaucrats' initial feelings about the policy are drawn from the range 0 to 1.

A vector (supobs, S_b) and a matrix (obsty, O) describe communication paths in the simulation. supobs (vector of length numburs) contains the probabilities for the supervisor observing each bureaucrat, drawn from a normal population with supobsparms (μ_s, σ_s^2). obsty (matrix numburs x numburs) contains ones and zeroes—if bureaucrat J sees bureaucrat I, then obsty(I,J)=1. The distribution of ones and zeroes is drawn from a normally distributed population with parameters burobsparms (μ_o, σ_o^2), then set to 0 or 1 based on a uniform random draw for each cell. The probability of bureaucrat J seeing bureaucrat I is the same as the probability of bureaucrat I seeing bureaucrat J, but the corresponding cells in obsty need not be equal. obsty, then, describes a directed graph of communications.

play: The second stage of the simulation has each bureaucrat performing his response and collecting rewards or punishment. Each bureaucrat acts his response, and receives the product of response and desire as his outcome (buroutc). The supervisor takes note of the mean and standard deviation of the responses. In other words, the supervisor has a crude measure of how relatively efficient the whole workforce is, although this measure is relative to the workforce and not to some "true" standard of efficiency. Although the response ranges from clear endpoints (total compliance or total defection), we do not mean this to imply that the policy's true efficiency would be total compliance from the workforce, nor would the supervisor necessarily know what response from his bureaucrats would be total compliance.

Once the supervisor records the mean and standard deviation of the response of the bureaucrats, she may discipline bureaucrats who respond below some deviation away from the mean. The rate of tolerance (punrate) varies from −2 (punish all those bureaucrats who respond less than two standard deviations greater than the mean or punish nearly all the workforce) to +2 (punish all those bureaucrats who respond less than two standard deviations less than the mean, or punish only a very small number of bureaucrats). Furthermore, the supervisor can only punish those defectors she catches: the simulation converts the vector supobs to ones and zeroes by draws from a uniform random distribution, corresponding to "seen" (1) and "unseen" (0). For those bureaucrats who defect below the rate of tolerance by the supervisor and are seen by the supervisor, they lose punconst from their outcome (buroutc). In this simulation of the model, we let punconst range as high as twice the maximum utility a bureaucrat might derive from the policy. (In alternate replications of this simulation, we let the punishment range as high as 100 times the maximum possible utility of the policy, with no effect to the parameter estimates of the effect of punishment. Further, in order to gauge the effect of reward in contrast to punishment, we reran the simulation with the supervisor adding punconst to those subordinates who exceed her tolerance level and were observed; again, this modification made no difference to the parameter estimates.) (punconst and punrate are global variables drawn from uniform random distributions in the bigloop function.)

adapt: the third stage of the policy function has bureaucrats imitating the response of the bureaucrat they saw who fared best. The routine has each bureaucrat identify the bureaucrat who received the best reward, of the bureaucrats they saw (obsty cell equals 1). If the bureaucrat's own outcome is the best visible to him, he retains his old response. This kind of imitation adapts on the basis of the other's utility: even if a bureaucrat hated a policy, if the most rewarded response visible to him is positive (complying with the policy), the bureaucrat will pick up that response. The policy function repeats the second (PLAY) and third (adapt) cycle until the maximum number of iterations is reached (maxiter=10). The bigloop function establishes the global parameters by draws from uniform random distributions, runs the policy function, then records the final responses and outcomes for supervisors and bureaucrats. bigloop made 1,000 trials of the policy function, with randomly chosen parameters. The section below contains the code (apl\11) for the functions in the simulation.

APL\11 Code for Simulation

Note <bs> denotes a backspace in order to generate overstrikes.

```
        bigloop1a trials; mincontvyin;popparms;
    varpop;ct;supobsparms;burobsparms;popparms;
    punrate;std;punconst;obsty;supobsty
[1]     C this routine randomly draws the assorted
    parameters
[2]     C and stores the final mean supoutc as a
    dependent var
[3]     C Version 1a calls policy1a (relative
    punishment) based on punrate
[4]     ct{1
[5]     C build a big matrix (x) of results
    per trial
[6]     x{(trials,17)R0
[7]     go: respin{mnandsd respparms{0.001X?2R999
```

```
[8]      C draw supobsparms randomly for policy
    1a/1b/2a/2b
[9]      supobsparms{0.001X?2R999
[10]     C uncomment line for policy 1c/2c
[11]     C supobsparms{1 0
[12]     burobsparms{0.001X?2R999
[13]     C observability matrix (for bureaucrats)
    dist'd unif(0,1)
[14]     C symmetric (x sees y sees x equally), where
    each entry is
[15]     C probability of seeing
[16]     C (obsty has to be global for the
    connectivity check)
[17]     obsty{(2Rnumburs)Rcrop((numburs*2)
    normal burobsparms)
[18]     test{(Robsty)RInumburs*2
[19]     obsty{(obstyXtest>\<bs>0test)+(\<bs>0
    obstyXtest>\<bs>0test)+test=\<bs>0test
[20]     C obsty is a constant network
[21]     obsty{Dobsty+0.001X?((2Rnumburs)R999)
[22]     C supervisor observability (see and be seen,
    here) dist'd unif(0,1)
[23]     supobsty{crop(numburs normal supobsparms)
[24]     popparms{('1+0.001X?1999),(0.001X?999)
[25]     C punrate is for policy1a/2a
[26]     punrate{'0.001X?1999
[27]     C std is for policy1b/1c/2b/2c
[28]     std{.001X?999
[29]     punconst{0.001X?1999
[30]     C change call below to switch policy
    variation
[31]     policy1a popparms
[32]     mincontvyin{analyze obsty
[33]     x[ct;I10]{supoutc[maxiter;],popparms,
    respparms,supobsparms,burobsparms
[34]     C will need to change punrate in line below
    to std for 1b/1c/2b/2c
[35]     x[ct;10+I5]{punrate,punconst,mincontvyin,
    (mnandsd response)
[36]     x[ct;15+I2]{(mnandsd buroutc[maxiter;])
[37]     }(trials&L{ct{ct+1)/go
```

```
        policyla mnpop;test;envy;catch;desire;do;
     s;c;iter
[1]     C this version of the policy routine
[2]     C assigns outcomes on the basis of dowhat
     Xresponse
[3]     C unless the saboteur is caught
[4]     C
[5]     C
[6]     C get initial conditions
[7]     C burs respond over '1 to 1, dist'd normally
[8]     response{'1+2Xcrop(numburs normal respparms)
[9]     C set counters to one, open result matrices
[10]    iter{1+catch{0
[11]    didwhat{buroutc{(maxiter,numburs)R0
[12]    supoutc{(maxiter,2)R0
[13]    getpolicy mnpop
[14]    play: C go from here
[15]    C dowhat ranges from '1 (complete defection)
     to 1 (complete compliance)
[16]    do{response
[17]    C outcome equals desire times do
[18]    buroutc[iter;]{desireXdo
[19]    C supervisor enforces against those she sees
     defecting
[20]    supoutc[iter;]{mnandsd do
[21]    s{Dsupobsty+0.001X?999
[22]    c{(((punrateXsupoutc[iter;2])>(do
     -supoutc[iter;1]))Xs)/Inumburs
[23]    C L{c{(((punrateXsupoutc[iter;2])>do
     -supoutc[iter;1])Xs/Inumburs)
[24]    }(0=Rc)/adapt
[25]    C}(0=Rc{(((punrateXsupoutc[iter;2])>do
     -supoutc[iter;1])Xs/Inumburs)/adapt
[26]    catch{catch+1
[27]    buroutc[iter;c]{buroutc[iter;c]-punconst
[28]    adapt: seenoutc{((2Rnumburs)Rburoutc[iter;])
     Xobsty
[29]    C choose response of the person you saw who
     did best
[30]    envy{S/(seenoutc=\<bs>0(2Rnumburs)
```

```
        R(S/seenoutc))X(2Rnumburs)RInumburs
[31]    response{do[envy]
[32]    C update didwhat (uncomment if you have
   didwhat set)
[33]    didwhat[iter;]{do
[34]    C play again, unless this iteration exceeds
   maxiter
[35]    }(maxiter&iter{iter+1)/play


        x{num normal params
[1]     x{((('2)X(O<bs>*0.001X?numR999))*0.5)
   X2O(O2X0.001X?numR999)
[2]     x{params[1]+params[2]Xx


        x{mnandsd str;mn;sd
[1]     mn{(%Rstr)X+/str
[2]     sd{((%Rstr)X+/(str-mn)*2)*0.5
[3]     x{mn,sd


        getpolicy mnpop
[1]     C fn returns vector of desirability to burs
   (dist'd norm)
[2]     desire{numburs normal mnpop


        h{analyze o;k;monads;ind
[1]     C set main diag to zero
[2]     o{o-oX((2Rnumburs)RInumburs*2)=\<bs>
   O(2Rnumburs)RInumburs*2
[3]     C count blind and invisible monads
[4]     monads{+/0=(+/[1]o)++/[2]o
[5]     C connected?
[6]     ind{ind[|<bs>Hind{+/o]
[7]     k{numburs-(S/ind)-1
[8]     }(0=h{^/(kYind)&Ik)/exit
[9]     go:k{numburs-1Y(h-1)Uind-1
[10]    }(~^/(kYind)&(Ik)+h-1)/out
[11]    }(0<h{h+1)/go
[12]    out:h{h-1
[13]    exit: C all done


        x{crop y
```

```
[1]        x{y
[2]        x[(x>1)/IRx]{1
[3]        x[(x<0)/IRx]{0
```

APPENDIX B

Distributions

Beta

The beta model is the appropriate choice for many of the models in the book for three distinct reasons. The underlying process that generates the beta distribution is one that is a parallel to the process generating the variation in compliance. One can generate a beta distribution by taking a fixed statistic from a bounded distribution. In the case of the imitation model, the statistic is the mean compliance level for a given replication, where mean compliance is bounded between -1 and 1.[1]

A second important reason for using a beta distribution is that the shape of the distributions of different aspects of influence vary significantly from the unimodal, symmetric normal distribution. Neither of the archetypal distributions generated by the imitation simulation remotely resembles the unimodal, symmetric Gaussian distribution. Under the three variations of random initial predispositions we see bimodal and skewed final responses. Under the three variations for positive initial predispositions, we see distributions which are skewed sharply right.

In fact, the beta distribution allows us to be agnostic about the underlying processes generating the varieties of distributions by reflecting the extraordinarily diverse predictions of different models of supervision. A model which postulated that subordinates uniformly prefer to shirk would be represented by a distribution sharply skewed to the left. A model which suggested middling levels of conformity would be represented by a unimodal model, which may or may not be symmetric, but where the mode appears somewhere in the middle of the range.

The beta distribution is defined over the interval 0–1, and may be skewed to either extreme, bimodal, unimodal, or uniform. Figure B.1 displays several

---

1. This is not a case where the central limit theorem applies. The central limit theorem refers to the sampling distribution of all possible means from some fixed size sample for a population. The present case concerns distributions of means for a range of different populations, with all manner of dispositions and initial reactions to the policy.

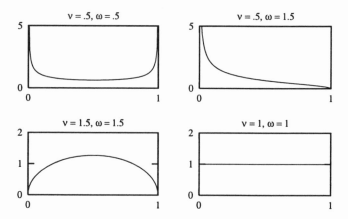

Fig. B.1. Manifestations of the beta distribution

typical variations of the beta distribution. Note that these variations of the beta distribution provide a reasonable fit to many of the skewed and asymmetric distributions of our dependent variables, fits that the OLS approach could never approximate. If the distribution is skewed (as in the upper right), it models the circumstances in which the norm of shirking is widely shared. It may also be skewed to the opposite direction, in which case the norm is for working, a pattern which closely replicates the simulation under the positive predispositions scenario. We can also generate a beta distribution which patterns after the scenario with random (both positive and negative) initial predispositions: the bimodal distribution (upper left) also describes circumstances where either extreme is possible. The beta distribution may also be uniform (lower right). Finally, our measures of bureaucratic responsiveness might be appropriately described by a unimodal and symmetric distribution much like the normal distribution (lower left).

A third reason to favor the beta distribution as the underlying stochastic process is that the two-parameter feature of the beta distribution adds yet another desirable property for the analysis of various measures of bureaucratic responsiveness: We can model factors leading towards sabotage as separate from those that lead toward high levels of work. In OLS, we are confined to two parameters: one describing the mean, the other describing variance. In fact, we will shortly demonstrate that there are asymmetric effects across compliance and defection for the range of initial predispositions, the connectivity of the subordinate's network, and the sanctions available to the supervisor.

We can then model the distribution of the supervisor's outcome by adding equations for the factors leading to compliance or defection. The beta distribution of y is a function of two parameters, v and ω:

$$\mathcal{L}(v, \omega | y) = \frac{\Gamma(v + \omega)}{\Gamma(v)\Gamma(\omega)} y^{v-1} (1 - y)^{\omega - 1} \qquad 0 \leq y \leq 1; \, v, \omega > 0 \quad \text{(B.1)}$$

The two parameters, v and ω, describe the tendency toward the low-end (defection) and the high-end (compliance), respectively. (Both parameters must be positive.)

One way to think of how the v and ω parameters affect the beta distribution is to imagine that parameters which are less than 1 "pull" the distribution toward that side, while parameters that are greater than 1 "push" the distribution. (It may be helpful to reexamine the plot of possible beta distributions for the present discussion.) For example, when $v < 1$ and $\omega > 1$, the distribution is pulled toward the low end (defection, v). The distribution is skewed in the opposite direction when $v > 1$ and $\omega < 1$. A bimodal distribution occurs when both parameters are less than 1.0. In this situation both the v and ω parameters "pull" the distribution toward their respective extremes. When both parameters equal 1, the distribution is flat. When both parameters are greater than one, the distribution is unimodal.

In fact, under certain values for the beta parameters, the beta distribution is *identical* to the gamma, Pearson VI, Student's t, F (Snedecor), and Cauchy distributions (Devroye 1986).

Let the systematic component of the supervisor's outcome be described by two equations:

$$v = \exp(Xv^*)$$
$$\omega = \exp(X\omega^*)$$

Since v and ω must be positive, we take the exponent of the linear equation.

Some of the interesting properties of the beta distribution become apparent when one looks at the mean and variance of the distribution. The mean of a beta distribution with parameters v and ω is given by $v/(v + \omega)$, and the variance is $v\omega/((v + \omega)^2(v + \omega + 1))$. Doubling v and ω by an equal amount leaves the mean unchanged, while it reduces the variance by about half (essentially, "pushing" the distribution in toward the middle equally). This means that effects of the coefficients must be calculated by taking both values for v and ω into account.

Ordered Probit

The ordered probit model assumes that the dependent variable falls into a set of ordered categories. That is, the dependent variable is measured at the ordinal rather than merely categorical or interval levels. The model used here assumes that the effect of the independent variables (X) can be summarized in a linear relationship $(\beta'X_i)$. Each level of the dependent variable would be determined by a series of threshold parameters (τ_i), each larger than the next. Conventionally, one fixes the first threshold at 0, so that if there are j categories, then there are $j-2$ threshold parameters to estimate. The generic likelihood for the ordered probit is as follows:

$$
\begin{aligned}
\log \mathcal{L}(\tau, \beta | y) \;=\; & \sum_{i=1}^{n} \big[y_{1i} \Phi(-\beta'X_i) \\
& + \sum_{k=2}^{j-1} y_{ki} \log \left[\Phi(\tau_k - X_i\beta, 1) - \Phi(\tau_{k-1} - X_i\beta, 1) \right] \\
& + y_{ji} \left[1 - \Phi(\tau_j - \beta'X_i) \right] \big]
\end{aligned}
\tag{B.2}
$$

where y_{ki} denotes a response in category k for respondent i, and $\Phi()$ denotes the cumulative normal density function.

Ordinarily, an ordered probit with many categories introduces a complication in that one must insure that the threshold parameters remain in order (i.e., that $\tau_{j+1} > \tau_j, \forall j > 1$). An approach used by King (1989) has been to insert penalty functions decrementing the estimated likelihood by an enormous amount any time an estimate for the threshold parameters falls out of order. Our case is fortunately simpler. Since we have collapsed the two extreme categories, we have a total of three categories to estimate over, and a single threshold parameter to locate. Our only requirement for the threshold parameter is that it be greater than zero, which we can accomplish through simple exponentiation. The actual likelihood that we estimate becomes:

$$
\begin{aligned}
\log \mathcal{L}(\tau, \beta | y) \;=\; & \sum_{i=1}^{n} y_{1i} \Phi(-\beta'X_i) \\
& + y_{2i} \Phi(e^{\tau_2} - \beta'X_i) \\
& + y_{3i}(1 - \Phi(e^{\tau_2} - \beta'X_i)).
\end{aligned}
\tag{B.3}
$$

Probit and Gompit

As long as we make two assumptions, the maximum likelihood function describing individual instances of brutality is relatively simple. First, each observation must be independent (this assumption permits us to use the simple product of the density functions as the likelihood). This first assumption would be violated if brutality in any one instance (say earlier in a shift) were related to brutality in other instances (perhaps later in a shift). The occasions of brutality are sufficiently sparse that this assumption appears to be reasonable. Second, the process generating brutality must be homogeneous (identically distributed) across police–citizen encounters (this assumption permits us to describe the probability of police brutality as a single parameter). This second assumption would be violated if the probability of brutality changed across the course of a shift. Both assumptions are reasonable, and quite commonly, if only implicitly, employed in dichotomous dependent variable models.

As noted above, we assume that each incident of brutality is independent; one case is not related to another. We also assume that the independent variables possess the same distribution across cases of brutality. Making these two assumptions, independence and homogeneity, we can describe the density function for the incidence of police brutality as a Bernoulli probability distribution:

$$\mathcal{L}(\pi|y_i) = \prod_{i=1}^{N} \Pr(y_i = \text{brutality}) \tag{B.4}$$

$$= \prod_{i=1}^{N} \pi_i^{y_i}(1-\pi_i)^{1-y_i}. \tag{B.5}$$

This Bernoulli probability distribution is conventionally used for probit and logit analyses of dichotomous dependent variables. In more formal terms, we use a "link function" (see McCullagh and Nelder 1983) to reparameterize π in terms of its systematic component:

$$\pi_i = F(\beta X_i) \tag{B.6}$$

where the function $F()$ is *any* monotonic function of X, bounded between 0 and 1. In the probit case, we substitute the cumulative normal density function, $\Phi()$, for $F()$; in the logit case, we substitute the log-odds function, $\log(1/1 + e^{-\beta X_i})$, for $F()$.

The probit link function, nevertheless, may not be the most appropriate function for analyzing brutality. The probit link is derived from the standard

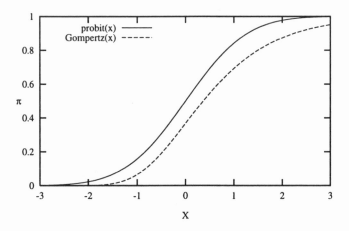

Fig. B.2. Comparison of Gompertz and probit link functions

normal distribution, which is symmetric. The probability process generating brutality or the absence of brutality is most likely not symmetric: thankfully, the vast preponderance of encounters between police and citizens are not brutal. Given the rare occurrence of brutality in our data, one might argue that brutality is an especially exceptional circumstance, and that the probability of brutality must be driven far across some threshold before the encounter becomes brutal. Look at the generalized linear model ($X\beta$) embedded in the link function (B.6): One might hypothesize that the effect of a unit change in $X\beta$ in the negative (nonbrutal) direction would be less than a unit change to $X\beta$ in the positive (brutal) direction.

In order to address the possibility of asymmetry of the effects of $X\beta$ on π, we suggest an alternative link function—the Gompertz curve. Figure B.2 displays the Gompertz curve and cumulative normal density function (probit) plotted for the same values of $X\beta$. The Gompertz curve is much slower to approach the upper asymptote (1) than the probit function. It is for this reason that some analysts suggest that the Gompertz curve is better suited to the analysis of "rare" dichotomous events than probit (Holden and Overall 1987, McDonald and Butler 1990). Following the tag Goldberger (1964) assigned to "Tobin's probit" (tobit), we refer to the use of the Gompertz curve as a link function in the binomial distribution as a "gompit" (in order to distinguish it from the use of Gompertz curves in hazard rate analysis).

To mark the comparison, the link function for the Gompertz curve is:

$$\pi_i = e^{-e^{-\beta x_i}} \tag{B.7}$$

We expect that the gompits will identify more statistically significant independent variables than the probit analysis. Moreover, we expect that the first differences from the gompits will be larger in absolute value than those produced by the probits. (Please refer to chapter 3 where we provide a more detailed discussion of first differences.)

How should the analyst interpret this observation? On what grounds would we prefer the gompit estimates over the probit estimates? (Simply being able to produce significant findings is hardly adequate.) The risk in this circumstance lies in the nature of hypothesis testing: We are never in the position, formally, of "accepting" the null hypothesis, only of "failing to reject" the null. In the current circumstances, the risk of falsely failing to reject the null is the risk of a "false negative," or failing to find an effect that would become apparent with a larger sample size. In public policy terms, the question is one of where we appropriately direct our prevention efforts. If our goal is to constrain police behavior such that brutality is not possible, then we would prefer to use statistical methods that detect important factors that other methods miss. If our goal is to tolerate "minor" deviations by officers, and to encourage active use of appropriate police behavior, then we should prefer more stringent statistical tests. This is an active aspect of the policy debate over the rights of suspects and the authority of police, a debate that can not be settled in the present chapter.[2]

Alternative link functions other than the Gompertz curve can be used for analysis of rare events, including the cumulative density functions for the Weibull and "J" distribution. Nagler (1992), for instance, advocates using the Burr-10 distribution to generate a scobit estimator as an alternative to logit and probit for models with dichotomous dependent variables. For the purposes of the present discussion, however, the Gompertz curve is a useful illustration. Note also that the Gompertz curve is the cumulative density function for Gumbel's extreme value distribution (Devroye 1986, 414).

Censored Probit

Dubin and Rivers (1990) develop the mechanics for handling selection bias in logit and probit models. The basic log-likelihood function resembles the Bernoulli log-likelihood:

---

2. Note that the goodness-of-fit measures are also of no help in resolving a choice between probit or gompit link functions. Both the probit and gompit functions are reparameterizations of the underlying probability, π_i, of brutality. One property of maximum likelihood estimation is invariance to reparameterization (see King 1989), and we should obtain almost exactly the same likelihood for the probit and gompit estimates across the same data. A desirable statistical test, although not feasible in the current data, is a "goodness-of-link" test. Pregibon (1980) develops one such goodness-of-link test, but only for link functions within the same "family" of links (e.g., variations on the logit link function). However, we are comparing two link functions that are wholly different and are not amenable to such tests.

$$\mathcal{L}(\beta_1, \beta_2, \rho) = \sum_{i=1}^{n} y_{2i}(y_{1i} \log(\Pr(\text{brutal}))$$
$$+ (1 - y_{1i}) \log(\Pr(\text{restraint})))$$
$$+ (1 - y_{2i}) \log(\Pr(\text{no brutality})) \qquad (\text{B.8})$$

where $\Pr(\text{brutal})$ is the joint probability that officers want to brutalize the citizen *and* actually brutalize that citizen, $\Pr(\text{restraint})$ is the joint probability that officers want to brutalize the citizen *but* restrain themselves from following through, and $\Pr(\text{no brutality})$ is the probability that the officer does not want to brutalize the citizen. The variables are y_1, incidence of brutality given predisposition to brutalize, and y_2, predisposition to brutalize. We seek the parameters β_2, the effect of the variables affecting predisposition to brutalize, β_1, the effect of the variables affecting the officers' following through on the predisposition, and ρ, the correlation between the error terms in the two stages of the decision tree.

Dubin and Rivers (1990) offer two different link functions for the probabilities in (B.8). In this chapter, we use the probit link functions. The joint cumulative density function for the error terms (u_1, u_2) to both stages of the decision tree (fig. 8.2)[3]:

$$F(u_1, u_2; \rho) = \frac{1}{2\pi\sqrt{1-\rho^2}} \times \int_{-\infty}^{u_2} \int_{-\infty}^{u_1} e^{-\frac{1}{2(1-\rho^2)}(u_1^2 - 2\rho u_1 u_2 + u_2^2)} du_1 du_2 \,(\text{B.9})$$

The probabilities in (B.8) are:

$$\Pr(\text{brutal}) = F(\beta_1' x_1, \beta_2' x_2, \rho) \qquad (\text{B.10})$$
$$\Pr(\text{restraint}) = \Phi(\beta_2' x_2) - \Pr(\text{brutal}) \qquad (\text{B.11})$$
$$\Pr(\text{no brutality}) = 1 - \Phi(\beta_2' x_2) \qquad (\text{B.12})$$

The model may be estimated in the appropriate maximum likelihood package (e.g., SST or Gauss).

Poisson

The Poisson distribution is especially appropriate when dealing with small numbers of events. The Poisson distribution describes the probability that an

---

3. This cumulative normal density function is actually slightly different from that used by Dubin and Rivers, adding a 2 to the interaction term.

event occurs λ times given that each occurrence is independent and has a constant probability. The shape of a Poisson distribution depends on the value of its mean (which is equal to its variance). If the mean is close to zero, then the distribution is skewed; if the mean is larger, the peak moves further from the vertical axis. (If the mean is very large, the Poisson distribution can be approximated with the normal distribution.)

The Poisson distribution for Y_i (Gourieroux 1984: 702–3; Lee 1986: 690–91) is a function of λ, the mean probability of an event occurring in fixed period:

$$\Pr(Y_i = \text{brutality event}) = f(y_i) = \frac{\exp(-\lambda_i)\lambda_i^y}{Y_i!}. \tag{B.13}$$

The base log-likelihood function is then:

$$\mathcal{L}(\lambda|y) = -\sum_{i=1}^{n}\lambda_i + \sum_{i=1}^{n}y_i\log\lambda_i - \sum_{i=1}^{n}\log(y_i!). \tag{B.14}$$

We reparameterize λ in terms of some set of explanatory variables, x, and coefficients b. Because λ must be positive, we chooose exponentiation as the link function, i.e.:

$$\lambda = \exp(x_i b). \tag{B.15}$$

This means that the log-likelihood that we estimate is:

$$\mathcal{L}(b|y) = -\sum_{i=1}^{n}y_i x_i b - \sum_{i=1}^{n}\exp(x_i b). \tag{B.16}$$

Numerous statistical packages (e.g., Shazam, Gauss, SAS, SST) now incorporate direct means for estimating Poisson models.

APPENDIX C

Estimates

TABLE C.1. Maximum Likelihood Estimates of the Effects of Supervision and Bureaucrats' Attitudes on Compliance

	Random Initial Predispositions					
	Relative Punishment		Fixed Standards		Omniscient and Fixed	
	v	ω	v	ω	v	ω
Constant	−.25	1.08*	−.42*	.91*	−.59	−.05
Mean desirabiliity (d_b)	.97*	−.65*	.92*	−.76*	1.06*	−.55*
Mean initial response (μ_w)	1.68*	−1.29*	1.74*	−1.22*	1.58*	−1.34*
Standard Deviation of Initial response (σ_w)	−1.85*	−2.04*	−1.79*	−1.77*	−1.62*	−2.02*
Connectivity	−.08*	−.03*	−.10*	−.07*	−.03	−.05*
Tolerance (T)	.20*	−.06				
Standard			.06	−.06	.37*	−.05
Sanction (P)	.08	−.07	−.05	−.01	.16*	.04
Probability supervisor observes	.24	−.13	.28	−.44		
χ^2	783.90		760.34		797.59	
	Positive Initial Predispositions					
	Relative Punishment		Fixed Standards		Omniscient and Fixed	
	v	ω	v	ω	v	ω
Constant	−2.13*	.64*	−1.63*	.44	−1.10	−.31
Mean desirabiliity (d_b)	1.51*	.21*	1.61*	.13	1.20*	−.11
Mean initial response (μ_w)	3.58*	−.77*	3.18*	−.59*	3.28*	−.55*
Standard Deviation of Initial response (σ_w)	−.57*	−2.62*	−.57*	−2.23*	−.11	−2.24*
Connectivity	−.01	−.03	−.05	−.04	−.03	−.05*
Tolerance (T)	−.01	−.11				
Standard			.20*	.04	.29*	−.02
Sanction (P)	.23	−.08	.08	.03	−.14	.02
Probability supervisor observes	.33	−.04	.05	−.03		
χ^2	758.58		631.69		683.73	

Note: The coefficients are Maximum Likelihood estimates for the model of the beta distribution. * $= p < .05, N = 1,000$.

TABLE C.2. Confirmatory Factor Scales for Preferences and Organizational Attributes, 1979 Federal Employee Attitude Survey

Variable	Loading
Working	
I don't have enough work to do to keep me busy (v77)	−1.00
I have too much work to do everything well (v83)	.29
I work hard on my job (v89)	.44
Pecuniary preferences	
(Importance of) your chances for getting a promotion (v112)	1.00
(Importance of) the amount of job security you have (v113)	.56
(Importance of) your chances for receiving a promotion award (v114)	.70
I am satisfied with my chances for getting a promotion (v115)	−1.21
I am satisfied with the amount of job security I have (v116)	−.11
Functional preferences	
In general, I like working here (v1)	1.00
What happens to this organization is really important to me (v10)	.02
My job makes good use of my abilities (v84)	.04
In the past I have been aware of what standards have been	
I enjoy doing my work for the personal satisfaction it gives me (v100)	.05
Working hard on my job leads to good job performance (v102)	.01
(Importance of) getting a feeling of accomplishment from your job (v109)	.62
(Importance of) the chances you have to accomplish something worthwhile (v111)	−.62
I am satisfied with the chances I have to accomplish something worthwhile (v117)	.02
I am satisfied with the recognition I receive for public service (v119)	.01
Solidary preferences	
Working hard on my job leads to gaining respect from coworkers (v103)	1.00
The people I work with generally do a good job (v41)	.84
I have confidence and trust in my coworkers (v42)	.99
My group works well together (v43)	1.02
I feel I am really part of my work group (v44)	.96
All in all, I am satisfied with my work group (v49)	.98
(Importance of) the friendliness of the people you work with (v108)	.18
(Importance of) the respect you receive from the people you work with (v110)	.21
I am satisfied with the respect I receive from the people I work with (v118)	.67

(continued)

TABLE C.2.—Continued

Strength of supervision

Disciplinary actions in this organization are avoided because of the paperwork that is required (v13)	−1.00
This organization moves its marginal and unsatisfactory workers to positions where they can be ignored (v20)	−.34
There is a tendency for supervisors here to give the same performance ratings regardless of how well people perform their jobs (v23)	−.32
I understand the performance appraisal system being used in this organization (v26)	.14
In general, disciplinary actions taken in this organization are fair and justified (v29)	.23
My job performance is carefully evaluated by my supervisor (v59)	.23
My supervisor gives me adequate information on how well I am performing (v63)	.21
Under the present system, it is very difficult to motivate employees with financial rewards (v3)	−.19
When an employee continues to do his/her job poorly, supervisors here will take the appropriate corrective action (v5)	.51
Supervisors in this organization take the time to help marginal and unsatisfactory workers improve their performance (v36)	.28
Performance appraisals do influence personnel actions in this organization (v38)	.23
My job duties are clearly defined by my supervisor (v54)	.21
My supervisor encourages me to help in developing work methods and job procedures (v55)	.17
My supervisor maintains high standards of performance for his/her employees (v56)	.22
My supervisor considers the performance appraisal of subordinates to be an important part of his/her duties (v57)	.25
My supervisor and I agree on what "good performance" on my job means (v58)	.19
My supervisor sets clear goals for me in my present job (v60)	.23
My supervisor insists that subordinates work hard (v64)	.19
My supervisor demands that subordinates do good work (v67)	.20
I will be demoted or removed from my position if I perform poorly (v104)	.28

Autonomy

My job is pretty much of a one-person job —there is little need for meeting or checking with others (v95)	1.00
I have to depend on work performed by coworkers in order to get the materials or information I need to do my job (v99)	−.25
All in all, I am satisfied with my work group (v48)	−.11

(continued)

TABLE C.2.—Continued

Working hard leads to pressure from coworkers not to work so hard (v97)	.16
I have the authority I need to accomplish my work objectives (v12)	1.00
I have a great deal of say over decisions concerning my present job (v93)	.69

Anomie

I am not sure what determines how I can get a promotion in this organization (v8)	1.00
New employees in this organization are well qualified to perform their jobs (v16)	−.49
Promotions or unscheduled pay increases here usually depend on how well a person performs on his/her job (v17)	−.80
Affirmative action policies have helped advance employment opportunities for women and minorities in this organization (v18)	−.41
There are adequate procedures to get my performance rating reconsidered, if necessary (v19)	−.66
Under the present system, financial rewards are seldom related to employee performance (v22)	.74
My supervisor evaluates my performance on things not related to my job (v74)	.47
In the past I have been aware of what standards have been used to evaluate my performance (v96)	−.57
I will be promoted or given a better job if I perform especially well (v120)	−.59

Organizational rigidity

It's really not possible to change things around here (v9)	1.00
I am told promptly when there is a change in policy, rules, or regulations that affects me (v11)	−.74
Employees do not have much opportunity to influence what goes on in this organization (v21)	.86
Management is flexible enough to make changes when necessary (v24)	−.82
In this organization, authority is clearly delegated (v32)	−.70
I am not afraid to "blow the whistle" on things I find wrong with my organization (v35)	−.31
It takes too long to get decisions made in this organization (v37)	.71

Note: Cell entries are factor loadings from a confirmatory factor analysis with all latent variables set to be orthogonal (have zero covariance). $N = 13,668$. All estimates statistically significant at $p < .01$.

TABLE C.3. Confirmatory Factor Scales for Preferences and Organizational Attributes, 1983 Federal Employee Attitude Survey

Variable	Loading
Working	
I don't have enough work to do to keep me busy (v34)	−1.00
I work hard on my job (v31)	.84
Rate the amount of effort you put into work activities during an average workday (v45)	.70
Pecuniary preferences	
(How important to start) Salary (v54)	1.00
(How important to start) Job security (v57)	.83
(How important to start) Fringe benefits (v55)	.88
(How important to stay) Job security (v62)	.80
(How important to stay) Fringe benefits (v60)	.84
(How important to stay) Salary (v59)	.73
Functional preferences	
In general, I like working here (v1)	1.00
Doing my job well gives me a feeling that I've accomplished something worthwhile (v32)	.28
(How important to stay) Opportunity for public service or to have an impact on public affairs (v63)	1.16
(How important to stay) Challenging work responsibilities (v61)	.64
(How important to start) Opportunity for public service or to have an impact on public affairs (v58)	1.11
(How important to start) Challenging work responsibilities (v56)	.61
Strength of supervision	
There is a tendency for supervisors here to give the same performance ratings regardless of how well people perform their jobs (v11)	−1.00
I understand the performance appraisal system being used in this organization (v2)	.44
In general, disciplinary actions taken in this organization are fair and justified (v14)	.57
My job performance is carefully evaluated by my supervisor (v24)	1.04
My supervisor gives me adequate information on how well I am performing (v25)	1.02
Under the present system, it is very difficult to motivate employees with financial rewards (v3)	−.25
If an employee performs his/her job poorly, supervisors here will take the appropriate corrective action (v4)	.56
Supervisors in this organization take the time to help marginal and unsatisfactory workers improve their performance (v15)	.65
Performance appraisals do influence personnel actions taken	

(continued)

TABLE C.3.—Continued

in this organization (v18)	.45
My supervisor maintains high standards of performance for his/her employees (v22)	.90
My supervisor and I agree on what "good performance" on my job means (v23)	.95
How often do you receive feedback from your supervisor that helps you to improve your performance (v29)	−.85

Autonomy

I have the authority I need to accomplish my work objectives (v5)	1.00
I have a great deal of say over what has to be done on my job (v35)	.40

Anomie

Promotions or unscheduled pay increases here usually depend on how well a person performs on his/her job (v7)	1.00
There are adequate procedures to get my performance rating reconsidered, if necessary (v8)	.39
My supervisor evaluates my performance on things not related to my job (v27)	−.24

Organizational rigidity

It's really not possible to change things around here (v6)	1.00
I am not afraid to "blow the whistle" on things I find wrong with my organization (v13)	−.14

Note: Cell entries are factor loadings from a confirmatory factor analysis with all latent variables set to be orthogonal (have zero covariance). $N = 19,721$. All estimates statistically significant at $p < .01$.

TABLE C.4. Confirmatory Factor Scales for Preferences and Organizational Attributes, 1992 Survey of Federal Employees

Variable	Loading
Working	
Generally, I don't have enough work to do to keep me busy (s2q3)	−1.00
When I don't feel well in the morning, I still try to come to work because I know my contribution will be missed (s2q12)	1.25
Pecuniary preferences	
I don't care what happens to this organization as long as I get my paycheck (s2q52)	.10
(Extent to which prefer as reward) Recognition (s2q80a)	−.02
(Extent to which prefer as reward) An outstanding performance rating (s2q80b)	.13
(Extent to which prefer as reward) An increase in base pay (s2q80c)	1.00
(Extent to which prefer as reward) A cash bonus (s2q80e)	.39
(Extent to which prefer as reward) A promotion (s2q80f)	.11
(Extent to which prefer as reward) Paid time off (s2q80g)	.16
(Extent to which prefer as reward) A training opportunity (s2q80h)	.15
I am satisfied with my pay (s7q1)	−1.10
My pay is fair considering what other people in this organization are paid (s7q2)	−.90
Considering the skills and effort I put into my work, I am satisfied with my pay (s7q3)	−1.13
My pay is fair considering what other places in this area pay for the same kind of work (s7q4)	−.88
Pay should be based on more than the knowledge and skills of the employee than on the duties and responsibilities of the position (s7q5)	.11
My pay is fair considering what people in similar jobs in this agency are paid (s7q6)	−.77
Functional preferences	
I like making decisions that affect other people (s2q17)	1.00
My job is challenging (s2q18)	.74
I am satisfied with the chances I have to accomplish something worthwhile (s2q51)	.90
My organization encourages employees to use their skills and abilities (s2q57)	.96
My organization makes attempts to keep employees challenged in their work (s2q60)	.99
Service to others (s2q75a)	.08
Challenging work (s2q75h)	.08
Solidary preferences	
My coworkers have the necessary skills and abilities to perform their jobs (s2q29)	1.00

(continued)

TABLE C.4.—Continued

People in my work unit cooperate to get the work done (s2q25)	.41
It's important for me to know where I rank among my coworkers (s2q30)	.10
I have confidence and trust in my organization (s2q47)	.27

Strength of supervision

My supervisor encourages me to help in developing work methods and job procedures (s2q40)	1.00
My supervisor works well with people (s2q43)	.82
I can expect to receive a pay raise or cash award if I perform exceptionally well (s2q7)	.53
People in my work unit are expected to work hard (s2q27)	.26
Pay raises and cash rewards around here depend on how well you perform (s2q49)	.59
In my organization, management gives everyone the same performance rating (s2q50)	−.11

Autonomy

I am required to get approval for decisions I can make myself (s2q15)	−1.00
Employees in my work unit are encouraged to participate in decisions affecting their work (s2q33)	−.29

Note: Cell entries are factor loadings from a confirmatory factor analysis with all latent variables set to be orthogonal (have zero covariance). $N = 33,896$. All estimates statistically significant at $p < .01$.

TABLE C.5. Beta Estimates for Working as a Function of Preferences and Organizational Characteristics, 1979 and 1983 FEA, 1992 SOFE

Variable	1979 v	1979 ω	1983 v	1983 ω	1992 v	1992 ω
Constant	-.58	-.36	.92	-.19	.15	.85
	(.16)	(.13)	(.10)	(.08)	(.06)	(.05)
Pecuniary preferences	.24	.19	.48	.43	-.11	-.71
	(.06)	(.05)	(.05)	(.04)	(.05)	(.04)
Functional preferences	1.48	.49	.02	-.97	.50	-1.69
	(.14)	(.11)	(.06)	(.04)	(.06)	(.05)
Solidary preferences	-.03	-.79			.06	.07
	(.10)	(.08)			(.06)	(.04)
Strength of supervision	1.21	.88	-.56	.15	.14	.07
	(.12)	(.09)	(.09)	(.06)	(.06)	(.04)
Autonomy	.14	.21	.21	.12	.12	.05
	(.08)	(.06)	(.06)	(.04)	(.04)	(.02)
Anomie	-.20	.15	-.12	.06		
	(.11)	(.09)	(.05)	(.03)		
Organizational rigidity	-.39	-.53	-.06	-.22		
	(.11)	(.08)	(.07)	(.05)		
χ^2	1269.76		1584.96		3961.54	
N	12182		17246		30046	

Note: Maximum likelihood estimates for the beta distribution of "work" (scale), standard errors in parentheses.

TABLE C.6. Ordered Probit Estimates of Work and Sabotage, from 1994 Survey of Durham County Social Services

Variable	Take Paperwork Home	Fudge Paperwork	Bend Rules	Others Break Rules
Constant	-0.49	1.89	1.42	2.68
My department rewards results and goal achievement both formally and informally.	0.03	0.21*	-0.04	-0.20*
Failure to treat customers fairly results in reprimands from supervisors.	-0.17*	-0.00	-0.13	-0.36*
Working hard on my job leads to gaining respect from coworkers.	-0.09	0.55*	0.16	0.02
A person gets the chance to develop good friends here	0.09	-0.17*	-0.25	-0.35*
Solidary like	0.08	0.87*	-0.01	0.38*
Doing my job well makes me feel good about myself as a person.	0.10*	-0.14	0.10	0.04
A person enters this profession because he likes the work.	0.21*	-0.18	-0.03	-0.05
"Helping" like	0.14*	0.37*	0.16	-0.09
"Paperwork" dislike	-0.79*	-0.36	-0.04	0.21
Pecuniary like/dislike	0.38*	0.55*	-0.32	-0.57*
Influence of immediate supervisor	0.01	-0.02	-0.01	-0.48*
Influence of coworkers	0.12*	-0.00	-0.08	0.03
Influence of customers	0.09	-0.04	0.12	-0.03
Influence of director	0.15	-0.29	0.02	0.49
τ_2	0.37*	1.16*	0.93*	0.88*
χ^2	38.44	37.34	29.44	68.98

Cell entries are ordered probit coefficients for the response to the Likert Scale questions about "taking paperwork home," "fudging paperwork," "bending the rules," and whether "others break the rules," where the scale is coded "strongly agree/agree" (1), "neither agree nor disagree" (2), and "disagree/strongly disagree" (3). * = $p < .05$, one-tailed test. $N = 126$.

TABLE C.7. Beta Estimates of Shirking by Police Officers, 1966 Police Behavior Data

Variable	ν	ω
Constant	.32	.67
	(.26)	(.25)
Boston	.02	.02
	(.15)	(.15)
Chicago	.17*	.06*
	(.02)	(.02)
Percent Black	.84*	.51*
	(.22)	(.20)
Percent White	.23	.13
	(.23)	(.24)
Professionalism	1.10*	2.74*
	(.41)	(.42)
Functional dislike	.56*	1.03*
	(.26)	(.25)
Solidary dislike	−.05	.64*
	(.19)	(.26)
Solidary like	−.05	−.44*
	(.19)	(.19)
Satisfaction with supervisor	−.70*	−.54*
	(.25)	(.24)
Mobile patrol	−.34	−1.15*
	(.23)	(.23)
χ^2	116.4	

Note: The dependent variable is the percentage of time that an officer shirks, as measured by an observer. Standard errors in parenthesis below coefficients. * $= p < .05$. $N = 486$.

TABLE C.8. Beta Estimates of Shirking by Police Officers, 1977 Police Behavior Data

Variable	ν	ω
Constant	-1.08^*	1.55^*
	(.06)	(.10)
Rochester metro	.46*	.25
	(.08)	(.12)
Tampa metro	.35*	.48*
	(.03)	(.05)
Solidary attachments	.04	$-.06$
	(.05)	(.04)
Satisfaction with Supervisor	$-.17^*$	.02
	(.05)	(.04)
Supervisor contact	.04*	.04*
	(.01)	(.01)
Contact with other officers	.02*	.06*
	(.01)	(.02)
Functional dislikes	$-.04$	.07*
	(.02)	(.02)
Functional likes	$-.05^*$	$-.27^*$
	(.06)	(.07)
χ^2	77.21	

Note: The dependent variable is the percentage of time that an officer shirks, as measured by an observer. Standard errors in parentheses below coefficients. * = $p < .05$. $N = 942$.

TABLE C.9. Beta Estimates of Shirking by Police Officers, 1977 Police Behavior Data

Variable	ν	ω
Constant	−1.03*	1.55*
	(.10)	(.15)
Rochester metro	.44*	.26
	(.11)	(.17)
Tampa metro	.33*	.48*
	(.05)	(.04)
Solidary attachments	.04	−.06
	(.05)	(.04)
Satisfaction with supervisor	−.17*	.02
	(.05)	(.04)
Supervisor contact	.04*	.04*
	(.01)	(.01)
Contact with other officers	.02*	.06*
	(.01)	(.02)
Functional dislikes	−.04	.07*
	(.02)	(.02)
Functional likes	−.05*	−.27*
	(.06)	(.07)
χ^2	517.45	

Note: The dependent variable is the percentage of encounters that an officer shirks, as measured by an observer. Standard errors in parentheses below coefficients. * = $p < .05$. $N = 942$.

TABLE C.10. Probit and Gompit Estimates of Effects of Officer Attributes, Preferences, and Circumstances on Measures of Brutality, 1966 Police Behavior Data

| | Unnecessary Force | | Unnecessary Frisks | |
	Probit	Gompit	Probit	Gompit
Constant	−2.71	−1.71	−2.57	−1.65
Boston	.72	.39*	.28	−.16*
Chicago	.77	.42*	−.08	−.05
Human relations skills	−.17	−.10	−.01	.02
Intellectual style	.02	−.02	−.04	−.03
Professional dimension	.03	.01	.22	.12*
Felony	.29	.16	.33	.19*
Violent	.43	.23*	−.14	−.07
Number of officers	.01	.004	.008	.006
Solidary likes	−.80	−.45*	.34	−.21*
Functional likes	−.80	−.45*	−.26	−.15
χ^2	4774	4774	4564	4564

| | Ridicule | | Threat | |
	Probit	Gompit	Probit	Gompit
Constant	−3.10	−1.99	−1.17	−.75
Boston	−1.09*	−.62*	.13	.09*
Chicago	−.51*	−.29*	.21*	.14*
Human relations skills	.11	.06	.05	.03
Intellectual style	−.008	−.04	−.16*	−.11*
Professional dimension	.28	.16*	−.05	−.03
Felony	.01	.05	−.13	−.09
Violent	.12	.08	.35*	.25*
Number of officers	.008	.007*	.007	.007*
Solidary likes	.18	.11	−.23*	−.17*
Functional likes	.54	.30*	−.21	−.15*
χ^2	4411	4411	3260	3260

Note: * = statistically significant at $p < .05$. $N = 3507$.

TABLE C.11. Probit and Censored Probit Estimates of Use of Unnecessary Force by Police Officers as a Function of the City of Residence, 1966 Police Behavior Data

	Probit Estimates		Censored Probit Estimates	
	Estimate	Effect	Estimate	Effect
Selection Model				
Constant			−2.45*	
Authoritarian			.51*	
Violent			.26*	
Number of officers			.004	
Outcome Model				
Constant	−2.71		−2.64	
Boston	.72*	.0044	.09*	.0114
Chicago	.77	.0034	.18*	.0195
Human relations skills	−.17	−.0002	−.28	−.0214
Intellectual style	.02	.0000	1.09*	.1420
Professional dimension	.03	.0000	−.42*	−.0225
Felony	.29	.0013	.03	.0051
Violent	.43	.0017	.53*	.0792
Number of officers	.01	.0250	.05*	.9103
Solidary likes	−.80*	−.0006	.11*	.0059
Functional likes	−.80*	−.0009	.15*	.0200

Note: * = statistically significant at $p < .05$. $N = 3507$. $\chi^2 = 4774$ with 15 d.f. for both probit and gompit models.

Confirmatory Factor Models for PUC Survey

The measures of the degree to which the governor, legislature, citizens' groups, and utilities were active in the PUC presented two problems for the analysis. Gormley asked only the PUC commissioners about the levels of activity of the four groups. This makes considerable sense for his research design, since the citizens' groups may not have adequate information to provide a reasonable guess at the involvement of political superordinates or of utilities. We impute the mean of a states' level of activity for the four scales to the rest of the sample. This method of imputation has the result of tending to depress covariation across related elements (Kalton 1983). It is a reasonable approach, theoretically, if one believes that the PUC commissioners are the respondents who are most likely to have the best information about the degree of activity from the four actors, and that it is the actual level of activity, not perceived activity, that should drive the different groups' perceived influence on the process. Our second research decision stems from an asymmetry between the questions. Gormley asked the commissioners to rate the activity of the governor and the state legislature in the PUC on a scale that ran from "very active" to "very inactive." Gormley also asked the commissioners to describe the frequency of visits by citizens' groups' members and utility companies' employees on a scale from "once a day" to "never." The first of these scales we coded from 0 for very inactive to 1 for very active. The second of these scales we coded from 0 for never through 1 for once a day. We do not know what difference the two codings should make for the comparability between the governor/legislature on the one hand, and the citizens' groups/utilities on the other. Presumably, our choice of scales for the two categories should not affect within-category comparisons.

Our confirmatory factor model drew upon questions assessing the usefulness of citizen participation. These indicators were coded from the open-ended responses to the question "What are the benefits and costs of citizen participation in P.U.C. proceedings?" There were up to three costs and three benefits coded for each respondent. Our confirmatory factor model used these dichotomous indicators as measures of three latent variables denoting the utility of citizen participation in the process: economic effect, aid to PUC, and expressive benefits. The results of the confirmatory factor model appear in table C.12. Note that the overall fit of the model is adequate (GFI=.87), and that the individual estimates for most factor loadings are statistically significant at $p < .01$.

Economic effects of citizen participation included lowering the price or improving quality ("improving services"). By this variable, we specifically intended to note the extent to which citizen involvement produced economic returns to the citizen. Although both of the factor loadings are in the anticipated (positive) direction, neither are statistically significant at conventional levels.

Several of the respondents mentioned costs or benefits to the Public Utility Commission itself ("improving regulation"). Two benefits were mentioned, an unspecified "helping the PUC" and "forcing the PUC to recognize certain issues." Both factor loadings were statistically significant and of the right sign, where forcing the PUC to recognize issues was twice the magnitude of the unspecified "helping PUC" loading. Most responses under this latent variable referred to costs: adding time, adding to the number of hearings, increasing regulatory burden, increasing PUC costs, or increasing Federal/state government costs. Only two were of the incorrect sign: the loadings on "adding number of hearings" and "increasing federal/state costs" were both positive, although only the latter was statistically significant, and both were quite small. The largest factor loading for this latent variable was on the cost of added time (−.81).

Most of the categories of response to the costs and benefits of citizen participation pointed to expressive benefits ("expressive benefits"). On the pos-

TABLE C.12. Confirmatory Factor Model of 1980 Politics of Public Utility Regulation Data

Indicator	Loading
Improve Services	
Price low	.16
Quality	.05
Improve Regulation	
Help PUC	.19*
Force PUC	.37*
Add time	−.81*
Add number	.01
Increase burden	−.38*
PUC cost	−.24*
Fed cost	.04*
Expressive benefits	
Voice	.51*
Balance utilities	.24*
Increase accountability	.17*
Increase understanding	.14*
Lack understanding	−.29*
Emphasize rhetoric	−.28*
Lowers credibility	−.06
Repeat testimony	−.11
Adverse PR	−.07
Disproportionate impact	−.003

Note: Estimates by maximum likelihood, convergence after 46 iterations, $N = 284$. Goodness-of-Fit Index = .87, * = $p < .01$.

itive side, respondents mentioned that citizen participation provided a "voice for the public," "counterbalances utilities views," "improves public acceptance of decisions," and "enhances citizens' understanding of decisions." All four factor loadings for these responses were of the correct sign and statistically significant at $p < .01$. The largest of the loadings was for the "voice" response, which is closest to the idea of expressive benefits. On the negative side, respondents noted that the costs of citizen participation included that "citizens lack full understanding of the issues," "emphasis on rhetoric at expense of reasoned debate," "lowers the credibility of the process," "repeat(s) testimony of proxy advocate or public utility commission staff," "adverse public relations," and "certain groups have a disproportionate impact." Although all of these loadings were of the correct sign, only the first two were statistically distinguishable from zero at $p < .01$.

TABLE C.13. Beta Model Estimates of the Respondents' Assessment of the Degree to Which a Group is Influential

Variable	Attorney General		Business Groups		Citizen Groups		Individuals	
	ν	ω	ν	ω	ν	ω	ν	ω
Constant	−0.629	−1.317*	0.576	1.138*	1.012*	1.292*	0.087	1.181*
Activity of								
Governor	−0.002	0.749	0.153	0.159	0.756*	0.486*	0.627*	0.422
Legislature	−0.110	0.882	−0.238	−0.636	−1.214*	−1.429*	0.046	0.387
Citizen groups	0.601	1.932	−1.590	−3.802*	3.379	3.960*	−0.824	−1.067*
Utilities	0.163	0.017	−0.474	−0.641	0.305	0.549	0.239	0.238
Expressive benefits	−0.084	−0.203	0.710	1.024*	−0.320	−0.384	−0.003	−0.083
Improve services	0.792	0.475	0.251	−0.165	−0.367	−0.148	−0.407	−0.777
Improve regulation	−0.129	−0.068	0.441	1.242*	1.565*	1.167*	1.199*	0.969*
χ^2	35.88		45.02		34.00		27.40	

Variable	Labor		Cities		PUC Staff		Utilities	
	ν	ω	ν	ω	ν	ω	ν	ω
Constant	−0.609	−0.224	0.587	1.881*	0.431	−1.015*	0.375	−0.742
Activity of								
Governor	0.446	0.179	0.702*	0.674*	0.963*	1.078*	0.115	0.534
Legislature	−0.437	−0.453	−0.299	−0.721	−0.525	−0.685	0.380	−0.385
Citizen groups	2.196	2.887	−1.264	−4.106*	0.717	−0.606	2.044	1.774
Utilities	0.399	0.405	1.137*	0.905*	0.390	0.172	0.003*	0.004*
Expressive benefits	−0.043	0.191	−0.033	0.180	0.150	−0.446	−0.101	0.612
Improve services	1.539*	2.512*	−0.633	−0.812	0.177	0.779	−0.403	−0.361
Improve regulation	0.557	0.261	0.112	−0.715*	1.152*	0.927*	0.007	0.376
χ^2	28.36		36.08		28.44		37.56	

Note: * = $p < .01$, N = 284.

References

Aberbach, Joel D. 1990. *Keeping a Watchful Eye: The Politics of Congressional Oversight.* Washington, DC: The Brookings Institute.

Aberbach, Joel D., Robert D. Putnam, and Bert A. Rockman. 1981. *Bureaucrats and Politicians in Western Democracies.* Cambridge, MA: Harvard University Press.

Achen, Christopher H. 1986. *The Statistical Analysis of Quasi-Experiments.* Berkeley and Los Angeles: University of California Press.

Adler, Seymour. 1983. "Subordinate Imitation of Supervisor Behavior: The Role of Supervisor Power and Subordinate Self-Esteem." *Social Behavior and Personality* 11:5–10.

Aitchison, J., and S. Silvey. 1957. "The Generalization of Probit Analysis to the Case of Multiple Responses" *Biometrika* 44:131–40.

Alchian, Armen, and Harold Demsetz. 1972. "Production, Information Costs, and Economic Organization" *American Economic Review* 62: 777–95.

Amemiya, Takeshi. 1985. *Advanced Econometrics.* Cambridge, MA: Harvard University Press.

Ansari, Mahfooz A. 1990. *Managing People at Work: Leadership Styles and Influence Strategies.* Newbury Park, CA: Sage Publications.

Arrow, Kenneth J. 1985. "The Economics of Agency." In *Principals and Agents: The Structure of Business*, edited by John W. Pratt and Richard Zeckhauser. Boston: Harvard Business School Press.

Arrow, Kenneth J. 1986. "Agency and the Market." In *Handbook of Mathematical Economics, vol. III*, edited by K.J. Arrow and M.D. Intriligator. Amsterdam: North-Holland.

Asch, Solomon. 1951. "Effects of group pressure upon the modification and distortion of judgment." In *Groups, Leadership, and Men,* edited by Harold S. Guetzkow. Pittsburgh: Carnegie.

Auman, Robert. 1981. "Survey of Repeated Games." In *Essays in Game Theory and Mathematical Economics in honor of Oscar Morgenstern*, edited by R. Auman. Mannheim: Bibliographisches Institut.

Axelrod, Robert. 1984. *The Evolution of Cooperation.* New York: Basic Books.

Bachman, Jerald G., David G. Bowers, and Phillip M. Marcus. 1968. "Bases of Supervisory Power: A Comparative Study in Five Organizational Settings." In *Control in Organizations,* edited by Arnold S. Tannenbaum. New York: McGraw Hill.

Balla, Steven J. 1994. "Information Provision, Agency Rulemaking, and Medicare Physician Payment Reform." Paper presented at the 1994 Annual Meeting of the Association for Public Policy Analysis and Management, Chicago, IL.

Bandura, Albert, Joan E. Grusec, and Frances L. Menlove. 1977. "Vicarious Extinction of Avoidance Behavior." *Journal of Personality and Social Psychology* 5:16–23.

Banks, Jeffrey, and Barry R. Weingast. 1992. "The Political Control of Bureaucracies under Asymmetric Information." *American Journal of Political Science* 36: 509–24.

Barker, Thomas. 1978. "An empirical study of police deviance other than corruption." *Journal of Police Science and Administration.* 6:264–72.

Barker, Thomas, and David L. Carter. 1991. *Police Deviance, Second Edition.* Cincinnati: Anderson Publishing.

Barnard, Chester. 1938. *The Functions of the Executive.* Cambridge, MA: Harvard University Press.

Baumeister, Roy F., and Dianne M. Tice. 1984. "Role of self-presentation and choice in cognitive dissonance under forced compliance: Necessary or sufficient causes?" *Journal of Personality and Social Psychology* 46:5–13.

Beavois, Jean-Léon, and Natacha Rainis. 1993. "Dissonance reduction and causal explanation in a forced compliance situation." *European Journal of Social Psychology* 23:103–7.

Becker, Gary S. 1965. "A Theory of the Allocation of Time." *Economic Journal* 75:493–517.

Bem, Daryl J. 1967. "Self perception: An alternative interpretation of cognitive dissonance phenomena." *Psychological Review* 74:183–200.

Bendor, Jonathan. 1988. "Review Article: Formal Models of Bureaucracy." *British Journal of Political Science* 18:353–95.

Bendor, Jonathan, and Terry Moe. 1985. "An Adaptive Model of Bureaucratic Politics." *American Political Science Review* 79:755–74.

Bendor, Jonathan, Serge Taylor, and Roland Van Gaalen. 1985. "Stacking the Deck: Bureaucratic Missions and Policy Design." *American Political Science Review* 81:873–96.

Bianco, William, and Robert Bates. 1990. "Cooperation By Design: Leadership, Structure, and Collective Dilemmas." *American Political Science Review* 84:133–48.

Bianco, William, Peter Ordeshook, and George Tsebelis. 1990. "Crime and

Punishment: Are One-Shot, Two-Person Games Enough?" *American Political Science Review* 84:569–88.

Bierhoff, Hans Werner, and Dorothee Bierhoff-Alfermann. 1976. "The Use of Psychological Theories by 'Naive' Judges: A Study of Implicit Personality Theory," *European Journal of Social Psychology*, 6: 429–45.

Bikhchandani, Sushil, David Hirshleifer, and Ivo Welch. 1992. "A Theory of Fads, Fashion, Custom, and Cultural Change as Informational Cascades." *Journal of Political Economy* 100:992–1026.

Bittner, Egon. 1971. *The Function of the Police in Modern Society.* Washington, DC: U.S. Government Printing Office.

Black, Donald. 1980. *The Manners and Customs of the Police.* New York: Academic Press.

Black, Donald, and Albert J. Reiss. 1967. "Patterns of Behavior and Citizen Transaction." In President's Commision on Law Enforcement and Administration of Justice, *Studies in Crime and Law Enforcement in Major Metropolitan Areas*, Field Studies III, Vol. II, Sec. I (Washington: U.S. Government Printing Office).

Blais, André, and Stéphane Dion. 1991. "Are Bureaucrats Budget Maximizers?" in Blais and Dion, eds., *The Budget Maximizing Bureaucrat*, Pittsburgh: University of Pittsburgh Press.

Blau, Peter. 1940. "A Theory of Social Integration." *American Journal of Sociology* 45:545–56.

Blau, Peter M., Wolf H. Heydebrand, and Robert E. Stauffer. 1966. "The Structure of Small Businesses." *American Sociological Review* 31:179–91.

Bollen, Kenneth A., and David P. Phillips. 1982. "Imitative Suicides: A National Study of the Effects of Television News Stories." *American Sociological Review* 47:802–9.

Brehm, John, and Scott Gates. 1990. "Supervision and Compliance." Paper presented at the annual meeting of the American Political Science Association, San Francisco, CA.

Brehm, John, and Scott Gates. 1992. "Policing Police Brutality," Paper presented at the Midwest Political Science Association meetings, Chicago.

Brehm, John, and Scott Gates. 1993a. "Donut Shops and Speed Traps: Evaluating Models of Supervision on Police Behavior," *American Journal of Political Science* 37:555–81.

Brehm, John, and Scott Gates. 1993b. "Adaptive Preferences in the Principal–Agency Context." Paper presented at the annual meeting of the Midwest Political Science Association, Chicago.

Brehm, John, and Scott Gates. 1994. "When Supervision Fails to Induce Compliance." *Journal of Theoretical Politics* 6:323–44.

Brown, Michael K. 1981. *Working the Street: Police Discretion and the Dilemmas of Reform.* New York: Russell Sage Foundation.

Brualdi, Richard A. 1977. *Introductory Combinatorics.* New York: North-Holland.

Calvert, Randall. 1987. "Coordination and Power: The Foundation of Leadership Among Rational Legislators." Paper presented at the APSA annual meeting, Chicago.

Calvert, Randall L., Mathew D. McCubbins, and Barry R. Weingast. 1989. "A Theory of Political Control and Agency Discretion." *American Journal of Political Science* 33:588–611.

Campbell, Colin, S. J., and Donald Naulls. 1991. "The Limits of the Budget-Maximizing Theory: Some Evidence from Officials' View of Their Roles and Careers." In A. Blais and S. Dion, eds., *The Budget-Maximizing Bureaucrat: Appraisals and Evidence,* Pittsburgh: University of Pittsburgh Press.

Cialdini, Robert. 1984. *Influence: The New Psychology of Modern Persuasion.* New York: Quill Books.

Clark, Peter B., and James Q. Wilson. 1961. "Incentive Systems: A Theory of Organizations." *Administrative Science Quarterly* 6:129–66.

Coase, Ronald N. 1937. "The Nature of the Firm." *Econometrica* 4:386–405.

Cohen, Michael, James March, and Johan Olsen. 1972. "A Garbage Can Model of Organizational Choice." *Administrative Science Quarterly* 17:1–25.

Cooper, Joel, and Russell H. Fazio. 1984. "A new look at dissonance theory." In L. Berkowitz (ed.), *Advances in Experimental Social Psychology* 17:229–267. San Diego, CA: Academic Press.

Crawford, Vincent P., and Hans Haller. 1990. "Learning How to Cooperate: Optimal Play in Repeated Coordination Games." *Econometrica* 58 571–95.

Cyert, Richard M., and James G. March. 1963. *A Behavioral Theory of the Firm.* Englewood Cliffs, NJ: Prentice-Hall.

Devroye, Luc. 1986. *Non-Uniform Random Variate Generation.* New York: Springer-Verlag.

Downs, Anthony. 1967. *Inside Bureaucracy.* New York: Harper-Collins.

Dubin, Jeffrey A., and Douglas Rivers. 1990. "Selection Bias in Linear Regression, Logit and Probit Models." *Sociological Methods and Research* 18:360–90.

Eagly, A. H., and S. Chaiken. 1993. *The Psychology of Attitudes.* San Diego, CA: Harcourt Brace Jovanovich.

Elster, Jon. 1989. *The Cement of Society: A Study of Social Order.* New York: Cambridge University Press.

Farrell, Dan. 1983. "Exit, Voice, Loyalty, and Neglect as Responses to Job Dissatisfaction: A Multi-dimensional Scaling Study." *Academy of Management Journal* 26:596–607.

Farrell, Dan, and Caryl E. Rusbult. 1981. "Exchange Variables as Predictors of Job Satisfaction, Job Commitment, and Turnover: The Impact of Rewards, Costs, Alternatives, and Investments." *Organizational Behavior and Human Performance* 28:79–95.

Fayol, Henri. 1949, 1916. *General and Industrial Management.* Trans. C. Storrs. London: Pitman.

Feldman, Martha S. 1989. *Order Without Design. Information Production and Policy Making.* Stanford: Stanford University Press.

Festinger, Leon. 1957. *A Theory of Cognitive Dissonance,* Stanford: Stanford University Press.

Festinger, Leon, Henry W. Riecken, and Stanley Schachter. 1956. *When Prophecy Fails.* Minneapolis: University of Minnesota Press.

Finer, Herman. 1941. "Administrative Responsibility in Democratic Government." *Public Administration Review* 1:335–50.

Fiorina, Morris P. 1977. *Congress: Keystone of the Washington Establishment.* New Haven: Yale University Press.

Fiorina, Morris P. 1981. *Retrospective Voting in American National Elections.* New Haven: Yale University Press.

Fiorina, Morris P. 1982. "Legislative Choice of Regulatory Forms: Legal Process or Administrative Process." *Public Choice* 39:33–66.

Fiorina, Morris P. 1986. "Legislative Uncertainty, Legislative Control, and the Delegation of Legislative Power." *Journal of Law, Economics, and Organization* 2:33–50.

Follett, Mary Parker. 1926. "The Giving of Orders." In Jay M. Shafritz and J. Steven Ott (eds.), *Classics of Organization Theory,* 3d ed. Belmont, CA: The Dorsey Press, 150–58.

Freedman, Jonathan L., John A. Cunningham, and Kristen Krismer. 1992. "Inferred values and the reverse-incentive effect in induced compliance." *Journal of Personality and Social Psychology* 62:357–68.

Friedrich, Carl J. 1941. "The Nature of Administrative Responsibility." In *Public Policy,* ed. Carl J. Friedrich. Cambridge, MA: Harvard University Press.

Friedrich, Robert J. 1980. "Police Use of Force: Individuals, Situations, and Organizations," *Annals of the American Academy of Political and Social Sciences* 452:82–97.

Fudenberg, Drew, and Eric Maskin. 1986. "The Folk Theorem in Repeated Games with Discounting or with Incomplete Information." *Econometrica* 54:533–54.

Fudenberg, Drew, and Jean Tirole. 1990. *Game Theory.* Cambridge, MA.: MIT Press.

Fuller, Raymond G. C., and Alan Sheehy-Skeffington. 1974. "Effects of Group Laughter on Responses to Humourous Material, A Replication and Extension." *Psychological Reports* 35:531–34.

Fyfe, James J. 1986. "The Split-Second Syndrome and Other Determinants of Police Violence." *Violent Transactions,* edited by A. Campbell and J. Gibbs. New York: Basil Blackwell.

Gates, Scott. 1991. "Working, Shirking, and Sabotage: Strategic Dissent in Organizations." Paper presented at the annual meetings of the American Political Science Association, Washington, DC.

Gates, Scott, and Robert E. Worden. 1989. "Principal–Agent Models of Hierarchical Control in Public Bureaucracies: Working, Shirking, Supervision in Police Agencies." Presented at the annual meetings of the American Political Science Association, Washington, DC.

Giola, Dennis, and Charles C. Manz. 1985. "Linking Cognition and Behavior: A Script Processing Interpretation of Vicarious Learning." *Academy of Management Review* 10:527–39.

Goldberger, Arthur. 1964. *Econometric Theory.* New York: Wiley.

Goldstein, Herman. 1977. *Policing in a Free Society.* Cambridge, MA: Ballinger.

Goodnow, Frank. 1900. *Politics and Administration.* New York: Russell and Russell.

Goodsell, Charles T. 1985. *The Case for Bureaucracy: A Public Administration Polemic.* Chatham, NJ: Chatham House Publishing.

Gormley, William T. 1982. "Alternative Models of the Regulatory Process: Public Utility Regulation in the States." *Western Political Quarterly* (September).

Gormley, William T. 1983a. "Policy, Politics, and Public Utility Regulation." *American Journal of Political Science* 27:86–105.

Gormley, William T. 1983b. *The Politics of Public Utility Regulation.* Pittsburgh: University of Pittsburgh Press.

Gormley, William T. 1985. *Politics of Public Utility Regulation in the United States, 1980.* ICPSR 8080.

Gormley, William T., John F. Hoadley, and Charles H. Williams. 1983. "Potential Responsiveness in the Bureaucracy: Views of Public Utility Regulation." *American Political Science Review* 77:704–17.

Gouriereux, C., A. Monfort, and A. Trognon. 1984. "Pseudo Maximum Likelihood Methods: Application to Poisson Models." *Econometrica* 52:701–20.

Graen, George B., and Terri A. Scandura. 1987. "Toward a Psychology of Dyadic Organizing." *Organizational Behavior* 9:175–208.

Graen, George B., Michael A. Novak, and Patricia Sommerkamp. 1982. "The Effect of Leader–Member Exchange and Job Design on Productivity and Job Satisfaction: Testing a Dual Attachment Model." *Organizational Behavior and Human Performance* 30:109–31.

Griffin, Russell W., Thomas S. Bateman, Sandy J. Wayne, and Thomas C. Head. 1987. "Objective and social factors as determinants of task perceptions and responses: An integrated perspective and empirical investigation." *Academy of Management Journal* 30:501–23.

Grossman, Sanford J., and Oliver D. Hart. 1983. "An Analysis of the Principal–Agent Problem." *Econometrica* 51:7–45.

Groves, Theodore. 1983. "Incentives in Teams." *Econometrica* 41:617–31.

Groves, Theodore. 1985. "The Impossibility of Incentive-compatible and Efficient Full Cost Allocation Schemes." In *Cost Allocation: Methods, Principles, Applications*, Peyton Young, editor. Amsterdam: Elsevier.

Groves, Theodore, and John O. Ledyard. 1977. "Optimal Allocation of Public Goods: A Solution to the 'Free Rider' Problem." *Econometrica* 45:783–809.

Gulick, Luther. 1937. "Notes on the Theory of Organization." In *Papers on the Science of Administration*, eds. L. Gulick and L. Urwick. New York: Institute of Public Administration.

Gummer, Burton. 1979. "On Helping and Helplessness: The Structure of Discretion in the American Welfare System." *Social Science Review* 53:215–28.

Hall, Richard H. 1968. "Professionalization and Bureaucratization." *American Sociological Review* 33:92–104.

Hall, Richard H. 1969. *Occupations and the Social Structure.* Englewood Cliffs, NJ: Prentice-Hall.

Hall, Richard H. 1976. "Professionalism and Bureaucracy, 1966." ICPSR 7314, Ann Arbor, MI.

Hammond, Thomas H. 1990. "In Defence of Luther Gulick's 'Notes on the Theory of Organization.' " *Public Administration* 68:143–73.

Hashimoto, Masanori, and John Raisian. 1985. "Employment Tenure and Earnings Profiles in Japan and the United States." *American Economic Review* 75:721–35.

Heckman, James J. 1976. "The common structure of statistical models of truncation, sample selection and limited dependent variables and a simple estimator for such models." *Annals of Economic and Social Measurement* 5/4:475–92.

Heclo, Hugh. 1977. *A Government of Strangers: Executive Politics in Washington.* Washington, DC: The Brookings Institute.

Heider, Fritz. 1946. "Attitudes and cognitive organization," *Journal of Psychology,* 21:107–12.

Heider, Fritz. 1958. *The Psychology of Interpersonal Relations.* New York: Wiley.

Hill, Jeffrey S. 1985. "Why So Much Stability? The Role of Agency Determined Stability." *Public Choice* 46:275–87.

Hirschman, Albert O. 1970. *Exit, Voice, and Loyalty: Response to Decline in Firms, Organizations, and States.* Cambridge, MA: Harvard University Press.

Hogarth, Robin M., Claude Michaud, and Jean-Louis Mery. 1980. "Decision Behavior in Urban Development: A Methodological Approach and Substantive Considerations." *Acta Psychologica* 45:95–117.

Holden, Kritina L., and John E. Overall. 1987. "Tests of Significance for Differences in Counts of Rare Events in Two Treatment Groups." *Educational and Psychological Measurement* 47:881–92.

Holmström, Bengt. 1979. "Moral Hazard and Observability." *Bell Journal of Economics* 10:74–91.

Holmström, Bengt. 1982. "Moral Hazard in Teams." *Bell Journal of Economics* 13:324–40.

Hummel, Ralph P. 1987. *The Bureaucratic Experience.* 3d edition. New York: St. Martin's Press.

Hurwicz, Leonid. 1973. "The Design of Mechanisms for Reserve Allocation." *American Economic Review* 63:1–30.

Janis, Irving Lester. 1972. *Groupthink: Psychological Studies of Policy Decisions and Fiascoes.* New York: Houghton Mifflin.

Jensen, Michael C., and William H. Meckling. 1976. "Theory of the Firm: Managerial Behavior, Agency Cost, and Ownership Structure." *Journal of Financial Economics* 3:305–60.

Johnson, Ronald N., and Gary D. Libecap. 1989. "Bureaucratic Rules, Supervisory Behavior, and the Effect on Salaries in the Federal Government." *Journal of Law, Economics, and Organization* 5:53–83.

Johnson, Ronald N., and Gary D. Libecap. 1994. *The Federal Civil Service System and the Problem of Bureaucracy: The Ecnomics and Politics of Institutional Change.* Chicago: University of Chicago Press.

Jones, Bryan D., Saadia R. Greenburg, Clifford Kaufman, and Joseph Drew. 1977. "Bureaucratic Response to Citizen-Initiated Contacts: Environmental Enforcement in Detroit." *American Political Science Review* 71:148–65.

Jones, Bryan D., Saadia Greenberg, and Joseph Drew. 1980. *Service Delivery in the City: Citizen Demand and Bureaucratic Rules.* New York: Longman, Inc.

Jones, Bryan D. 1985. *Governing Buildings and Building Government: A New Perspective on the Old Party.* University, AL: University of Alabama Press.

Jones, Stephen R. G. 1984. *The Economics of Conformism.* Oxford: Basil Blackwell.

Kadushin, Alfred. 1992. *Supervision in Social Work.* 3d ed. New York: Columbia University Press.

Kahneman, Daniel, and Amos Tversky. 1979. "Prospect Theory: An Analysis of Decisions Under Risk." *Econometrica* 47:263–91.

Kalton, Graham. 1983. *Compensating for Missing Survey Data.* Ann Arbor: Institute for Social Research.

Kanter, Rosabeth Moss. 1977. *Men and Women of the Corporation.* New York: Basic Books, Inc.

Kaplan, Robert E. 1984. "Trade Routes: The Manager's Network of Relationships." *Organizational Dynamics* 12:37–52.

Kaufman, Herbert. 1960. *The Forest Ranger.* Baltimore: Johns Hopkins Press.

Kaufman, Herbert. 1975. *The Limits of Organizational Change.* University, AL: University of Alabama Press.

Kaufman, Herbert. 1985. *Time, Chance, and Organizations: Natural Selection in a Perilous Environment.* Chatham, NJ: Chatham House Publishers.

Kiesler, Charles A. 1971. *The Psychology of Commitment: Experiments Linking Behavior to Beliefs.* San Diego, CA: Academic Press.

Kiewiet, D. Roderick, and Mathew D. McCubbins. 1991. *The Logic of Delegation: Congressional Parties and the Appropriations Process.* Chicago: University of Chicago Press.

Kinder, Donald R., and Janet A. Weiss. 1978. "In lieu of rationality." *Journal of Conflict Resolution* 22:707–35.

King, Gary. 1989. *Unifying Political Methodology.* Cambridge: Cambridge University Press.

Klockars, Carl B. 1980. "The Dirty Harry Problem." *Annals of the American Academy of Political and Social Sciences* 452:33–47.

Koford, Kenneth J., and Jeffrey B. Miller, editors. 1991. *Social Norms and Economic Institutions.* Ann Arbor: University of Michigan Press.

Kohn, Art, Wendy K. Kohn, and J. E. R. Staddon. 1993. "Preferences for constant duration and constant sized rewards in human subjects." *Behavioural Processes* 26:125–42.

Krehbiel, Keith. 1991. *Information and Legislative Organization.* Ann Arbor: University of Michigan Press.

Kreps, David M. 1984, 1990. "Corporate Culture and Economic Theory," in *Perspectives on Positive Political Economy,* edited by JE. Alt and KA. Shepsle, 90–143. New York: Cambridge University Press.

Lazear, Edward P. 1989. "Pay Equity and Industrial Politics." *Journal of Political Economy* 87:561–80.

Lazear, Edward P. 1994. *Personnel Economics.* Cambridge, Mass.: MIT Press.

Lazear, Edward P., and Sherwin Rosen. 1981. "Rank-Order Tournements as Optimum Labor Contracts." *Journal of Political Economy* 89:841–64.

Lee, In Ho. 1993. "On the convergence of informational cascades." *Journal of Economic Theory* 61:395–411.

Lee, Lung-Fei. 1986. "Specification Test for Poisson Regression Models." *International Economic Review* 27:689–706.

Leibenstein, Harvey. 1982. "The Prisoners' Dilemma in the Invisible Hand: An Analysis of Intrafirm Productivity." *American Economic Review* 72:92–97.

Leibenstein, Harvey. 1987. *Inside the Firm: The Inefficiencies of Heirarchy.* Cambridge, MA.: Harvard University Press.

Leippe, Michael R., and Donna Eisenstadt. 1994. "Generalization of dissonance reduction: Decreasing prejudice through induced compliance." *Journal of Personality and Social Psychology* 67:395–413.

Lipsky, Michael. 1980. *Street-Level Bureaucracy: Dilemmas of the Individual in Public Services.* New York: Russell Sage Foundation.

Locke, Edwin A., Judith F. Bryan, and Lorne M. Kendall. 1968. "Goals and intentions as mediators of the effects of monetary incentives on behavior." *Journal of Applied Psychology* 52:104–21.

Long, Norton E. 1949. "Power and Administration." *Public Administration Review* 9:257–64.

Lupia, Arthur, and Mathew D. McCubbins. 1993. "Designing Bureaucratic Accountability." Unpublished manuscript.

Malcolmson, James M. 1984. "Work Incentives, Hierarchy, and Internal Labor Markets." *Journal of Political Economy* 92:486–507.

Manning, Peter K. 1977. *Police Work.* Cambridge, Mass.: MIT Press.

Manning, Peter K. 1982. "Organizational Work: Structuration of Environments." *British Journal of Sociology* 33:118–32.

March, James G., and Herbert Simon. 1958. *Organizations.* New York: Wiley.

Mashaw, Jerry L. 1990. "Explaining Administrative Process: Normative, Positive, and Critical Stories of Legal Development." *Journal of Law, Economics, and Organization* (special issue) 6:267–98.

Matza, D. 1964. *Delinquency and Drift.* New York: John Wiley.

Mayo, Elton. 1945. *The Social Problems of an Industrial Civilization.* Cambridge, MA: Harvard University Press.

McCubbins, Mathew, and Arthur Lupia. 1993. "Learning from Oversight: Fire Alarms and Police Patrols Reconstructed." Unpublished paper.

McCubbins, Mathew, Roger Noll, and Barry Weingast. 1987. "Administrative Procedures as Instruments of Political Control." *Journal of Law, Economics, and Organization* 3:243–77.

McCubbins, Mathew, Roger Noll, and Barry Weingast. 1989. "Structure and Process, Politics and Policy: Administrative Arrangements and the Political Control of Agencies." *Virginia Law Review* 75:431–82.

McCubbins, Mathew, Roger Noll, and Barry Weingast. 1990. "Positive and Normative Models of Procedural Rights: An Integrative Approach to Administrative Procedures." *Journal of Law, Economics, and Organization* (special issue) 6: 307–32.

McCubbins, Mathew, and Thomas Schwartz. 1984. "Police Patrols vs. Fire Alarms." *American Journal of Political Science*, 28:165–79.

McCullagh, P., and J. A. Nelder. 1983. *Generalized Linear Models.* 2d ed. London: Chapman and Hall.

McDonald, James B., and Richard J. Butler. 1990. "Regression Models for Positive Random Variables," *Journal of Econometrics*, 43:227–51.

Merton, Robert. 1940. "Bureaucratic Structure and Personality." *Social Forces* 18:560–68.

Migué, Jean-Luc, and Gérard Bélanger. 1974. "Towards a General Theory of Managerial Discretion." *Public Choice* 17:24–47.

Milgram, Stanley. 1974. *Obedience to Authority.* Harper Torchbooks: New York.

Milgrom, Paul, and John Roberts. 1992. *Economics, Organization, and Management.* Englewood Cliffs, New Jersey: Prentice Hall.

Miller, Gary J. 1987. "Administrative Dilemmas: The Role of Political Leadership." Washington University, Political Economy Working Paper 118.

Miller, Gary J. 1992. *Managerial Dilemmas. The Political Economy of Hierarchy.* New York: Cambridge University Press.

Miller, Gary J., and Terry M. Moe. 1983. "Bureaucrats, Legislators and the Size of Government." *American Political Science Review* 77:297–322.

Mintzburg, Henry, and Alexandra McHugh. 1985. "Strategy Formation in an Adhocracy." *Adminstrative Science Quarterly* 30:160–97.

Mitnick, Barry M. 1973. "Fidicuiary Rationality and Public Policy: The Theory of Agency and Some Consequences." Paper presented at the 1973 Annual Meeting of the American Political Science Association, New Orleans, LA.

Moe, Terry M. 1982. "Regulatory Performance and Presidential Administration." *American Journal of Political Science* 26:197–224.

Moe, Terry M. 1984. "The New Economics of Organization." *American Journal of Political Science* 28:739–777.

Moe, Terry M. 1985. "Control and Feedback in Economic Regulation: The Case of the NLRB." *American Political Science Review* 79:1094–116.

Moe, Terry M. 1990. "Political Institutions: The Neglected Side of the Story." *Journal of Law, Economics, and Organization* (special issue) 6:213–53.

Muris, Timothy J. 1986. "Regulatory Policymaking at the Federal Trade Commission: The Extent of Congressional Control." *Journal of Political Economy* 94:881–89.

Nagler, Jonathan. 1992. "Scobit: An Alternative Estimator to Logit and Probit for Models with Dichotomous Dependent Variables." Paper presented at the Midwest Political Science Association meetings, Chicago.

Nelson, Richard R., and Sidney G. Winter. 1982. *An Evolutionary Theory of Economic Change.* Cambridge: The Belknap Press.

Niskanen, William A., Jr. 1971. *Bureaucracy and Representative Government.* Chicago: Aldine-Atherton, Inc.

Niskanen, William A., Jr. 1975. "Bureaucrats and Politicians." *Journal of Law and Economics* 18:617–44.

Nexis News Service. October 1996.

Ostrom, Elinor, Roger B. Parks, and Gordon Whitaker. 1988. "Police Services Study, Phase II, 1977: Rochester, St. Louis, and St. Petersburg." ICPSR 8605.

Palmer, Bryan. 1975. "Class, Conception and Conflict: The Thrust for Efficiency, Managerial Views of Labor and the Working Class Rebellion, 1903–22." *Review of Radical Political Economics* 7:31–49.

Pate, Antony M., and Lorie E. Fridell. 1994. "Police Use of Forece (United States): Official Reports, Citizen Complaints, and Legal Consequences: 1991–1992." ICPSR 6274.

Perrow, Charles. 1987. *Complex Organizations: A Critical Essay,* Third ed. New York: Random House.

Petty, Richard E., and John T. Cacioppo. 1986. *Communication and Persuasion: Central and Peripheral Routes to Attitude Change.* New York: Springer-Verlag.

Pittman, Thane S., Jolee Emery, and Ann K. Boggiano. 1982. "Intrinsic and Extrinsic Motivational Orientations: Reward-Induced Changes in Preference for Complexity." *Journal of Personality and Social Psychology* 42:789–97.

Pratt, John W., and Richard J. Zeckhauser. 1985, 1991. *Principals and Agents: The Structure of Business.* Boston: Harvard Business School Press.

Pregibon, Daryl. 1980. "Goodness of Link Tests for Generalized Linear Models." *Applied Statistics* 29:15–24.

Pressman, Jeffrey L., and Aaron Wildavsky. 1973. *Implementation.* Berkeley: University of California Press.

Radelet, Louis A. 1986. *The Police and the Community,* 4th ed. New York: Macmillan Publishing.

Rahim, M. Afzalur, and Gabriel F. Buntzman. 1989. "Supervisory Power Bases, Styles of Handling Conflict with Subordinates, and Subordinate Compliance and Satisfaction." *Journal of Psychology* 123:195–210.

Rasmusen, Eric. 1989. *Games and Information.* Oxford: Basil Blackwell.

Reiss, Albert J. 1971. *The Police and the Public.* New Haven: Yale University Press.

Rosenstone, Steven J., and John Mark Hansen. 1993. *Mobilization, Participation, and Democracy in America.* New York: MacMillan Publishing Company.

Ross, Stephen A. 1973. "The Economic Theory of Agency: The Principal's Problem." *American Economic Review* 63:134–39.

Rousseau, Denise M. 1985. "Issues of Level in Organization Research: Multi-level and Cross-level Perspectives." *Research in Organizational Behavior* 7:1–37.

Rubin, Donald B. 1987. *Multiple Imputation for Nonresponse in Surveys.* New York: Wiley.

Rubinstein, Jonathan. 1973. *City Police.* New York: Farrar, Straus, and Giroux.

Rusbult, Caryl E., Isabella Zumbrodt, and Lawanna K. Gunn. 1982. "Exit, Voice, Loyalty, and Neglect: Responses to Dissatisfaction in Romantic Involvements." *Journal of Personality and Social Psychology* 43:1230–42.

Salancik, Gerald, and Jeffrey Pfeffer. 1978. "A social information processing approach to job attitudes and task design." *Administrative Science Quarterly* 23:224–53.

Salisbury, Robert H. 1969. "An Exchange Theory of Interest Groups," *Midwest Journal of Political Science* 13:1–32.

Saltzstein, Grace Hall. 1992. "Explorations in Bureaucratic Responsiveness." *The State of Public Bureaucracy*, edited by Larry B. Hill. Armonk, NY: M. E. Sharpe.

Scharfstein, David S., and Jeremy C. Stein. 1990. "Herd Behavior and Investment." *American Economic Review* 80:465–79.

Schelling, Thomas C. 1960. *The Strategy of Conflict.* Cambridge, MA: Harvard University Press.

Schnake, Mel E., and Michael P. Dumler. 1987. "The social information processing model of task design." *Group and Organization Studies* 12:221–40.

Schweiger, David M., Carl R. Anderson, and Edwin A. Locke. 1985. "Complex Decision Making: A Longitudinal Study of Process and Performance." *Organizational Behavior and Human Decision Processes* 36:245–72.

Scott, W. Richard. 1965. "Reactions to Supervision in a Heteronomous Professional Organization." *Administrative Science Quarterly* 20:65–81.

Selznick, Phillip. 1948. "Foundations of the theory of organization." *American Sociological Review* 13:25–35.

Simon, Herbert A. 1945. *Administrative Behavior.* New York: Free Press.

Simon, Herbert A. 1946. "The Proverbs of Administration." *Public Administration Review* 6:53–67.

Smith, Douglas A., and Christy A. Visher. 1981. "Street-Level Justice: Situational Determinants of Police Arrest Decisions." *Social Problems* 29:167–78.

Stackelberg, Heinrich von. 1934. *Marktform und Gleichgewicht.* Berlin: J. Springer.

Staten, Michael E., and John Umbeck. 1982. "Information Costs and Incentives to Shirk: Disability Compensation of Air Traffic Controllers." *American Economic Review,* 72:1023–37.

Steele, Claude M. 1988. "The psychology of self-affirmation: Sustaining the integrity of the self." In L. Berkowitz (ed.), *Advances in experimental social psychology.* 17:261–302. San Diego, CA: Academic Press.

Steele, Claude M., and J. T. Liu. 1983. "Dissonance processes as self-affirmation." *Journal of Personality and Social Psychology* 16:65–78.

Stein, Robert M. 1990. "The Budgetary Effects of Municipal Service Contracting: A Principal–Agent Explanation." *American Journal of Political Science* 34:471–502.

Steinbruner, John D. 1974. *The Cybernetic Theory of Decision: New Dimensions of Political Analysis.* Princeton: Princeton University Press.

Sykes, Gary W. 1985. "The Functional Nature of Police Reform: The 'Myth' of Controlling the Police." *Justice Quarterly* 2:52–65.

Taylor, Frederick W. 1911. *The Principles of Scientific Management.* New York: W. W. Norton.

Taylor, Frederick W. 1916. "The Principles of Scientific Management." In Jay M. Shafritz and J. Steven Ott (eds.), *Classics of Organization Theory,* 3d ed. Belmont, CA: The Dorsey Press, 69–80.

Tedeschi, James T. 1981. *Impression Management Theory and Social Psychological Research.* New York: Academic Press.

Tesser, Abraham, and David P. Cornell. 1991. "On the confluence of self-processes." *Journal of Personality and Social Psychology* 27:501–26.

Tsebelis, George. 1989. "The Abuse of Probability in Political Analysis: The Robinson Crusoe Fallacy." *American Political Science Review* 83:77–92.

United States Office of Personnel Management. 1979, 1980. *Federal Employees Attitude Survey.*

Van Maanen, John. 1983. "The Boss: First-Line Supervision in an American Police Agency." In M. Punch, ed., *Control in the Police Organization.* Cambridge, MA.: MIT Press.

Veblen, Thorstein. 1921. *The Engineers and the Price System.* New York: BW Huebsch, Inc.

Verba, Sidney, and Norman H. Nie. 1972. *Participation in America: Political Democracy and Social Equality.* New York: Harper and Row.

Weber, Max. 1947. *The Theory of Social and Economic Organization.* New York: The Free Press.

Weick, Karl E. 1979. *The Social Psychology of Organizing,* 2d ed. Reading, MA: Addison-Wesley.

Weingast, Barry R., and Mark J. Moran. 1983. "Bureaucratic Discretion or Congressional Control?: Regulatory Policymaking by the Federal Trade Commission." *Journal of Political Economy* 91:765–800.

Weiss, Howard M., and Christine E. Nowicki. 1981. "Social influences on task satisfaction: Model competence and observer field dependence." *Organizational Behavior and Human Performance* 27:345–66.

Weiss, Howard M., and James B. Shaw. 1979. "Social influences on judgments about tasks." *Organizational Behavior and Human Performance* 24:126–40.

Welch, Ivo. 1992. "Sequential Sales, Learning, and Cascades," *The Journal of Finance.* 47:695–732.

White, Kenneth J. 1978. "A General Computer Program for Econometric Methods — SHAZAM." *Econometrica* 46:239–40.

White, Theodore Harold. 1969. *The Making of the President, 1968.* New York: Atheneum Publishers.

Williamson, Oliver. 1975, 1983. *Markets and Hierarchies: Analysis and Antitrust Implications.* New York: Free Press.

Williamson, Oliver. 1981. "The Modern Corporation: Origins, Evolution, and Attributes." *Journal of Economic Literature* 19:1537–70.

Wilson, James Q. 1968. *Varieties of Police Behavior: The Management of Law and Order in Eight Communities.* Cambridge, MA: Harvard University Press.

Wilson, James Q. 1989. *Bureaucracy: What Government Agencies Do and Why They Do It.* New York: Basic Books, Inc.

Wilson, Woodrow. 1887. "The Study of Administration." *Political Science Quarterly* 2:197–222.

Wood, B. Dan. 1988. "Principals, Bureaucrats, and Responsiveness in Clean Air Enforcements." *American Political Science Review* 82:213–34.

Wood, B. Dan. 1990. "Does Politics Make a Difference at the EEOC?" *American Journal of Political Science.* 34:503–30.

Wood, B. Dan. 1991. "The Dynamics of Political Control of the Bureaucracy." *American Political Science Review* 85:801–28.

Wood, B. Dan, and Richard W. Waterman. 1991. "The Dynamics of Political Control of the Bureaucracy," *American Political Science Review* 85:801–28.

Wood, B. Dan, and Richard W. Waterman. 1993. "The Dynamics of Political-Bureaucratic Adaptation." *American Journal of Political Science* 37:1–39.

Wood, B. Dan, and Richard W. Waterman. 1994. *Bureaucratic Dynamics: The Role of Bureaucracy in a Democracy.* Boulder, CO: Westview Press.

Worden, Robert E. 1989. "Situational and Attitudinal Explanations of Police Behavior: A Theoretical Reappraisal and Empirical Assessment." *Law and Society Review* 23:667–711.

Yukl, Gary. 1981. *Leadership in Organizations.* Englewood Cliffs, NJ: Prentice-Hall.

Index